THE HISTORY OF THE BRITISH 'U' CLASS SUBMARINE

THE HISTORY OF THE BRITISH 'U' CLASS SUBMARINE

by

DEREK WALTERS

Pen & Sword
MARITIME

First published in Great Britain in 2004 by
Pen & Sword Maritime
an imprint of
Pen & Sword Books Ltd
47 Church Street
Barnsley
South Yorkshire
S70 2AS

ISBN 1 84415 131 X

Typeset in Meridien by
Phoenix Typesetting, Auldgirth, Dumfriesshire

Printed and bound in England by
CPI UK

Pen & Sword Books Ltd incorporates the imprints of Pen & Sword Aviation,
Pen & Sword Maritime, Pen & Sword Military, Wharncliffe Local History,
Pen & Sword Select, Pen & Sword Military Classics and Leo Cooper.

For a complete list of Pen & Sword titles please contact
PEN & SWORD BOOKS LIMITED
47 Church Street, Barnsley, South Yorkshire, S70 2AS, England
E-mail: enquiries@pen-and-sword.co.uk
Website: www.pen-and-sword.co.uk

CONTENTS

I	The Small and Simple Submarine	1
II	British Submarines in Home Waters	18
III	The Mediterranean: Pre *Operation Torch*	41
IV	The Mediterranean: *Operation Torch* to the Italian Armistice	88
V	The Mediterranean and Beyond	126
VI	The Allied Navies' Contribution	155
VII	Special Operations	184
VIII	Accidental Losses of Submarines and Lives	204
IX	In Conclusion	224

Appendix I	Gallantry Medals awarded to officers and men serving in British 'U' class submarines	232
Appendix II	Gallantry Medals awarded to officers and men of the Allied Navies serving in 'U' class submarines	248
Appendix III	Submarine pennant numbers	251

Abbreviations	252
Bibliography	253
Acknowledgements	254
Index	256

TYPICAL 'U' CLASS SUBMARINE GENERAL LAYOUT

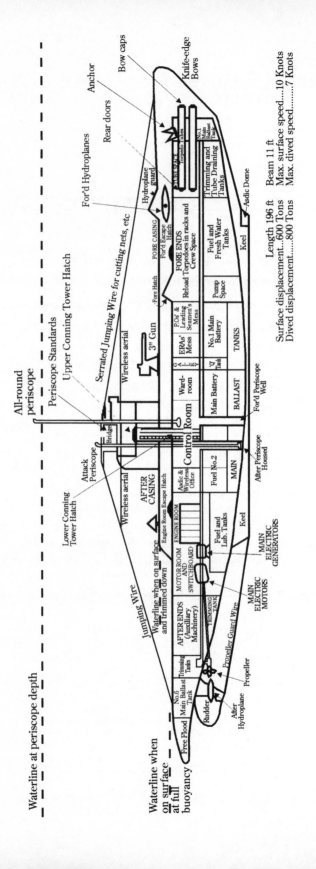

Waterline at periscope depth

All-round periscope

Periscope Standards

Upper Conning Tower Hatch

Lower Conning Tower Hatch

Attack Periscope

Serrated Jumping Wire for cutting nets, etc

Wireless aerial

Rear doors

Ford Hydroplanes

Anchor

Bow caps

Knife-edge Bows

Hydroplane guard

3" Gun

FORE CASING

Fore Hatch

FORE ENDS
Reload Torpedoes in racks and Crew Space

TUBE SPACE
Torpedo tubes

No.1 Main Ballast Tank

Trimming and Tube Draining Tanks

Asdic Dome

Keel

Fuel and Fresh Water Tanks

Pump Space

TANKS

No.1 Main Battery

Ford Periscope Well

BALLAST

Main Battery

Ward-room

Q Tank

GALLEY

ERAs' Mess

P.O.s & Leading Seamen's Mess

Ford Escape Hatch

Ford Casing

Wireless aerial

Control Room

Bridge

AFTER CASING

Asdic & Wireless Office

Engine Room Escape Hatch

ENGINE ROOM

Fuel No.2

MAIN

After Periscope Housed

Fuel and Lub. Tanks

MOTOR ROOM AND SWITCHBOARD

AFTER ENDS (Auxiliary Machinery)

TRIMMING TANK

Keel

MAIN ELECTRIC GENERATORS

MAIN ELECTRIC MOTORS

Propeller Guard Wire

Jumping Wire

Waterline when on surface and trimmed down

Waterline when on surface at full buoyancy

Free Flood

No.6 Main Ballast Tank

Trimming Tanks

Rudder

After Hydroplane

Propeller

Length 196 ft   Beam 11 ft

Surface displacement....600 Tons   Max. surface speed....10 Knots

Dived displacement.....800 Tons   Max. dived speed........7 Knots

HULL DEVELOPMENT OF 'U' & 'V' CLASS SUBMARINE
UNITY CLASS SMALL PATROL SUBMARINES

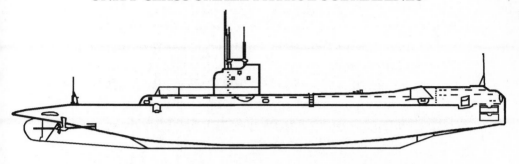

U CLASS GROUP I SMALL PATROL SUBMARINES

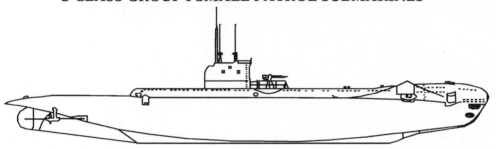

U CLASS GROUP II SMALL PATROL SUBMARINES

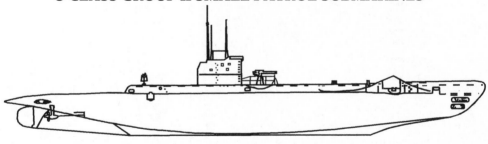

V CLASS SMALL PATROL SUBMARINES

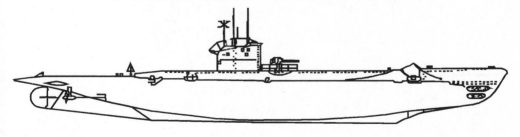

Seeing a submarine for the first time was a depressing experience.
The submarine designer must have been a genius. In such a
small amount of space he had found room for torpedoes,
ammunition and food stores, hundreds of pipes, boilers,
valves, engines and batteries. Only one small detail
had escaped his attention – room for thirty crew
who were to live, breathe and maybe die there.

Captain Andrzej Klopotowski
June 1993

I

THE SMALL AND SIMPLE SUBMARINE

Until I have got a great number of destroyers on the station I
would not spend a shilling on submarines.
Admiral Arthur Cheveson, 1924.[1]

During the First World War, the use of submarines delivered an exceptional level of success. However, on cessation of hostilities the development of the submarine as an accepted war tool did not receive the unanimous support of British senior naval officers. Admiral Cheveson in his capacity as C.-in-C. of the Far Eastern Fleet commented in his memo of October 1924:

> Submarine thinking officers, as well as the others, are beginning to admit that their capabilities in their pet line are a good deal over-rated. They know that a FAST, well-handled, alert cruiser has very little to fear from them if the cruiser wants to force a passage through a strait or get to her destination. It requires so very many submarines as to be prohibitive on account of cost, and also even then there is the liability of getting in each other's way and colliding with each other.[2]

These comments gave support to opinions previously expressed by Admiral Sir Charles Madden in his report *The Capital Ship* of January 1921. He wrote:

> When the submarine approaches the surface ship in mobility (surface speed and radius action combined) and has a higher submerged speed approximating to the war

1

cruising speed of surface vessels, so that the chances of the submarine being able to make a submerged attack are increased, and, further, when submarines can co-operate tactically in squadrons, while submerged, then they will become a serious threat to a fleet comprising of all types.

Submarines can be effective for commerce destruction only if of considerable size; or if they sink ships on sight, a policy which this country, dependent as we are on trade with foreign countries, cannot afford to pursue, even for a temporary advantage.[3]

These strongly expressed views did not prevent the slow development of the submarine but construction was concentrated on the larger type of submarine intended as a multi-functional vessel.

The London Naval Treaty of 1930 restricted the total tonnage of the British submarine fleet to 52,700 tons, which gave rise to consideration being given to producing smaller submarines. This policy was encouraged by the experiences learned during naval exercises when the previously constructed large submarines were easier to locate with the introduction of anti-submarine screens and easier to attack due to lack of manoeuvrability. It was also recognised that in 1933 the small 440-ton 'H' class submarines being used for all anti-submarine training were nearing the end of their life, the last one being launched in 1918. It was at this time that Rear Admiral N.F. Laurence, Rear Admiral Submarines, recommended that a small, cheap submarine should be designed with the primary purpose of anti-submarine training but having a torpedo capability to be used for short-distance patrols in case of war. In March 1934, Rear Admiral Laurence followed up his original recommendation and submitted the specifications for a small submarine under the title 'Small, Simple Submarine for Anti-Submarine Training etc.'[4] This was to be the catalyst for the design and production of the 'Unity' class submarine and subsequently the 'U' class.

On 5 November 1936 the Admiralty placed an order with Vickers-Armstrong of Barrow-in-Furness for three submarines of the new 'Unity' class design. In keeping with the recommendations of the Hopwood Committee of 1926, the submarines were given names beginning with the same letter of the alphabet. Thus *Undine, Unity* and *Ursula* became the first three submarines in the lead-up to the new 'U' class submarine.

These three submarines were to have very different histories. *Unity* was lost after she collided with the merchant ship *Atle Jarl* in thick fog in the approaches to the River Tyne. *Undine* was lost when she was scuttled after being depth-charged in Heligoland Bight. *Ursula* served throughout the war, including a period on loan to the Russian Navy from 30 May 1944 to 10 February 1949 when she operated as *B4*, before being returned and broken up for scrap in 1950.

Although larger than the 'H' class they were intended to replace, they were still the smallest submarines constructed since the end of the 1914–1918 war. The initial design was a small vessel of just 191 feet in length (an increase of twenty feet from the 'H' class) with a sixteen-foot maximum beam. The standard displacement was 540 tons rising to 600 tons when fully loaded and to 730 tons when submerged. The riveted pressure-hull was of half-inch thick steel and divided into five watertight compartments with a recommended safe diving depth of 200 feet. This was underestimated as, during the imminent conflict, the submarines had on many occasions to dive to greater depths. The pressure hull had a light metal casing covering the top fitted with free-flooding holes, and the conning tower was also free flooding. This provided a safe operating area for the gun crew and deck party and cover for the conning-tower party when at sea. It also provided ample storage for cables, anchors and miscellaneous objects such as collapsible boats which were to prove essential during landing operations.

The original specification set out by Rear Admiral Laurence was for a submarine to be armed with four forward-facing torpedo tubes and two Lewis guns. During the planning process this was amended to six forward-facing torpedo tubes to include two external tubes. There was also the capacity for a reload capability of four torpedoes giving it a payload of ten torpedoes. In addition, provision was made to mount a 3-inch gun at short notice should this be necessary. The submarine, originally intended for training purposes, was being prepared for war and the role of a multi-purpose, short-patrol vessel. The gun, when fitted, proved to be a great asset during later operations.

Power was provided by a dual diesel/electric system. Whilst on the surface, two 400-horsepower Paxman diesel engines drove the two propellers via the two generators which ensured the main battery remained fully charged. When submerged, the propellers were driven by two electric motors of 825 horsepower supplied directly from the main battery consisting of 112 high-capacity cells and situated under the control room and accommodation space. The fuel capacity of thirty-eight tons of diesel gave the submarine a range of 3,800 nautical miles at 10 knots on the surface and 120 nautical miles at 2 knots submerged. The time submerged and operating on the battery was not infinite as it was necessary for the submarine to return to the surface on a regular basis and run on main engines to recharge the batteries. This was obviously a disadvantage and the later development of the snorkel, which allowed the submarine to remain submerged for a longer period, was to be a great asset. The first snorkels fitted to these submarines came in late 1944 and were purely dummy snorkels fitted to assist in exercises carried out with aircraft from the Royal Air Force. None of the British-operated 'U' class submarines was fitted with a fully operational snorkel. This was not so of the submarines operated post-war by the Norwegian and Danish Royal Navies. All these submarines did have operational snorkels fitted during refits in the early 1950s.

To assist in underwater observation, two periscopes were fitted: an 8-inch bifocal search periscope with high- and low mag-nification; and a smaller 6-inch attack periscope with low magnification only. The periscopes could only be raised some twelve feet forcing the submarine to operate at this depth just under the surface. At such a shallow level, the submarine could be identified from the air either by the shape of the boat itself or, more significantly, by the sight of the periscope. This placed the larger submarines at even greater risk during operational conditions.

To give the submarine an underwater listening facility, three hydrophones were installed, one each side of the pressure hull near the bows and facing to port and starboard, the third being

4

fitted in the conning tower structure and facing aft. Type 129 Asdic was also fitted forward of the keel to be used for echo detection and underwater communication. This was first introduced in 1937 and became a standard piece of equipment on all Allied Second World War submarines. Two radio aerials ensured communication: one, a jumping wire fitted to the conning tower, allowed reception of Very Low Frequency transmissions whilst at periscope depth; raising the W/T mast clear of the water spread the second aerial facilitating the reception and transmission of messages. Naturally, whilst on the surface all communications were made by conventional methods.

Accommodation was sparse for the twenty-seven crew consisting of four officers, four petty officers, four engine room artificers and fifteen other ratings. The officers were accommodated in the small wardroom with the artificers' and petty officers' messes adjacent, both being about the size of an old railway passenger compartment. The petty officers were the Coxswain, Torpedo Gunner's Mate, Petty Officer Telegraphist and Stoker Petty Officer. The other ratings were all accommodated in the torpedo stowage compartment, also known as the 'fore-ends', sharing this with the torpedo reload, bread, potatoes and all victualling and ancillary equipment. One additional petty officer and three other ratings made a crew total of thirty-one for operational conditions. Sanitary arrangements for the whole ship's company were two toilets with a complex operating procedure and just two hand basins. Captain Klopotowski of the Polish Navy best describes these arrangements:

> There were two wash basins, one for the officers and one for the crew, both with running water pumped directly from the sea. This has a nasty habit of stopping soap from making a lather. There were also two toilets. Their operating instructions were so complicated – twelve rules to read before and twelve rules to read after use – that there existed a real danger of sinking the submarine or at best having your face showered had a wrong valve been opened. It seemed a good idea to avoid the toilet at all cost, not to mention the fact that we had to have special permission

from the officer of the watch to use it if the boat was under-water.[5]

Access to the submarine was gained by any of four methods: day-to-day access was via the torpedo-loading hatch forward and the engine-room hatch to the stern. Access could also be gained via the conning tower with an additional hatch being provided in the torpedo stowage compartment to provide an escape route. Escape is a major consideration for all submariners and the design recognised the need for this by incorporating an escape facility at both ends of the submarine. Escape could be carried out from the torpedo stowage compartment forward and from the engine room aft. Both escape hatches were fitted with drop-down canvas trunking that, after closing all watertight doors, was lowered and secured to the deck before the hatch was loosened to allow water to enter the watertight compartment. As the water rose in the compartment, the air/water pressure equalled out, preventing the water from completely filling the compartment and allowing the crew to breathe the trapped air prior to escape. The crew used the Davis Submerged Escape Apparatus (DSEA) which comprised a nose clip and a mouthpiece connected to an oxygen bag. The first man would enter the trunking, fully open the escape hatch and make good his escape to the surface. He would be followed by each man in turn, all making for the surface by non-assisted free ascent. The only alternative to the two specifically designed escape hatches was via the conning tower. The drawback to this escape procedure was the control of the water entering the control room. The procedure to use this method was that the lower hatch was opened, two men then entering the conning tower, closing the lower hatch after them. Once the lower hatch was closed and secured they then opened the upper hatch, flooding the conning tower and made good their escape. At least one successful escape was made using this method during the Second World War and this will be mentioned later.

These small submarines were easily manoeuvrable and very handy under water but unfortunately they did have some design faults. They were very slow on the surface in contradiction of the requirements previously set out on many occasions by Senior

Naval officers but, as they were originally designed for short patrols, it was considered to be of little consequence. This was to prove a handicap during the oncoming conflict. The fitting of the two external torpedo tubes was also a mistake. The high bulbous fore casing enclosing the external tubes caused a prominent bow wave when the submarine was operating on the surface. It was also evident when operating at periscope depth making the submarine easily discernible from the air or by surface vessels when manoeuvring to commence an attack. Lieutenant J.F.B. Brown, RN, Commanding Officer of *Unity* highlighted this in October 1939 on his return from patrolling off the coast of Denmark. He reported that the bow wave and very loud noise from the engine exhaust placed the submarine at a great disadvantage when operating on the surface. He also reported that, to reduce the bow wave whilst travelling at speed, it was necessary to travel at full buoyancy; also the engine exhaust could be heard from a range of three-quarters of a mile. These defects were quickly rectified by ensuring that future constructions omitted the external tubes, and during her refit in 1942 *Ursula* had them removed with her bows being fined and lengthened. There was an additional buoyancy problem: when making an attack it was impossible to keep the submarine submerged after firing a full salvo of six torpedoes.

In 1938 it was learned that Germany was constructing submarines to their total tonnage of 70,000 tons in accordance with the terms of the agreement between all nations in the London Naval Treaty of 1936. The German-designed U-boat was much lighter than any submarine in service with the Royal Navy and consequently would give the German Navy an obvious advantage in any forthcoming conflict. However, having considered these facts, Parliament decided to maintain submarine construction at the agreed level, ensuring that seventy-one submarines would be in service with the Royal Navy by 1941. Obviously events overtook this decision and many more submarines were to be constructed in the ensuing years.

In September 1939, a further assessment was made of the need to produce a particular-sized submarine as naval warfare had changed considerably since 1914 – 1918. With the introduction of Asdic and the development of radio communications, surface forces were now able to take up a more offensive anti-submarine role with a reasonable chance of success. Whilst the submarine had until this time been the principal menace, this would not necessarily be so in the future. The Royal Navy surface forces had improved its anti-submarine procedures and the Germans had strengthened their forces, introducing the pocket battleship with which no surface cruiser could compete. It was realised that many British submarines were unsuitable for their task, again citing the size of the submarines compared with the smaller German U-boat.

This assessment went on to recommend that small submarines should be used in the North Sea and areas similar to the Skagerrak and the Norwegian coast. They should be used in waters where the Royal Navy had no surface control. In this type of area it was considered that they should have some success both against enemy surface vessels and submarines. This was not always to be appreciated by the crews of the submarines operating off the Norwegian coastline. They were small craft and were subjected to heavy buffeting in the northern seas off Norway. On more than one occasion the submarines were to 'poop' and water was to pour into the control room soaking everything therein. Also, members of the crew on lookout duty on the bridge were dashed off their feet and injured. In addition, the length of time they spent at sea in such conditions drained the resources of all crew members which caused senior submarine officers to report that they had on occasions reached the limit of their endurance and recommended that rest periods be introduced. Whilst these problems were highlighted, there were never any doubts expressed as to the general seaworthiness of these submarines.

On 4 September 1939, a further twelve submarines were ordered, being financed from the War Supplementary Emergency Programme. Two of these, *Umpire* and *Una*, were built at His Majesty's Dockyard, Chatham; the remaining ten were to be built at Vickers-Armstrong at Barrow-in-Furness, these being *Unbeaten, Undaunted, Union, Unique, Upholder, Upright, Urchin, Urge, Usk* and *Utmost*.

Other than the omission of the external torpedo tubes, these were constructed initially to the same specifications as the 'Unity' class, but the later constructed submarines were increased in length as a finer bow was fitted in an attempt to further reduce the bow-wave effect. The fuel capacity was increased together with the engine rating (to 615 horsepower). These submarines were initially fitted with a 12-pounder gun of First World War design, which was replaced by the 3-inch quick-firing gun as each individual submarine was refitted. They were also fitted with Type 291W combined air and surface warning equipment.

Mixed fortunes were to meet these submarines: one, *Umpire*, was never destined to see any active service and was sunk in a collision whilst en route from Chatham to join the 3rd Submarine Flotilla at Dunoon. During her passage, she was rammed by the armed trawler *Peter Hendriks*, with the loss of twenty-two lives. Three, *Una, Upright* and *Urchin*, survived the war and were eventually scrapped. *Urchin* was to enjoy an exemplary war record as *Sokol*, manned by personnel of the Free Polish Navy. The remaining eight perished by various means during the conflict.

A further ten submarines were ordered from Vickers-Armstrong on 11 March 1940. These were *P34 (Ultimatum), P35 (Umbra), P37 (Unbending)* and *P31 (Uproar)*, these being the ones that survived to be named, and *P32, P33, P36, P38* and *P39*, all of which were lost before they could be named. The one remaining submarine, *P41*, was manned by servicemen from the Free Norwegian Navy from November 1941, renamed *Uredd* and served with distinction. The four that survived to be named were lucky enough to see service throughout the conflict and were eventually scrapped after peace had been restored.

This was followed up by an order for twelve additional submarines on 23 August 1940, again, all to be constructed by Vickers-Armstrong at their Barrow-in-Furness yard. These were *P53 (Ultor), P42 (Unbroken), P43 (Unison), P44 (United), P45 (Unrivalled), P46 (Unruffled), P49 (Unruly), P51 (Unseen), P54 (Unshaken), P47, P48* and *P52*. These twelve submarines were to have chequered careers serving in four Allied navies in addition to the Royal Navy. Of this group, just one, *P48*, failed to see the end of hostilities, and was lost before any naming ceremony could take place. *P47* was manned by the Royal Netherlands Navy and operated throughout the war as *Dolfijn*. *P52* was manned by personnel of the Free Polish Forces as *Dzik* until the end of the war, and in 1947 she was loaned to the Royal Danish Navy. Initially identified as *U1*, she was renamed *Springeren* after Denmark joined NATO. *P42 (Unbroken)* and *P43 (Unison)* initially served with the Royal Navy until July 1944 when they were loaned to the Russian Navy and operated under the titles of *B2* and *B3* respectively.

The final group of twelve submarines was ordered from Vickers-Armstrong on 12 July 1941, four to be constructed at Barrow-in-Furness and the other eight at their Naval Yard, High Walker, Newcastle-upon-Tyne. Amongst this group was the *Untamed* that foundered and was lost off the west coast of Scotland during acceptance trials; she was salvaged, refitted and renamed *Vitality*. The *Vandal* also was lost during acceptance trials but on this occasion the submarine was never traced until much later, towards the end of the twentieth century. The remaining ten were *P57 (Universal)*, *P55 (Unsparing)*, *P63 (Unswerving)*, *P59 (Untiring)*, *P65 (Upstart)*, *P56 (Usurper)*, *P62 (Uther)*, *P61 (Varangian)*, *P66 (Varne I)* and *P67 (Vox I)*. Once again some of these submarines were to see service with the Allied navies. The *Varne* was loaned to the Royal Norwegian Navy in March 1943; renamed *Ula* she was to assist in patrolling off the coast of Norway and home waters. *Vox I* was loaned to the Free French Forces in May 1943 and renamed *Curie*; she was to see service in both home waters and the Mediterranean. In 1945, after the end of the war, *Untiring* and *Upstart* were loaned to the Royal Hellenic Navy and renamed *Xifias* and *Amfitriti* respectively.

The revised design ensured that, with the removal of the external torpedo tubes, the bows were reshaped, making them finer, and the submarine length extended to 196 feet. Number 5 main tank was converted for oil storage, thus increasing the fuel capacity to fifty-five tons, which extended the submarines' range from 3,800 to 5,500 nautical miles. There was also an increase in crew numbers of two ratings, giving a wartime complement of four officers and twenty-nine crew.

As the production of these submarines increased, they were not given names but identified purely by their pennant numbers.

This procedure was maintained until November 1942 when, after the direct intervention of the Prime Minister, Winston Churchill,[6] it was decided to give names to all submarines either already in service or under construction. On 4 November the First Lord of the Admiralty wrote to the Prime Minister in answer to a query:

> You raised with me the question of the dropping [of] the practice of naming submarines. The decision was taken early in June 1940 on the recommendation of the Controller, concurred in by F.O. (S). It was made in order to avoid the confusion which it was expected would arise owing to the very large building programme of destroyer flotillas which, as you know, are usually recognised by the initial letter of their names. The system of numbering was adopted on the basis of experience with submarines in the last war, but I do not think that at the time, in the midst of all the other pressure upon us, it was realised how different the circumstances would be compared with the last war when the number of submarines were small and E9 or E11 stood out prominently in the public minds. In this war the numbers are beginning to run into hundreds and it is much more difficult to follow the career of a particular submarine.
>
> Agreeing with Wellington's expressed opinion that it is better to be right than to be consistent, I think there is no doubt it might do a great deal of good to revert to the practice of allotting names to submarines, and F.O. (S) agrees with me. He is looking into the matter to how it can best be dealt with.'

The Prime Minister replied:

> Let me see the list of the ones that will come into service by December 31 1942, in their classes and also those at present in service with no names.
>
> I have no doubt whatever that names should be given and I will myself make some suggestions which may stimulate others.

It took so long to organise that on 19 December 1942 the Prime Minister sent a further note to the First Lord of Admiralty and the First Sea Lord that was short and to the point. He wrote:

I am grieved to see our submarines described as 'P.212' etc, in daily returns. I thought you told me that you would give them names. It is in accordance with the tradition of the Service and with the feelings of the officers and men who risk their lives in these vessels. Not even to give them a name is derogatory to their devotion and sacrifice.

This note spurred on the effort to allocate names and several notes were exchanged between the various offices with proposals of suitable names for all the unnamed submarines. It was brought to the attention of the Prime Minister that there were insufficient reasonable names beginning with 'U' and the Admiralty Naming Committee suggested that they should run over into the next letter 'V'. This accounts for the overlap of names in the later development of the class that has ensured the 'V' class is included in this analysis. A list of proposals was provided and on 27 December the Prime Minister returned this note with his own suggestions and the comment:

I have no doubt a little more thought, prompted by the dictionary, would make other improvements possible. Now do please get on with it and let them be given their names in the next fortnight.

Shortly after this, all submarines both in commission and under construction were named, which included many of the Prime Minister's own suggestions. In the interest of continuity, the names eventually allocated to each submarine, in addition to the pennant number, have been used throughout this account. Unfortunately, some of the submarines brought into service before the end of 1942 were lost before this naming policy could be implemented and were never given names.

The final developments came in the form of the 'V' class submarines. Of thirty-four originally ordered, only twenty-two

12

were completed, as the Admiralty cancelled the remainder when the need for such a submarine declined as the phases of the war changed. The first eight of these were ordered on 5 December 1941, followed by another twelve on 21 May 1942, with the final two being ordered on 17 November 1942. All these submarines were to be built by Vickers-Armstrong, split between their two construction yards.

The design was again developed in line with the experiences of the submarines in service. The overall length was again increased, to 204 feet, by further fining of the bows, together with the lengthening of the stern. The modification of the stern was done in an attempt to improve the angle of approach of water to the propellers to further reduce propeller noise. The problem known as 'singing propellers' had been constant throughout the history of the 'U' class submarines. On more than one occasion, enemy warships had detected patrolling submarines both in the Mediterranean and home waters by this excessive noise. Just one week in October 1940 was to highlight the problem as both *Utmost* and *Upright,* patrolling off the coastline of France, were put at risk by this defect. 3 October found *Utmost* patrolling off Fechamp, and as she started her approach to attack a small convoy, two armed trawlers located her. Fortunately they lost contact as the submarine slowed to reduce the propeller noise. Just five days later *Upright* was patrolling on the same coastline when she was subjected to an anti-submarine hunt by a French Chasseur attracted by the noise of the 'singing propellers'; fortunately this hunt was also unsuccessful. The departure of both submarines to patrol in the Mediterranean was delayed for attention to this very problem. Throughout the lifetime of the 'U' class submarines, propellers were the most consistent problem requiring to be modified and replaced at regular intervals in an attempt to eradicate the 'singing propellers', but without complete success. Even as late as March 1944, *Visigoth* reported the problem during her acceptance trials.

The operational diving depth was increased to 300 feet by increasing the thickness of the pressure hull from half an inch to three-quarters of an inch and by welding the pressure hull frames. The diesel power was increased to give an additional 1.5

13

knots surface speed. In addition the crew was increased by four, taking the total crew of officers and men to thirty-seven.

Twelve were built in Barrow-in-Furness – *Veldt, Venturer, Vigorous, Viking, Virtue, Visigoth, Vox II, Upshot, Variance, Vengeful, Vineyard* and *Virulent*. None of these submarines was lost in combat and seven served with Allied navies. *Variance* was renamed *Utsira* when loaned to the Royal Norwegian Navy on 4 August 1944. In July 1946 she was purchased by the Norwegian Government and continued to be of service until sold and broken up in December 1965. In addition to *Variance*, the Norwegian Government also purchased *Venturer* and *Viking. Venturer* served from 5 November 1946 under the name of *Utstein* until being broken up in January 1964, and *Viking* served as *Utvaer* from 5 September 1946 to December 1964 when she was broken up for scrap. *Veldt, Vengeful* and *Virulent* were loaned to the Royal Hellenic Navy: *Veldt* from 28 October 1943 to 10 December 1957 and renamed *Pipinos; Vengeful* from 23 April 1945 until 10 December 1957 operating under the name of *Delfin;* and *Virulent* from 29 May 1946 until 2 May 1958 and renamed *Argonaftis. Vineyard* was loaned to the Free French Navy and renamed *Doris* on 30 July 1944 to be returned to British control on 18 November 1947.

At the High Walker Yard, Newcastle-upon-Tyne, Vickers-Armstrong built *Vampire, Urtica, Varne II, Vivid, Volatile, Voracious, Vortex, Vulpine, Vagabond* and *Votary*. Again, none of these submarines was lost in conflict and four of the ten were loaned out to Allied navies. *Vortex* was renamed *Morse* and loaned to the Free French Forces on 15 November 1944. On 17 September 1946 she was returned to Admiralty control by the French authorities. She was then loaned to the Royal Danish Navy in January 1947 and renamed *U3*, only to be changed to *Saelen* in 1951. In January 1958 the Danish authorities returned her to the Admiralty. In addition to *Vortex* the Danish Government also took *Vulpine* on loan, initially identifying her as *U2* before being renamed *Storen* on joining NATO; she served from September 1947 until being returned to the Admiralty in January 1959. The Royal Hellenic Navy took *Volatile* on loan from 29 May 1946 and renamed her *Triaina* until she was returned to British control on

2 October 1958. Finally, the Norwegian Government agreed in July 1946 to purchase *Votary* which, having been renamed *Uthaug*, served with the Royal Norwegian Navy from 5 September 1946 until being sold for scrap on 3 July 1965.

As with the construction of any vessel, problems and the inevitable delay in delivery were experienced. Even from the beginning this was so, an examination of the original three 'Unity' class submarines after a short time in operation revealing extensive frame cracks, and necessitating additional work which took all three submarines out of action for four to six weeks. The *Untamed* was lost whilst exercising off Sanda Island, south of Kintyre, with the anti-submarine training yacht *Shemara*, when at 13.45 she reported a leak in the periscope. The Commanding Officer, Lieutenant G.M. Noll, RN, decided it was possible to continue the exercises and dived just three minutes later. She was never to surface and all the crew perished. She was subsequently salvaged and after a refit was commissioned under her new name *Vitality.* This loss, following so quickly after the loss of *Vandal,* caused questions to be asked of the workforce employed by Vickers-Armstrong. A memorandum from Rear Admiral C.B. Barry listed problems experienced in 'U' class submarines which included *Untiring* damaged by explosion and *Unswerving* falling from her blocks, which delayed completion of both submarines by more than one month. Both incidents occurred at High Walker, and Barry suggested that there was sufficient suspicion to warrant investigation into the possibility of malicious intent or sabotage, and a close watch was to be kept for the activity of any possible saboteurs in the construction yards. In July 1943 *Unsparing* arrived in Bizerta from patrol to report abnormally high temperatures on the main generator bearings together with other defects. Captain (S) First Submarine Flotilla commented:

> This is the first 'U' class submarine built at Vickers Yard on the Tyne and this almost certainly accounts for the fact that she is at present suffering from heavier incidence of breakdown than other 'U' class of about the same period. It is felt that a more intimate liaison between the experienced Barrow Yard and the Tyne Yard building their first modern

15

submarine might well have lessened these early troubles. The views of the Commanding Officer, who stood by *Unsparing* while building confirm this view.[7]

In June 1943 a review of the submarine strength was under-taken as a result of the anticipated change in the war's circumstances. This review was to change the thinking in respect of the production of further 'U' class submarines. In 1941 the primary tasks for these submarines were patrols to prevent invasion of Britain and short-range patrols in the Mediterranean. Consequently, on 14 June 1941, the Prime Minister issued an instruction that speed of construction and a quick increase in numbers was the first priority. It was accepted that the 'U' class, whilst having several limitations, was by far the quickest to build. However, by 1943 the reach of the war was slowly spreading to the Far East and it was accepted that a submarine designed for inshore work with a limited range would not be suitable for this type of patrol. The 'U' class submarine patrols of the Norwegian coastline had highlighted their unsuitability for distant and prolonged patrols making them totally unsuitable for work in Far Eastern waters. This review suggested that the primary role for the 'U' class submarine should be restricted to training purposes and recommended that the construction of further 'U' class submarines be halted. The spare capacity at the construction yards used to construct the 'S' class submarines accepted that fewer submarines would be constructed. Admiral (Submarines) Rear Admiral C.B. Barry, concluded:

> I feel that to continue with the 'U' class just because this would produce greater numbers is not warranted, and on all counts it would be better to have (say) six submarines which could be used to effect than ten 'U' class which could not.[8]

In January 1944 the Admiralty cancelled the final twelve submarines of this particular class. Of the eighty-three originally ordered, seventy-one were completed and accepted for service in the Royal Navy and seven different Allied navies. Eighteen were lost, fifteen due to enemy action in both home waters and the Mediterranean campaigns, two in collision with friendly merchant ships and one, *Vandal*, disappeared in unexplained circumstances during independent exercises off the western coast of Scotland.

To return to November 1936 and the original order for three submarines of which HMS *Undine* was the first to be accepted for service in the Royal Navy: ion the afternoon of 8 July 1938, a cool dull summer day, she slipped her berth under the command of Lieutenant E.R.J. Oddie, RN. As he sailed into Morecambe Bay and a strong north-westerly gale en route for Gare Loch, one wonders if, even in his wildest dreams, he thought that this boat was the beginning of an era, an era that would see these submarines make a major contribution to naval operations to counteract the Axis forces. Or that, having been designed for training and short patrols that they would see service in seven Allied navies and would serve in areas as far apart as Australia, Canada, the Mediterranean and the West Indies.

Notes
1. National Archives Kew Reference: ADM 116/316.
2. National Archives Kew Reference: ADM 116/3164.
3. National Archives Kew Reference: ADM 1/8597/9.
4. National Archives Kew Reference: ADM 1/9389.
5. Captain Klopotowksi – Tribute to Tadeuz Noworol.
6. National Archives Kew Reference: ADM 1/12500.
7. National Archives Kew Reference: ADM 199/1818.
8. National Archives Kew Reference: ADM 1/15333.

II

BRITISH SUBMARINES IN HOME WATERS

The primary object of submarines is to report movement of German war vessels, but no favourable opportunity of attacking them should be neglected.[1]
Submarine War Orders for the North Sea.

On 1 September 1939 Germany invaded Poland, which immediately requested assistance in accordance with the guarantees both Britain and France had previously given them. Both countries issued Hitler with ultimatums to withdraw from Poland, but to no avail. At 11.15 a.m. on Sunday, 3 September 1939, the Prime Minister, Neville Chamberlain, broadcast to the nation and war was declared on Germany. At this time there were just the three 'U' class submarines in commission. On 4 September, a further twelve were ordered.

Whilst the diplomatic efforts were still being made *Ursula, Unity* and *Undine* sailed from Blyth on 31 August to patrol in the North Sea and in Heligoland Bight, the first patrols of many to be performed in the coming years. On 9 September *Ursula*, under the command of Lieutenant Commander G.C. Phillips, RN, threw the first punch in the campaign when, from a distance of 1,000 yards, she fired a full salvo of four torpedoes at the U-boat *U35*; none found the target. Ten minutes later she fired a further torpedo, but again was not to hear the sweet sound of success as the *U35* proceeded on her way. This was the only contact made by all three submarines during their first patrols. On their return to port it was discovered that all three were suffering from extensive frame cracks and were withdrawn from service.

December 1939 saw the first strike by a 'U' class submarine

18

when Lieutenant Commander Phillips in *Ursula* sighted the damaged German cruiser *Leipzig* being escorted along the Danish coast by six vessels. A salvo of four torpedoes was dispatched at the cruiser but none found their intended target. The torpedo tracks were sighted by the 650-ton escorting torpedo boat *F9* and her Commanding Officer placed her between the torpedoes and the *Leipzig*, causing her to be hit and sunk by one of them. Another torpedo sank an unidentified 'R' boat of about 200 tons. Thus *Ursula* opened the account both personally and for the 'U' class in general. On 1 January 1940 the *London Gazette* announced the first awards to be given to personnel of the 'U' class submarine in recognition of the action taken by Lieutenant Commander George Chesterton Phillips, RN, when he received the Distinguished Service Order.

This early success was quickly followed by disaster. On 7 January 1940 Lieutenant Commander A.S. Jackson, RN, in *Undine* was patrolling twenty miles west-south-west of Heligoland when he sighted two trawlers. *Undine* altered course and attacked the leading trawler by firing one torpedo, which missed the target. According to the German coxswain on the trawler, the torpedo passed just one or two metres astern, the trawler's speed having been underestimated. The trawlers commenced their counter-attack and *Undine* dived to fifty feet and turned away from them. At this time both Asdic and hydrophone equipment were out of order, rendering her incapable of underwater direction finding. The Asdic dome had flooded and the hydrophone had been defective for some time prior to this patrol, but Lieutenant Commander Jackson stated that there had been no opportunity to carry out the extensive repairs required.

As a result of these defects it was necessary for *Undine* to return to periscope depth and the attack periscope was raised to find one of the trawlers at very close range. The order was given to dive to sixty feet but before any action could be implemented, three depth-charges exploded, one aft, one forward and one very close to the control room amidships. This resulted in the submarine being blown upwards with considerable flooding forward, which necessitated the fore-ends being abandoned. The upward movement continued unabated and the Commanding Officer went to

19

the bridge to be joined by the Leading Signalman, and the order was given to burn the Confidential Books whilst the Negative Flag, symbolising the 'white flag' for surrender, was waved. The crew was ordered to abandon ship and all exited the submarine via the control room hatch and gathered on the fore casing. After ensuring that the confidential books were all destroyed, the crew was ordered into the water and the First Lieutenant, Lieutenant E.M. Harvey, RN, opened all the main vents to sink the submarine. This flooding procedure was necessary, as it was not possible to use the scuttling charge, as that was stored in the fore ends and inaccessible. Unfortunately the submarine was slow at settling and a German officer was able to gain access to the boat only to be driven back by gas and nothing worthwhile was found. After some time the submarine finally disappeared from view. The water was very cold, only just above freezing point, and the crew, having been picked up by the trawlers, was shivering violently and very close to exhaustion. Again Lieutenant Harvey was to display his bravery when, having been picked up by the German trawler, he checked all the crew was safe only to see Chief Petty Officer Telegraphist Jordan was still in the water and in difficulties. Lieutenant Harvey immediately dived back into the freezing water, towed the Chief Petty Officer to a nearby rescue boat, helped him onboard and then returned to the trawler. This act of courage was to earn Lieutenant Harvey an award from the Royal Humane Society.

The patrols in the North Sea were maintained together with patrolling the coastlines of Norway and Denmark including Skagerrak. Many minor incidents were recorded but it was not until March 1940 that some real activity was experienced. On 6 March *Unity* (Lieutenant Brown) sighted the German supply ship *Altmark* being escorted along the coast of Norway by three destroyers. The escorts ensured that they did not leave Norwegian territorial waters but *Unity* attempted to maintain contact should they attempt so to do. No such luck, so *Unity* withdrew to send an 'enemy sighting' report. Due to damage to the radio aerial this report was delayed, the *Altmark* was lost and a subsequent aerial reconnaissance failed to locate her.

On 21 March *Ursula* (Lieutenant Commander Phillips) was

patrolling in the straits between the Skagerrak and the Kattegat and sighted the 4,949-ton German merchant vessel *Heddernheim*. When challenged she gave her nationality as Estonian, but as *Ursula* crossed her stern the name of her base port, Bremen, could be seen easily. *Heddernheim* was forced to heave-to after a practice round had been fired from the submarine's 3-inch gun. The crew was ordered to abandon ship but they were so slow at reacting to this instruction that it was necessary to fire a further round to encourage them to act with a little more alacrity. After the *Heddernheim* had been abandoned and the Chief Engineer had been taken prisoner, *Ursula* commenced the task of dispatching her to the depths. This was done despite considerable problems with *Ursula*'s torpedo functions. Three of the torpedo tubes had been damaged by ice earlier in the patrol and were inoperable. One torpedo was fired prematurely due to poor drill and another failed to run. The remaining torpedo ran true and struck the target amidships and sank her. The two lifeboats containing the ship's crew were towed towards the Danish coast. They were released when *Ursula* felt the need to withdraw, suspecting German patrol craft may approach, drawn to the incident by distress signals sent out by *Heddernheim* prior to being abandoned.

Ursula was again engaged when she intercepted the Danish steamer *Sejro* on the 22nd, stopped her, examined her papers, established she was carrying coal from Swansea to Copenhagen, and allowed her to proceed.

The month ended with a humanitarian mission performed by Lieutenant Brown in *Unity*. On 20 March 1940 the Dutch trawler *Protinus*, fishing in the North Sea out of Ijmuiden, Holland, was bombed by a German monoplane. The aeroplane flew over the trawler, machine-gunning on the first run, then returned and dropped a string of seven bombs, one of which hit the *Protinus*. On a third run the crew of the trawler waved a large Dutch flag, but this was to no avail as the aeroplane continued the attack, scoring a further hit which destroyed the engine room and killed the ship's captain and one crew member. The remainder of the crew took to the open boat and the trawler was seen to sink. They had no compass but they attempted to steer towards the Danish coast. On the 25th *Unity* (Lieutenant Brown) sighted the small boat, approached and established they were no threat to the submarine before picking up the eight survivors. Between abandoning the *Protinus* and being picked up by *Unity* they had spent five days in a small, open boat with no food and only a little brackish water. They had suffered the ordeal of losing two shipmates and had to abandon their bodies to the sea. They were all in a poor physical state and three were so weak it was necessary to haul them aboard. They were suffering from exposure and had no feeling in their limbs. Hot drinks were quickly provided with all the men being given warm clothing and a good rub down. They were given initial medical attention and *Unity* diverted to Rosyth to land them.

Having resumed her patrol, *Unity* was in the North Sea on 5 April 1940 when, in a rough sea and heavy swell, she sighted an unidentified U-boat. She manoeuvred into position and fired three torpedoes and the sound of two explosions raised hopes that a hit had been made. This was not to be, as shortly afterwards HE was heard as the U-boat proceeded on her way.

On 9 April 1940 *Unity*, still in the North Sea, sighted a 3,000-ton merchant ship similar to the *Casablanca*. She was allowed to proceed as the Commanding Officer decided that in pursuit of International Law she was not a legitimate target for attack without warning, and he did not wish to compromise the submarine's position at this time. Royal Navy submarines were still operating under international rules that required the target vessel to be inspected to ensure the occupants were hostile with the crew being given time to escape before being subjected to any attack. These operational rules, based on international agreements, were not particularly beneficial to the submarine commander, as in the incident involving the *Heddernheim*, when their implementation gave the crew the opportunity to trade under an assumed neutral flag and radio their position and situation, putting the submarine at risk. The German U-boats did not adhere to these rules of engagement and without warning attacked many ships carrying innocent people to safety across the Atlantic. However, April 1940 was to see the shackles removed from our submarines when they were informed of the political decisions made by Cabinet with regard to submarine warfare. Any hostile ship, either merchant or otherwise, within ten miles of the Norwegian coast east of six degrees east and operating between fifty-four and sixty-one degrees north, were to be attacked on sight. Ships at anchor could be attacked if identified as enemy. In addition, all German merchant ships encountered in the Kattegat and Skagerrak east of eight degrees east were to be treated as transports and sunk without warning.

April 1940 was a month of congratulations for the action of submarines of all classes to date. The Admiralty made the following signal to all submarines on patrol: 'You are all doing a wonderful job.'[2] This reinforced the signal made by C.-in-C., Home Fleet to Vice Admiral Submarines, which read: 'Well done. We on the surface are very proud of our comrades who fight under the surface.'[3] A far cry from the opinions expressed by Admiral Cheveson in 1924.

The end of the month saw the contribution to the war effort by the 'U' class submarines significantly reduced. On 29 April 1940 *Unity* (Lieutenant F.J. Brown) sailed from Blyth for her patrol area when thick fog prevailed and visibility was reduced to just half a cable length. As she proceeded down the main swept channel she encountered the merchant ship *Atle Jarl* inbound. A collision occurred and within four minutes the *Unity* was lost, along with the lives of the First Lieutenant and three ratings. As a result of their actions in this incident the First Lieutenant, Lieutenant J.N.A. Low, RN, and Able Seaman H.J. Miller were awarded the George Cross, both posthumously. This event will be covered more comprehensively in a later section.

May 1940 was a month of consolidation of policy with regard to submarine activity. It opened with a further relaxation of available targets when Admiralty instructions were received that any warship showing Danish colours could be attacked on sight and all Danish merchant shipping was to be treated as enemy shipping. A war memorandum setting out in full the terms of engagement further illustrated this policy. It identified the areas along the coasts of Norway, Denmark, Holland and Belgium where all ships could be attacked whether under way, at anchor or alongside, which also applied to ships in the Bay of Biscay. In

Swedish waters it restricted the attack to vessels under way. Quite naturally it included vessels encountered in home waters, ensuring that due regard be paid to the possibility that friendly shipping would also be operating in this area. Thus the submarine's terms of reference were well documented.

Ursula continued to patrol throughout the summer of 1940 but without incident. September saw an increase in the availability of 'U' class submarines as the next phase of construction started to come on-line. *Upright, Utmost* and *Unique* were all accepted for service and became available for deployment. *Upright* and *Utmost* were allocated to the Fifth Submarine Flotilla based at Portsmouth and were later joined by *Ursula*, all to patrol off the coast of France between Dieppe and Le Havre.

In October 1940 it was decided that the 'U' class submarines would deliver a more beneficial service in the Mediterranean Sea with *Ursula, Upright* and *Utmost* nominated to fulfil this role. The sailing of *Upright* and *Utmost* was delayed for attention to the 'singing propeller' problem. By 7 November all three submarines were in Gibraltar preparing for service with the First Submarine Flotilla in the Mediterranean, albeit *Utmost* was in dry dock being repaired after a collision with the destroyer HMS *Encounter* as both vessels neared Gibraltar. The circumstances were that *Utmost* sighted a cruiser and three destroyers and fired a yellow smoke-candle signal, this being the usual identification procedure for a submerged submarine. The expectation of the submarine commander was that the surface ship would stop engines and tell the submarine to surface, but when this did not occur a further two smoke candles were fired and the submarine surfaced – only to collide with *Encounter*. This collision damaged both ships with the submarine's starboard foreplane damaging the destroyer, which was described by Lieutenant J.H. Eaden, RN, (*Utmost*) as being cut open like a tin-opener opening a tin of sardines. On arrival at Gibraltar, both vessels needed dry dock and Admiral (Gibraltar) was reported to have said: 'Put them in the same dock and let them sort it out between themselves.'[4]

During the months September to December 1940, further 'U' class submarines became available for deployment. As previously

24

stated, September saw *Upright, Utmost* and *Unique* enter service and these were joined in October by *Usk* and *Upholder*, and November saw *Unbeaten* join the fleet. With more 'U' class coming on-line *Unique, Usk* and *Upholder* were dispatched to the Mediterranean. *Urge* and *Undaunted* replaced them in home waters in December.

In January 1941 *Urchin* was loaned to the Free Polish Services and renamed *Sokol*, a submarine which was to serve the cause with distinction. This was the first of many to be loaned to the Allied navies and was not unique in providing excellent support in the fight against the Axis forces. The number of boats was steadily increasing and in February 1941 *Union* joined the fray. The home-based submarines continued to patrol the coastlines of northern France and Norway in particular, but no success against enemy shipping was reported during this time.

These patrols were interspersed with their intended usage in providing anti-submarine training. It was from this very activity that on 21 March 1941 both *Unbeaten* and *Union* were diverted to patrol off Brest together with thirteen other submarines to create an 'iron ring' around the port. This was intended to inter-cept the German battlecruisers *Gneisenau* and *Scharnhorst*, as they were reported to be heading in that direction. One of the deficiencies of the 'U' class was its slow surface speed, and as a result of this both submarines arrived on station too late and the German warships were already safe and sound in Brest, having sailed directly through the patrol area designated to be patrolled by *Union*. They were joined later by *Undaunted* as Flag Officer (Submarines) signalled that all submarines manning this 'ring of iron' were to remain on patrol to the limit of their endurance. However, on 10 April 1941, with both battlecruisers still safely tucked up in Brest, the vigil was abandoned and all the submarines were recalled.

April 1941 was to see some success for the submarines patrolling in home waters. *Urge*, under the command of Lieutenant E.P. Tomkinson, RN, sailed from Portsmouth on 14 April, to patrol en route to Gibraltar and service in the Mediterranean. On 18 April, whilst patrolling northern Biscay in position 46 degrees 51 minutes north and 8 degrees 29 minutes west, she sighted a tanker. The submarine manoeuvred to attack and fired three torpedoes, two of which hit and sank the Italian blockade-running tanker *Franco Martelli*, of 10,535 tons.

The patrols in home waters were maintained throughout April, May and June 1941, again without success. Submarines were consistently re-deployed as the search for the enemy pocket battleships continued, but all to no avail. In fact the direct opposite was almost achieved when, on 13 June, Lieutenant J.B. Kershaw, RN, in *Uproar* was diverted after RAF Bomber Command reported that a German pocket battleship had been bombed and damaged. As *Uproar* approached the position, she sighted an unidentified aircraft and immediately dived to safety with no explosion or any other activity being experienced. The submarine had, in fact, been attacked by a friendly aircraft, which reported: 'Am over enemy submarine, have attacked enemy with bombs. Estimate one hit.'[5] Fortunately this was not so; the aircraft returned to base only to find that its bombs had failed to release, thus saving *Uproar* from becoming an ignominious loss.

The production of new vessels continued, and during the months between April and July 1941, five more submarines, including *Umpire*, joined the fleet. The operational life of *Umpire* was quickly curtailed by an incident that occurred just two days after sailing from His Majesty's Dockyard, Chatham. Prior to sailing to join the fleet the Commanding Officer, Lieutenant M.R.G.S. Wingfield, RN, created the ship's motto 'Keep On Keeping On'. However, this was not to be as, en route north, the *Umpire* was in collision with the requisitioned armed trawler *Peter Hendriks*. The circumstances leading up to this collision and subsequent action will be covered more fully later.

Submarines out on patrol experienced many unusual incidents, most of which did not warrant a mention in the Commanding Officer's report. Lieutenant Commander Boris Karnicki, commanding the Polish-manned submarine *Sokol*, whilst patrolling in the south-east corner of the Bay of Biscay, experienced what could have been just another routine unusual incident. The submarine was patrolling submerged when she became aware that a trawler had located her. Nothing untoward

26

in that, but Lieutenant Commander Karnicki was suspicious and made several alterations to course and speed only to find the trawler maintained station some 2,000 yards away and matched the submarine with every variation. Lieutenant Commander Karnicki reported this incident as he suspected that the enemy was trying out some new type of listening device. It may have been just another case of the 'singing propellers'.

September 1941 saw a further development in the Allied navies' contribution to the war effort together with acceptance of three more 'U' class submarines to the fleet. The Royal Norwegian Navy initially agreed to man one submarine and meet the costs of the crew with the British Royal Navy meeting the running costs of the submarine. The *P41*, being constructed by Vickers-Armstrong at Barrow-in-Furness, was allocated for this role. She was to be manned by Norwegian personnel from the Norwegian submarine *B1* and named *Uredd*. During this same month the Dutch authorities made a request to take over three 'T' class submarines. This request was declined but the Royal Netherlands Navy agreed to accept two 'U' class submarines.

The last quarter of 1941 saw the 'U' class submarine strength rise by a further six boats, one of which was the Norwegian-manned *Uredd*. Patrols of home waters from the northern coast of Spain to the Norwegian coastline were maintained and these duties were interspersed with anti-submarine training. After a few patrols in home waters they were dispatched to the Mediterranean where their particular attributes were better suited, the continuity in Home waters being provided by *Uredd*. The patrols saw very little success as the German warships maintained a low profile, with the main units being reported to be at Brest. The major problem to be addressed was the effect the German U-boat was having on Atlantic convoys. Only five contacts with German U-boats had been reported by Allied 'U' class submarines, four attacks having been made but no U-boat destroyed.

Many of these patrols were concentrated on the Norwegian coast where the submarines operated under various constraints that made life frustrating for their Commanding Officers. They operated under orders to provide intelligence on the description of merchant shipping together with their movements and to restrict any aggression to attacking enemy cruisers and above, or U-boats. An additional hazard was placed on them when instructions were given that all submarines patrolling off the Norwegian coast should refrain from surfacing to take navigational sights during daylight hours due to the increased German air reconnaissance in that area. Whilst Flag Officer Submarines accepted that this would prohibit submarines from attacking identified targets, it created additional navigational problems already high due to the short days, fog and snow flurries. This was the time when the (future) snorkel would have been invaluable. The problems were such that several incidents occurred when friendly submarines were in accidental contact, situations that could have had disastrous consequences for the patrolling submarine. On 18 February *Unbending*, with Lieutenant H. Winter, RN, in command, surfaced and immediately met up with the submarine *Tuna*, even though their designated patrol areas were miles apart. Again on 24 May 1942, *Uredd* was patrolling off the north-western coast of Norway in support of the Russian convoys when she encountered *Unruffled* which was some ninety miles off station. *Uredd* was involved in a similar incident on 22 November 1942 when she was patrolling in support of Russian convoys and sighted the Russian submarine *K3*. The original belief was that this submarine was proceeding without the knowledge of Flag Officer Submarines and the matter was taken up with the Senior British Naval Officer, North Russia via the Admiralty. On *Uredd*'s return to harbour it was discovered that, once again, navigational problems had been highlighted, as it appeared that she was well off station and the Russian submarine was operating correctly. This caused embarrassment to the Admiralty resulting in an apology being made to the Russian authorities. A message was sent to that effect instructing the Senior British Naval Officer to express such regrets as he deemed desirable. An increased risk was experienced when the patrolling submarines regularly encountered floating mines – sometimes as many as fourteen or fifteen in one day. Operating under all these restrictions made life very uncomfortable and frustrating particularly when Commanding

Officers saw merchant ship after merchant ship pass by unmolested.

These restrictions were criticised by Lieutenant Winter,
commanding *Unbending*, after two consecutive patrols when he
had passed up the opportunity to attack forty merchant ships
totalling more than 100,000 tons, several destroyers and a
number of anti-submarine vessels. His one clear opportunity of
attack was when he fired two torpedoes at a passing U-boat with
no success. In reply Admiral (Submarines) wrote:

> I am in full sympathy with the Commanding Officer of *P37*
> in that so many tempting targets had to be left unmolested,
> but a success on such targets would have prevented HM
> Submarine *P37* from achieving a success against the enemy
> main units. The threat to our vital communications to
> North Russia exercised by enemy main units at Trondheim
> cannot be diverted from that of attacking the main units
> only, in particular during the passage of convoys.[6]

The uncertainty of a submarine's position in these Norwegian
waters may have led to a missed opportunity for Lieutenant
H.B. Turner, RN, in *Unrivalled*. He was patrolling off the
Norwegian coastline on 26 June 1942 when the officer on watch,
Sub Lieutenant Jones, reported the sighting of a periscope.
Signalman W. Pearce confirmed the sighting but it was not seen
by the Commanding Officer who had recently arrived on the
bridge. *Unrivalled* dived and Able Seaman G. Simmonds confirmed HE. As the other submarine had not been positively
identified, and with knowledge that friendly submarines had
been located out of position, Lieutenant Turner delayed attacking
until he had been convinced it was not a 'friendly'. When it was
established that the submarine was taking evasive action he fired
just one token torpedo set at a running depth of forty-four feet –
which failed to find the target.

The month of July 1942 brought no luck for Lieutenant Turner
or *Unrivalled* as they patrolled off the Norwegian coastline and
encountered no fewer than five submarines. The first was
unidentified but was suspected as being the Russian submarine

K29. (The Russians were in the habit of deploying submarines in this area to support their convoys. Unfortunately this <u>did</u> lead to confusion at times, as they did not always cooperate with the divulgence of information on deployment.) On 11 July she encountered two U-boats, both surfaced. The first was attacked by a full salvo of four torpedoes, all of which missed as the U-boat dived to safety. On sighting the second she engaged her with gunfire but again the U-boat dived and made good her escape. Later in the patrol, two further U-boats were seen but were at long range and due to the slow speed of the 'U' class it was not possible to close for an attack. *Unrivalled* had not seen the end of her bad luck for the month. As she arrived at Scapa Flow at the end of her patrol on 22 July she collided with the destroyer HMS *Douglas* causing holes in the seam and sprung rivets along the starboard side. The ship's pumps were able to cope with the inflow of water until she was dry-docked to effect repairs.

All submarines were constantly at risk when on operational patrol, not only from enemy attention but also from lack of concentration. This can be illustrated by the problems experienced by *Unseen* as she attempted a routine surface procedure to facilitate a navigational sun sighting and a catalogue of errors put the submarine at risk. The Commanding Officer, Lieutenant M.L.C. Crawford, RN, ordered 1 and 6 ballast tanks to be blown but the panel watchkeeper, who had mistaken the instruction, blew the emergency 'Q' tank instead of number 6 ballast tank. At that time the Kingston valve was shut, as orders had been given to the First Lieutenant for 'Q' tank to be flooded immediately the submarine reached the surface. This was to allow him to dive should an emergency arise. On his arrival on the bridge, Lieutenant Crawford observed that the submarine appeared to be sinking from the stern. The reduction in buoyancy by flooding 'Q' tank and number 1 ballast tank only being blown was drawing the submarine down stern first. Only the quick intervention of the Commanding Officer in ordering the submarine to be dived was a disaster avoided. As a result of this the 'Q' tank was damaged and it was discovered that water had leaked into number 1 battery. Once the damage had been identified, the controls for 'Q' tank were lashed in the shut position. Whilst the Commanding Officer was happy to continue the patrol, Captain (S) Third Submarine Flotilla, Captain H.M.C. Ionides, was not and *Unseen* was recalled from patrol. Lieutenant Crawford was instructed to explain what action he had taken in respect of the case of bad drill and he replied that the rating concerned had been stopped three weeks' pay and ten days' submarine pay; he further stated that he felt that sufficient punishment had been given. He also recommended that the 'Q' tank HP Blow handle be milled (or some similar treatment) to avoid a repetition of this accident.

August 1942 was to see the first real success of the summer for the patrolling 'U' class boats. Lieutenant C.E. Oxborrow, RN, in *Unshaken* was patrolling off the Norwegian coast when on 12 August he sighted a convoy of three merchant ships under escort from an armed trawler. Lieutenant Oxborrow closed to attack and fired a full salvo of four torpedoes, one of which hit and sank the merchant ship *George L M Russ*, of 2,980 tons.

Patrols were maintained in an attempt to restrict the German main units' use of Norwegian ports and protect the Russian convoys. It was not always possible so to do and this was well illustrated on 10 September 1942 when both *Unshaken* and *Uredd* were patrolling off Andfjord in the north of Norway. The submarines both sighted German main units, but both were not able to close to attack and both were frustrated in their attempts to transmit an enemy-sighting message due to the attentions of enemy aircraft. Thus two main units, identified as the *Admiral Scheer* and possibly *Tirpitz*, made good their escape into the open seas and were not located by Allied aircraft due to the delay in receiving the sighting message.

November 1942 was to see the loss of *Unbeaten* under the command of Lieutenant D.E.O. Watson, RN. She had success-fully completed the landing of agents off Vigo, Spain and had been re-deployed to intercept an enemy supply ship. A sighting of the enemy vessel was received from *Unbeaten* on 6 November, this being the last communication received. On 11 November a Wellington aircraft of 172 Squadron sighted and attacked a submarine on the surface only ten miles from the estimated position of *Unbeaten*. Although there is no proof that this was in fact *Unbeaten* (and this was the conclusion of a Board of Enquiry held by Coastal Command, as the enemy never reported losing a submarine in that area) it is likely that it was.

As 1942 drew to a close the Vickers-Armstrong yard maintained its high level of production. Throughout the year a further thirteen 'U' class submarines had been accepted into the fleet and this included two for the Allied navies. The first was *Dolfijn* manned by personnel from the Dutch Navy followed by *Dzik* – the second submarine to be operated by Free Polish personnel. All the 'U' class submarine operations were to follow the same pattern. On completion of their 'work-up' period they were deployed on one or two patrols in home waters mainly to hone their operational abilities before being deployed to the Mediterranean. The one exception was *Uredd*, manned by Norwegian personnel, which provided continuity as the mainstay of patrols off the Norwegian coast. However, this was to be short-lived as, on 5 February 1943, she sailed for an operation off Norway, never to return. The details will be referred to later in the report on actions by the Allied navies' submarines. *Uredd* was eventually replaced in the Norwegian organisation by *Ula*, which was constructed by Vickers-Armstrong at Barrow-in-Furness.

The first six months of 1943 saw the introduction of a further ten 'U' class submarines which included two destined for the Allied navies. *Ula* was the first and *Curie*, to be operated by Free French personnel, followed. Eight were destined for service with the British Royal Navy but two of these were not to see any service. *Vandal*, under the command of Lieutenant J.S. Bridger, RN, was lost with all hands whilst going through her work-up procedures and *Untamed*, having sunk during her work-up, was salvaged. She was then returned to service, being renamed *Vitality*.

The final six months of 1943 saw more results from the Vickers-Armstrong production line as eight more 'U' class submarines joined the fleet, including *Pipinos*, loaned to the Royal Hellenic Navy and operated by Greek personnel. In addition to the anti-submarine training role (for which they were intended) the new submarines were deployed on work-up patrols off the Norwegian coast before making their way to the

Mediterranean for a much more active role in the hostilities. Unfortunately these patrols were not to see much success as, during the six months in question, only two confirmed contacts with enemy shipping were reported. The first was on 27 August when Lieutenant R. Boyd, RN, patrolling north-east of the Faeroe Islands in *Untiring*, sighted the fishing vessel *Habist II* and, after taking the seven Norwegian crew members off, sank it by gunfire.

The second success fell to Lieutenant P.C. Chapman, RN, on 14 September when *Upstart*, patrolling en route to Gibraltar for service in the Mediterranean, sighted two French ketches in the 'sink on sight' area of the Bay of Biscay. The *Grotte de Bethlehem* (forty-nine tons) and the *Torpille* (forty-six tons) were intercepted and each crew of eight was taken aboard *Upstart*, following which both ketches were sunk by gunfire. Lieutenant Chapman felt he should justify this action on his arrival in the Mediterranean. He had been informed that fishing vessels were still operating in a forbidden area and this was not to be tolerated and they were to be sunk on sight. He was aware that *Untiring* was due to take the same route about a week later and the presence of a British submarine in this area should not be compromised. Although Lieutenant Chapman reported that the French fishermen were all well behaved, sixteen extra mouths to feed for eighteen days was a severe drain on the submarine's food supplies. The bread and biscuits were exhausted ten days before their arrival in Gibraltar.

This was also a period that highlighted mechanical problems and, as an example, during November 1943 four submarines' operational capabilities were affected by engine failure. *Umbra*, whilst operating with the RAF, was stuck in Fishguard with both main engines out of action. Just six days later Captain (S) Ninth Submarine Flotilla reported that both *Uther* and *Varangian* had problems with their main engines that would take some time to complete. A further six days on, the Norwegian-manned *Ula*, whilst on patrol off the Norwegian coastline, lost the use of the port main engine but was able to complete her patrol on just one engine but with a greatly reduced capacity.

British 'U' class submarines reported no further successes

on patrol in home waters until March 1944. The first of these successes came on the 2nd, when *Venturer*, commanded by Lieutenant J.S. Launders, RN, on patrol off Stadlandet, western Norway, sighted a convoy of two merchant ships under escort from four anti-submarine trawlers. Lieutenant Launders closed the convoy and fired a full salvo of four torpedoes, one of which hit and sank the 2,526-ton merchant ship *Thor*. As the ship was heard breaking up, the submarine was subjected to a counter-attack by the escorting vessels forcing her to go deep and, in doing so, she lost trim and bottomed at 305 feet, a good test for a submarine with a recommended safe diving depth of just 300 feet. *Venturer* made a further attack on a Danish merchant ship on 6 March and although the Commanding Officer recorded one hit, no such success could be confirmed then or since that time.

The submarines continued their anti-submarine exercises both with surface forces and aircraft of the Royal Air Force. Whilst these were normally routine it was not always so. Lieutenant J.C. Ogle, RN, was exercising *Vigorous* out of Larne on 1 March when he saw her 'adversary' aircraft crash into the sea astern of the submarine. The submarine quickly closed the scene and was able to rescue all the aircrew and return immediately to Larne.

April was to bring more success for *Venturer* and Lieutenant Launders. On the 15th, whilst patrolling off Egersund, she sighted a convoy of two merchant ships under the escort of four anti-submarine trawlers. A salvo of four torpedoes was fired and the 1,923-ton *Friedrichshaven* was dispatched to the bottom of the sea. This was particularly pleasing as earlier in the day *Venturer* had failed in her attack on a much larger merchant ship. This increased the success rate for the month, as on 7 April Lieutenant J. Whitton, RN, in *Unshaken* had been able to report a success. She was patrolling off Lister with Lieutenant Whitton feeling a little frustrated after failing to hit a passenger ship leaving the port, when she sighted the 3,894-ton merchant ship *Asien* under heavy escort of three minesweepers and four armed trawlers. *Unshaken* closed, attacked and sank the *Asien* – one of the four torpedoes fired finding its target.

Patrols were maintained along the Norwegian coastline

throughout the summer of 1944 and during this time many contacts were made with German U-boats. Unfortunately these sightings were not always profitable, as the chances to close and attack were not always possible. In July *Viking* had three sightings of U-boats on consecutive days. After the frustrating experiences of the previous two days, on 5 July she was patrolling off the northern coast of Norway when the officer of the watch sighted the conning tower of a 500-ton U-boat at three-and-a-half miles distance. The Commanding Officer, Lieutenant Commander R. Bannar-Martin, RN, closed to attack. The target was zigzagging about forty degrees every six minutes in a flat calm sea. A full salvo of four torpedoes was fired but none found the target. The German lookouts must have been particularly alert; having identified the torpedo runs, the U-boat took immediate evasive action and foiled the attack. Yet another unsuccessful patrol!

The next success was to be at the hand of *Venturer* and her Commanding Officer Lieutenant Launders on 11 September, as they patrolled off Lister in south-west Norway. Early that morning they sighted the 678-ton merchant ship *Vang*, tracked her for some time, then attacked and sank her with three of the four torpedoes fired finding their target – an excellent result from such a patient approach. Just two days later she attempted to repeat the success when she made an unsuccessful torpedo attack on the 499-ton merchant vessel *Force* under escort from two armed trawlers. Again a full salvo was fired, but on this occasion without initial success, as one torpedo exploded prematurely and the remainder failed to find the target. This was not to be the end of the affair because the crew of the *Force*, having identified the torpedo tracks, immediately abandoned ship. *Venturer* surfaced and engaged the vessel by gunfire but after firing just five rounds the submarine was obliged to abort the attack and dive to avoid the attention of the shore batteries. Whilst the initial torpedo attack had not been successful they had the satisfaction of knowing that the brief gun engagement had been sufficient to sink the *Force*.

Viking and *Venturer* were to continue the fight throughout the final months of 1944 with some degree of success. On 14 October

Viking was on patrol off Fleinvaer in the Bodo area of the Norwegian coast when she sighted a convoy northbound under escort from three armed trawlers. The convoy was closed and attacked, which resulted in the 1,287-ton merchant vessel *Standard* being torpedoed and sunk. This attack was followed by a counter-attack by the escorting trawlers and a hunt of one-and-a-half hours was maintained, but they made contact with the submarine on just two occasions. Six depth charges were dropped but they were so far from the submarine that she was never in jeopardy.

More joy came for Lieutenant Launders and *Venturer* on 11 November as she stood off Tromsø waiting to commence a special operation (the details of which will be covered later). At 08.45 she sighted the 769-ton U-boat *U771* under the command of *Oberleutnant* H. Block. *Venturer* quickly moved into an attacking position and fired off four torpedoes – one of which hit and sank the *U771*. The quick and deadly attack had taken just six minutes from the sighting to the sinking of the U-boat.

Venturer was to continue this sort of success throughout the winter months of 1945 and on 20 January, whilst patrolling the southern approaches to Stavanger, a convoy of three medium-sized merchant ships, under escort from four armed trawlers, was located hugging the snow-covered coastline. At this time *Venturer* had one engine out of operation due to defects, which was likely to make any attack very difficult and force Lieutenant Launders to decide quickly on his plan of attack. Should he fire from a distance whilst on the surface giving him the best visibility or should he dive and close with the hope that the visibility would be good enough for him to attack submerged? The decision was to attack from a distance, and a full salvo of four torpedoes was fired from 3,500 yards. It is believed a hit was made but this has never been confirmed.

Just two days later, in the bright winter moonlight of 20 January, another convoy consisting of three merchant ships and four armed trawlers was sighted, this time off Skudesnes. Lieutenant Launders dived the submarine and attacked submerged. He fired his remaining four torpedoes and reaped the reward when the merchant vessel *Stockholm* of 618 tons was hit and sunk. Having expended her full quota of torpedoes *Venturer* turned and headed for home.

February 1945 saw *Venturer* maintain her luck as she returned to patrol off Bergen. At 09.32 on 9 February, whilst patrolling the approaches to Bergen, the very faint HE of a diesel-powered vessel was heard by Leading Seaman Head, the Asdic's operator. Further reports of this were made but nothing was seen until 10.50 when the officer of the watch, Lieutenant A.T. Chalmers, RN, made a prolonged search on the reported bearing. He saw what he described as a thin mast, which turned out to be the periscope of *U864* under the command of *Korvettenkapitän* R.R. Wolfram. For the next one-and-a-half hours, Lieutenant Launders and Leading Seaman Head tracked the *U864* until, at 12.12, four torpedoes were fired. The *U864* was hit and a loud explosion was heard in *Venturer* followed by breaking-up noises and later the sound of three of the torpedoes exploding some distance away as they struck the shore. Not to worry – one torpedo had done its job. *Venturer* approached the position of the target to discover a large amount of oil and debris on the surface, which included a container carried by larger U-boats to store helicopter lookout kites. Ben Bryant, Captain (S) Third Submarine Flotilla, commented upon this attack by reporting:

> Lengthy remarks have been made about this attack since it is believed to be unique. *Venturer*'s was a carefully thought out and finely judged attack, lasting two hours, and owing to the education of the enemy she was unable to transmit, and therefore had no assistance from Asdic ranges. Whilst good fortune must inevitably play its part in this sort of attack which cannot expect to be often repeated, nevertheless, the highest skill and efficiency was required. That the British submarine proved so superior to her German counterpart at every move of the game is most satisfactory.[7]

This is the only time in history that a submarine has sunk another whilst both vessels were submerged. *Venturer* is also the only submarine in history to sink two German U-boats whilst on active service. There being no further incident, *Venturer* returned to base.

This was not the last the Germans were to hear of *Venturer* and Lieutenant Launders, as she sailed from Lerwick on 14 March to patrol off Frohavet and the approaches to Trondheimfjord. It was in this position at 05.45 on 19 March that she sighted the 998-ton merchant vessel *Sirius* in convoy with three more merchant ships, all being escorted by five anti-submarine vessels. Lieutenant Launders was called from his bunk and, after manoeuvring into an attacking position, a full salvo of four torpedoes was dispatched at 06.33. The submarine then dived deep and withdrew along the coastline. As she did so the crew heard the results of their labours. First was one large explosion as a torpedo found its target followed by the noises of a ship breaking up. Then they heard another very loud explosion followed by loud rumbling sounds as the ship continued to break-up. The convoy escorts made a search for the submarine lasting over an hour but they had anticipated she would withdraw seawards and so failed to locate her.

That was the final target to be sunk by British 'U' class submarines in the Second World War. One last patrol was carried out by *Venturer* and Lieutenant Launders. It was her thirteenth and as such was to prove unsuccessful. Having sailed from Lerwick on 17 April 1945, the only targets worthy of attack were trawlers, until 24 April when a small merchant ship under escort was sighted. A full salvo of four torpedoes was fired but all missed and exploded on the coast astern of the convoy, which continued on its way unperturbed. The final attack came on 25 April with *Venturer* patrolling the mouth of the Skudenesfjord, when she sighted two anti-submarine trawlers. The submarine manoeuvred inshore of them and found them to be at anchor alongside each other. One torpedo was fired but no explosion was heard and the Asdic operator reported the torpedo HE to have ceased, which indicated a torpedo failure. Thus a faulty torpedo thwarted the final attack on enemy shipping. At the conclusion of this patrol Captain Ben Bryant, Captain (S) Third Submarine Flotilla commented:

This patrol was carried out with Lieutenant Launders' usual skill and determination; but on this his thirteenth patrol in *Venturer* fortune was unkind. The attack on the trawlers showed determination of a high order, and is considered a fitting end to the operational activities of the Third Submarine Flotilla, which has a proud record of endeavour since 1939, which has cost the enemy dear. It seems probable that it is the last operational patrol of our very successful 'U' class.[8]

On 8 May 1945 German High Command signalled the German Navy with the order that the German land, sea and air forces were to surrender unconditionally. This brought an end to both the hostilities in Europe and the need for further production of 'U' class submarines. Nine already in commission were placed in immediate reserve and the remainder were deployed throughout the world to perform their principle role in anti-submarine training activities.

On 13 May Rear Admiral (Submarines) sent the following message:

> At the close of the German War, Admiral (Submarines) contemplates with pride the contribution which our submarines, in this and especially previous years, have been able to make to the disruption of the German sea communications in Home Waters.[9]

The 'U' class submarines contributed to this success by the sinking of two escort vessels accompanying *Tirpitz*, one of which deliberately protected *Tirpitz* by placing herself in the line of torpedo fire. Two U-boats and fourteen merchant ships with a total tonnage of more than 31,000 tons were sunk, a modest return for operating in an area which regularly had little daylight and with sea conditions which did not lend themselves to the particular strengths of these submarines. Losses were also suffered as two submarines, *Undine*, and the Norwegian-manned *Uredd*, were lost in conflict. Mishaps accounted for the loss of three further submarines, *Unity*, *Umpire* and *Vandal*.

Notes

1. National Archives Kew Reference: ADM 234/380.
2. National Archives Kew Reference: ADM 199/373.
3. National Archives Kew Reference: ADM 199/373.
4. *The Fighting Tenth* by John Wingate, DSC, RN Rtd.
5. National Archives Kew Reference: ADM 199/1825.
6. National Archives Kew Reference: ADM 199/1225.
7. National Archives Kew Reference: ADM 199/1815.
8. National Archives Kew Reference: ADM 199/1815.
9. National Archives Kew Reference: ADM 234/380.

III

THE MEDITERRANEAN: PRE *OPERATION TORCH*

The Allied Invasion of North Africa 8 November 1942

The 'U' class submarines at Malta continue to take a steady toll of shipping proceeding on the Italy – Tripoli Route.
Admiral Sir Andrew Cunningham,
C.-in-C., Mediterranean, June 1941.[1]

Having completed their period of work-up and one or two war patrols in home waters, the British-operated 'U' class submarines were dispatched to the Mediterranean – a far more productive hunting ground with a restricted patrol time. This theatre of operations was to see many successes and losses as the full story unfolded. In pursuit of the original objective there were some spectacular successes in the interception of enemy supplies (both men and materials) that inhibited the Axis forces in North Africa, a fact acknowledged in a report by German Naval Command dated 9 September, 1941 when they wrote: 'Now, as formerly, the most dangerous British weapon in the Mediterranean is the submarine.'[2]

It was in October 1940 when the decision was taken to deploy three 'U' class submarines to the Mediterranean – *Ursula, Upright* and *Utmost*. The sailing of *Upright* and *Utmost* was delayed pending the result of their 'singing propeller' trials and so *Ursula* led the way to Gibraltar, arriving on 30 October to join the 1st Submarine Flotilla. However, the honour of carrying out the first

Mediterranean war patrol fell to *Upright* which patrolled the north-west coastline of Sicily en route from Gibraltar to Malta, arriving in Malta on 4 December 1940. On completion of this first patrol the Commanding Officer, Lieutenant J.E. Brooks, RN, made several constructive comments in the General Section of his patrol report. He wrote:

> Seamen and stokers mess in the torpedo compartment which is also the only available stowage for the majority of the three weeks provisions carried for patrol. This compartment suffers from excessive 'sweating' and is permanently damp. The cortiscene of the deck is completely sodden and requires constant renewal. Hammocks cannot be kept dry and bunks are not provided. Under these conditions it is considered that 12 days at sea is a maximum compatible with any degree of efficiency. In the North Sea patrols were normally 12 days from harbour to harbour with 14 days provisions on board. Bad weather has a noticeable depressing effect on the ship's company as sleep becomes impossible and even the old hands are seasick.[3]

Captain (S) First Submarine Flotilla, Captain S.M. Raw, RN, responded thus:

> This is the first patrol carried out by one of the 'U' class since their arrival in the Mediterranean and the remarks as to their performance and endurance are of great interest but will require confirmation. Living conditions seem to be most unsatisfactory, but there is no alternative accommodation; these difficulties will be increased in the hot weather.[4]

A further three submarines quickly followed as *Unique, Upholder* and *Usk* arrived in Gibraltar on 23 December 1940. These were to have very different introductions to the Mediterranean. *Usk* limped into Malta from her first patrol with a main bearing out of action having run hot and been shut down. Inspection of the problem found that carborundum had been put into the reserve lubricating oil tank as deliberate sabotage, which was suspected to have taken place at the builder's yard. *Unique* on the other hand was to mount the first attack by a 'U' class submarine in the Mediterranean but, unfortunately, it did not lead to the first success. She was patrolling the Kerkenah Bank on the western approaches to Tripoli when she attacked a 2,000-ton coaster by firing just one torpedo that missed the target. Captain S.M. Raw, commanding the First Submarine Flotilla, had some very strong views on submarine attacks by one torpedo. He commented on this attack thus:

> It is my considered opinion that, if a target is worth attacking at all, two torpedoes should always be used unless the target vessel is stopped.[5]

January 1941 started with the arrival in Malta of Commander George Simpson to assume the role of Commander (Submarines) Malta on a day when there were no submarines in attendance. The month ended with success for the new 'U' class submarines in the Mediterranean when *Upholder* struck the first blow. She was patrolling the western approaches to Tripoli (again along the Kerkenah Bank) when she sighted the German ship *Duisburg*, of 7,889 tons. Two torpedoes were to inflict such damage that the target required a tow back into Tripoli where she was out of action for four months under repair. This was particularly pleasing for the Commanding Officer, Lieutenant Commander Malcolm David Wanklyn, RN, as just two days before he had made an unsuccessful attack on a convoy of three merchant ships by firing four torpedoes from an undesirable range. He had not been able to reach the optimum attacking position due to the lack of surface speed. This lack of speed of the 'U' class submarine was to frustrate other submarine commanders in future attacks.

In February 1941 Captain S.M. Raw, RN, assumed operational control of all submarines in the Mediterranean, deploying the submarines along the Tunisian coastline between Tripoli and Misurata to intercept all vessels on the western approaches to Tripoli. The C.-in-C., Mediterranean proposed all submarines should have their rest periods in Malta thus reducing the distance to and from their patrol areas and consequently the length of time spent at sea.

At the beginning of the month many target vessels were sighted, but of the five separate attacks mounted none were successful due to torpedo malfunction or incorrect estimations of speed and course. *Utmost*, Lieutenant Commander R.D. Cayley, RN, having recently assumed command, was to see the first success of the month when, on 12 February, whilst patrolling off the eastern coast of Tunisia, she sighted a three-ship convoy with one destroyer in attendance. She attacked and damaged the 8,000-ton *Galilea*, with a depth-charge counter-attack of more than ninety minutes, but no damage was inflicted. Three hours later she returned to the scene and saw the *Galilea* down by the stern with all engines stopped. Lieutenant Commander Cayley believed she was going to sink but this was not so and the *Galilea* was salvaged to be repaired. It was certainly unfortunate as this was the only successful attack during this period when there were so many targets available. *Unique* arrived in Malta on 18 February and her Commanding Officer, Lieutenant A.F. Collett, RN, reported sighting thirty-eight vessels between 8 and 16 February, of which thirty were considered to be viable targets. Only on one occasion was he able to mount an attack that was not only unsuccessful but could easily have been fatal. Four torpedoes were fired at a merchant vessel, apparently unescorted at the time; three were heard to explode as they hit the seabed. The fourth torpedo had gyro failure and turned back on *Unique* and was heard to career over the after-casing before running out of control – a near miss and almost an own goal.

The next success came to Lieutenant A.R. Hezlet, RN, commanding *Ursula* when, on the 22nd, he attacked and damaged the 5,788-ton *Sabbia* in the Gulf of Gabes. The *Sabbia* was repaired and carried on in service until July 1943 when she was sunk by the Dutch-manned *Dolfijn*, an incident that will be referred to later. Further success was to follow on the very next day. *Upright*, commanded by Lieutenant E.D. Norman, RN, was in the Gulf of Gabes south-east of Sfax when he attacked and damaged the 2,365-ton tanker *Silvia Tripcovitch*. The tanker was not as lucky as the *Sabbia* because her life was only extended a few hours before being sunk by the submarine *Regent*.

Lieutenant Norman was to have greater success later in the patrol. At 2.30 in the morning of 25 February as they patrolled the Kerkenah Bank, the officer of the watch, Sub Lieutenant D. Swanston, sighted a convoy of warships consisting of two cruisers – *Armando Diaz* and *Barbiano* – in company with one destroyer. He fired a full salvo of four torpedoes and the 5,000-ton 6-inch cruiser *Armando Diaz* was dispatched to the seabed. An insignificant counter-attack took place before the accompanying destroyer returned to the scene to assist in the recovery of survivors from the cruiser. This major strike resulted in congratulatory telegrams for the submarine from both the C.-in C. Mediterranean and the Admiralty.

In March 1941 Captain (S) First Submarine Flotilla reported that he intended operating the majority of submarines during dark nights to give them better opportunities to charge their batteries and to become more productive. This resulted in some spectacular interceptions of German troops being ferried to the North African campaign in accord with the primary objective. The first to strike was *Utmost*, commanded by Lieutenant Commander Cayley, when on 9 March he was on patrol in the Gulf of Hammamet. During the forenoon, a convoy of two merchant ships with one escorting vessel was sighted. The escort was allowed to pass just 200 yards from the submerged submarine before *Utmost* fired three torpedoes that resulted in one hit, which sank the 5,775-ton *Capo Vita* in just twelve minutes. The explosion was such that *Utmost* was lifted bodily and shaken from stem to stern. Lieutenant Commander Cayley believed that this explosion was the result of explosives on board the *Capo Vita* being detonated by the torpedo. There was no counter-attack of any consequence, as this would have caused more damage to the survivors in the water than the submarine. The escorting vessel dropped just six depth charges and made off to assist the survivors. This was a particularly telling attack as the *Capo Vita* had been carrying a substantial number of troops to assist the German African campaign – a significant loss to Rommel.

This was compounded on 28 March when, as a result of intelligence that German units were to embark on transports at

Salerno en route for North Africa, *Utmost* was re-deployed to patrol the western approaches to Tripoli off Kuriat Island. At 21.35 the convoy was sighted; it consisted of six heavily laden merchant vessels under escort from two destroyers. An attack was mounted and a full salvo of four torpedoes was fired as the ships formed an unbroken line against the horizon. Two torpedoes found their mark; the German troop ship *Heraklea*, of 1,927 tons was sunk and the German ship *Ruhr* was damaged. There was no counter-attack as the escorts were busy stopping and starting as they tried to rescue the survivors from the sea.

Not to be outdone, Lieutenant Collett in *Unique* sank the merchant ship *Felicia*, 2,548 tons, by torpedo off the Kerkenah Islands on 10 March. March was such a successful month that the BBC announced the successes on the Tripoli shipping route by the submarines based at Malta. This was to the chagrin of the C.-in-C., Mediterranean who immediately signalled his regret at this announcement. He pointed out that this type of reporting would only increase the difficulties experienced by the Malta-based submarines. They were already having their rest periods disturbed by the intensive air attacks by the Luftwaffe, which were later to cause serious damage to submarines alongside in the harbours.

With the successes of March 1941 the 'U' class submarine had started to show its teeth. The effect on enemy shipping was to be increased as their strength increased. April saw four more of their class join in the fight as *Undaunted*, *Unbeaten*, *Union* and *Urge* passed through Gibraltar to join the First Submarine Flotilla. This was against the loss of *Usk*. On 18 April 1941, the day before *Usk* sailed to patrol off Cape Marittimo, Sicily, Able Seaman Ivor Gwyn Williams wrote a letter to his girlfriend Betty to be opened in the event of his death:

Dearest Betty,
    Betty, my darling, I think that you won't mind me calling you that for the last time, as I expect by now my sister has informed you that I have died in fighting for ours and other countries. But I may say, darling, that my last thoughts

46

were of my family and you, and I love you while there is a breath in my body.

I take this, the last opportunity of wishing you the happiest married life which it is possible for two people to have. And only wish it was I. Also give my wishes for a happy and long life to your relations, and with these few words I close, wishing you all the very best.

Your most loving friend.

Gwyn.[6]

Usk sailed from Malta on 19 April 1941 to patrol off Cape Marittimo and was presumed lost off Cape Bon, Tunisia. Whilst the circumstances of this loss are purely conjecture, it has been established that the submarine had been subjected to intense anti-submarine activities off Cape Marittimo. At 21.00 on 25 April the Commanding Officer, Lieutenant G.P. Darling, RN, signalled to the Commander First Submarine Flotilla:

IMMEDIATE.
Commander S.1 from HMS *Usk*.
Intense A/S activity in area. Withdrawing to CAPE BON or further south as directed.[7]

The loss has never been confirmed as there was no claim of success by the Italian or German authorities but it is reasonable to presume that *Usk* struck a mine off Cape Bon. The decision that the confidential books had not been compromised and did not need replacing reinforced this opinion. This was Lieutenant Darling's first patrol in command of *Usk* and Commander George Simpson stressed that he was fully conversant with all the relevant intelligence and the submarine was 100 per cent ready for war. Unfortunately the minefield between Cape Bon and Sicily had been recently reinforced and extended by the laying of an additional 1,500 mines between 20 and 24 April.

Action during the first two weeks of April was not blessed with success. Five targets were attacked using sixteen torpedoes but none found the target. The reasons given were poor estimations of speed and course together with torpedo failures and malfunctions. Much of these failures were put down to the type of torpedo being used. With all these submarines based at Malta it had created a shortage of torpedoes designed specifically for submarines. Type IV torpedoes, designed for use by destroyers, were being adapted.

Lieutenant Commander Wanklyn in *Upholder* was en route to Malta on 21 April when he sighted a convoy of five large ships escorted by three destroyers off Pantellaria Island. All torpedoes had been expended but Lieutenant Commander Wanklyn felt he must take some action against such an enemy force. It was midway through the middle watch when the convoy was sighted and at 02.12 he fired two star shells which fell in front of the convoy. The convoy immediately turned and ran for cover as they believed this to be the forerunner of a surface force attack.

Wanklyn continued to take the fight to the Germans and sailed from Malta on 21 April to patrol the areas around Kerkenah and Lampedusa Islands. *Upholder*'s first attack came on the 25th when she sighted the *Antonietta Laura*, 5,428 tons, fully laden with nitrates bound for Italy. Just two torpedoes were necessary. One found the target and the resultant explosion was so ferocious that most of the light bulbs in the submarine were smashed, but it was six hours before the *Antonietta Laura* sank. *Upholder* was instructed to investigate the possibilities of destroying a merchant vessel and destroyer that had been located aground on Kerkenah Bank. The following day she sighted the 2,452-ton German motor transport vessel *Arta* but Wanklyn waited for the appropriate time to attack. After dark he took *Upholder* alongside and had the *Arta* boarded. She was fully laden with lorries, cars and motor cycles and had two holds converted to accommodate troops who had obviously suffered heavy casualties. The boarding party took possession of all the papers in both the captain's cabin and radio room together with samples of arms, flags and helmets, and a Staff Officer's abandoned picnic basket. The demolition charges were set and the ship abandoned with *Upholder* standing off to watch the fire spread to the lorries and, with the *Arta* obviously well alight, the submarine withdrew. The following day *Upholder* attempted to approach the abandoned destroyer but the water was too shallow so it was not possible to board her and it was also considered impracticable to use torpedoes. The attack was aborted, *Upholder* withdrew seawards and resumed her patrol duties.

Upholder was not finished and as May 1941 began she opened her account. She was on patrol in the Gulf of Gabes when a large convoy of five merchant ships under the escort of four destroyers was sighted, apparently en route from Sfax. A full salvo of four torpedoes was fired as the silhouettes of the two largest ships of the convoy converged; both ships were hit. The 2,586-ton *Arcturus* sank immediately and it was obvious that the 7,836-ton *Leverkusen* had been seriously damaged. *Upholder* retired graciously from the scene albeit temporarily since, returning three hours later, she found the *Leverkusen* still afloat and accompanied by one destroyer. They were trailed for three hours before two further torpedoes were put into *Leverkusen* and within the hour she was lost. *Upholder* withdrew and set course for Malta to complete a successful patrol. Commander George Simpson commented:

> Lieutenant Commander Wanklyn has always acted with skill and determination in his operations in the Mediterranean, and I consider that this successful patrol is deserving of immediate recognition, and recommendations for awards are being forwarded.[8]

However, Wanklyn and *Upholder* were to suffer a loss of personnel during their time in Malta. On 9 May, whilst preparing for sea, they were loading torpedoes when the torpedo loaded into Number 3 tube had a hot run resulting in the deaths of Lieutenant C.H. Read, RN, and Petty Officer J.F. Carter.

In his Operational Appreciation for the month of April, C.-in-C., Mediterranean wrote:

> The 'U' class submarines working from Malta started to get their hands in and to be more successful and a number of enemy ships were sunk.[9]

In future months he was to enjoy a far greater level of damage inflicted on enemy supply lines as the number of submarines operating in the Mediterranean increased along with the greater expertise of the Commanding Officers.

Undaunted, under the command of Lieutenant J.F. Livesay, RN, became the second 'U' class to be lost in the Mediterranean conflict when on her first patrol she went down patrolling off Tripoli. On 1 May 700 mines were laid by enemy forces on the western approaches to Tripoli and there was a submarine sighting report received on 7 May giving the location as thirty-four miles north of Tripoli. So whilst the actual reason for the loss has never been confirmed, it is most likely that she struck a mine some time between 7 and 10 May.

On 11 May *Unbeaten* sailed from Malta to patrol off Khoms on the eastern approaches to Tripoli. This was the first patrol in the central Mediterranean for Lieutenant E.A. Woodward, RN, and he was instructed that all schooners were suspect as they could be acting as 'Q' ships, and it was inadvisable to engage them with gunfire unless conditions were to the advantage of the submarine. His first encounter came on 14 May when a convoy of schooners under escort by an armed trawler was sighted off Khoms. The largest schooner, of some 1,000 tons, bringing up the rear was attacked by torpedo; three were fired and one hit the schooner. Subsequent periscope examination established that the schooner had disappeared with the remaining vessels continuing on their way. The next day *Unbeaten* stood off and watched another schooner of about 800 tons anchor at Khoms. Lieutenant Woodward took the boat within 700 yards, surfaced and engaged the schooner by gunfire, sinking it after five of the twenty rounds fired found their target. Another six rounds were seen to ricochet into the town itself.

Lieutenant Woodward was not yet finished, and on 19 May he sighted the 6,000-ton *Giovinezza* escorted by one destroyer. He carried out an attack that almost ended with disastrous results. Three torpedoes were fired at the *Giovinezza*. The first exploded on the seabed just eight seconds after being fired, forcing the submarine to lift some fifteen feet, although fortunately she was able to remain submerged. The second ran true, hitting and sinking the *Giovinezza*. The third torpedo was fired whilst the submarine's trim was affected by the explosion from the first; as

50

a result the torpedo went straight down to the bottom, exploded and forced the stern of the submarine to break the surface. The subsequent counter-attack lasted for over one hour with twenty-seven depth charges being dropped. The submarine was hunted continually for the next eight hours as she lay silent on the seabed, unable to make any movement or sound without drawing the destroyer towards her. Lieutenant Woodward later reported that the morale of the crew had been exceptional and that they spent these hours enjoying a meal and getting some rest. The incident *did* result in some slight damage to lights and fittings but nothing too serious.

Urge (Lieutenant Tomkinson commanding) was next to take up the cudgels as she patrolled off Cape Bon. On the morning of 20 May the discharge of a single depth charge was heard to the north, the sign that a convoy was due, obviously en route to Tripoli. It had become common knowledge that the Italian Navy used this system of dropping depth charges in front of a convoy in the hope of dissuading submarines from attacking. Commander George Simpson described this system of convoy defence as ridiculous as it served no purpose other than to give Allied submarines early warning of an approaching convoy. This convoy was of particular value, consisting as it did of one troop ship, a medium-sized merchant ship and two tankers. The importance of this convoy to the enemy could be seen from the escorting vessels; these four transports were being escorted by five destroyers in close escort with a covering force of two cruisers and a further three destroyers. This was the heaviest escort to have been observed up to that time. *Urge* closed the convoy and fired a full salvo of four torpedoes, just 300 yards from the nearest destroyer, and scored three hits. These hits led to the sinking of the 5,165-ton troop ship *Zeffiro* and serious damage to the 4,800-ton merchant ship *Perseo*. The submarine was then taken to 278 feet (well below the recommended diving depth of 250 feet) to avoid the short, sharp, depth-charge counter-attack that followed. Lieutenant Tomkinson was later to comment that he felt the curtailment of the depth-charging was due to the troops from the transports being in the water.

The next day was to see further success for *Urge*. As she

patrolled off Lampedusa she attacked a naval unit comprising two cruisers, three destroyers and one torpedo boat. This attack resulted in the loss, to the enemy, of the torpedo boat *Curtatone*. Having expended her full quota of torpedoes, *Urge* returned to Malta leaving *Upholder* patrolling the eastern coast of Sicily on the southern approaches to the Straits of Messina.

This patrol was to see the remainder of the successes for the month of May – starting on the 23rd – when she sighted two southbound tankers fully laden, believed to be Vichy French. Lieutenant Commander Wanklyn had just thirty seconds to decide on an attack and in his usual aggressive pose, he fired three torpedoes, hitting the 5,000-ton tanker *Capitaine Damiani*, causing such damage that she had to be towed into Messina for repairs. *Upholder* went deep and withdrew.

The next day was to see even greater success for Lieutenant Commander Wanklyn and *Upholder* as they patrolled off Cape Passero, Sicily. A convoy of three large liners was sighted sailing southwards under the protection of at least four destroyers. *Upholder* closed and fired the last two torpedoes at the largest liner as she was silhouetted against the afterglow of the setting sun. Both struck the liner *Conte Rossee* (17,879 tons) as she carried 2,729 Italian soldiers to North Africa. The liner sank with the loss of 1,300 of these troops. The submarine was then subjected to a concerted depth-charge attack during the first fifteen minutes, in which thirty-seven depth charges were dropped – none too close to inflict much damage. These types of attacks had different effects on the submarine personnel. On one occasion the submarine sat it out on the bottom and the crew enjoyed a meal and took the chance of getting some rest, but on this occasion, with the submarine at 150 feet and taking avoiding action, the signalman was so stressed he tried to get out of the conning-tower hatch.

Upholder returned to Malta, closing the activities for the month, to receive the following comment from the C-in-C:

HMS *UPHOLDER*, under Lieutenant Commander M.D. Wanklyn's command, is inflicting heavy losses on the enemy. Great credit is due to all on board.[10]

He went on to include the matters in his Monthly Operational Assessment when he wrote:

> Submarines had scored very successful results during the month. In particular *UPHOLDER* sank 7 ships including the *CONTE ROSSO*. *URGE* sank 2 merchant ships and a destroyer. *UNBEATEN* sank 2 ships. There were losses; *USK* with 32 crew and *UNDAUNTED* with 34 crew.[11]

June 1941 saw the consolidation of submarine operations in the Mediterranean. The C.-in-C. requested as many submarines as could be spared to be made available, as there were so many opportunities to inflict considerable losses on enemy shipping as they attempted to supply the Afrika Korps through its narrow channels. The result was that during the month the strength of 'U' class submarines was increased by two: *P32* and *P33*. Unfortunately *P32* arrived at Gibraltar having been damaged from an air attack whilst off Cape Finisterre, and which required a considerable amount of repair work lasting six weeks before she was able to join the fray. The C.-in-C., Mediterranean congratulated the submarines on their contribution to date. He sent a message that said:

> I fully appreciate the heavy call which is being made on you all but I am confident you will realise the necessity and meet it with the ready efficiency you have always displayed.[12]

He did, however, sound a warning regarding the availability of torpedoes at Malta when he reported the stock to be just sixty-four, when the monthly requirement for the 'U' class submarines operating from Malta was sixty.

The Admiralty originated the following signal:

1. The steadily increasing scale of success achieved by submarines operating in the Mediterranean indicates a very high standard of accuracy and resolution.

2. If this scale of attack can be maintained or increased it is probable enemy operations will be hampered owing to lack of shipping.

3. Congratulations to crews and all Naval Attachés whose efforts contribute to such successful results.[13]

The submarines continued to patrol the routes from Italy to North Africa and on 3 June Lieutenant Collett, in *Unique*, was off the island of Lampedusa when he noticed various small merchant vessels entering the harbour. On reconnoitring the harbour he saw one particular merchant ship lying in a vulnerable position if he could breach the boom. He fired two torpedoes; one passed the boom and exploded on the shore, but the second found its target and hit and sank the 736-ton *Arsia* as she lay at anchor in the harbour.

June was not a good time to operate submarines in the Mediterranean with the sea flat calm and as smooth as glass. These conditions were the reason for submarines being sighted early as they made their approaches to convoys, only to be driven away by concerted depth-charge attacks from the escorting ships. Both *Urge* and *Unique* became the recipients of such attacks, each consisting of more that sixty depth charges; fortunately neither attack was accurate and neither submarine suffered any damage.

The conditions, whilst not conducive to submarine warfare, did not deter submarine commanders from plying their trade on enemy shipping. Lieutenant R.M. Galloway, RN, in *Union* was patrolling off the island of Pantellaria on 22 June when he heard the usual intermittent depth-charging which announced the approach of a convoy. He located the convoy and saw a fully laden Italian merchant ship southbound under escort. Closing, he fired three torpedoes that struck and sank the 1,004-ton *Pietro Querini*. Lieutenant Commander Cayley, in *Utmost*, was to continue the fight as he patrolled the north Sicilian coast off Cape Orlando and on the 26th he torpedoed and sank the 4,080-ton *Enrico Costa*.

The experiences of submarine commanders were not always concerned with attack and counter-attack, as Lieutenant Woodward was to learn during his June patrol in the southern approaches to the Straits of Messina. When *Unbeaten* sailed from Malta on 11 June there were some doubts over the health of Leading Stoker Sturman. He had been ill for some time prior to sailing but had insisted he was perfectly well and specifically requested to remain with the boat as she sailed to patrol. Unfortunately this was not the case and just two days out it became apparent all was not well when the Leading Stoker collapsed and died, subsequently to be buried at sea. Although everything had been done to save Leading Stoker Sturman, his death had a detrimental effect on crew morale. The opinion of the base Medical Officers was that he died of haemorrhage of the brain.

The opening days of July showed more success with *Urge*, under Lieutenant Tomkinson, opening the account on the 2nd. He was checking the progress of work on the damaged railway line outside Taormina on the eastern coast of Sicily when he sighted the 6,696-ton *Brarena*. A full salvo of four torpedoes committed *Brarena* to the depths. This was followed the next day when Lieutenant Commander Wanklyn in *Upholder* attacked and sank the 5,870-ton *Laura C.*

Patrols were maintained along the western approaches to Tripoli that resulted in more successes for the submarines. *P33*, under Lieutenant R.D. Whiteway-Wilkinson, RN, was off the island of Pantellaria on 15 July on her first patrol out of Malta when five northbound merchant ships, escorted by six destroyers, were sighted. These were attacked and the 5,293-ton merchant ship *Barbarigo* was sunk. The attack was followed by a ferocious counter-attack by the escorting warships lasting one-and-a-half hours and consisting of 116 depth charges. This was more accurate than usual and the submarine was damaged, spiralling down to 350 feet, deeper than any 'U' class submarine had gone before. The pressure hull creaked and rivets sprang but the submarine survived. She cut short the patrol and returned to Malta. Whilst closer to Tripoli, at Marsa Zuaga, Lieutenant Woodward in *Unbeaten* intercepted two schooners and engaged them with gunfire. Forty-three rounds were fired; fifteen hit one schooner, which immediately sank, and five hit the second, but Lieutenant Woodward was not able to observe the final result as he was forced deep by an approaching aircraft.

The month of July saw another deep dive take place, again inadvertently. Lieutenant J.S. Wraith, RN, was on his second patrol in *Upright* off Cape Spartivento, Sicily, when he came upon the most unusual target. About 1,500 yards off the coast he found a large floating dock being towed under escort. He closed and attacked, firing a full salvo at what he considered to be an important economic target; he heard two explosions and believed he had scored a hit. He was not able to observe the result as he was busy avoiding the counterattack from the escorting torpedo boats. As Lieutenant Wraith avoided the counter-attack he became subject to an unusual Mediterranean phenomenon of freshwater springs off the coast of Italy. This decreased the density of seawater and sent the submarine plummeting to 340 feet which had to be countered by blowing main ballast, putting the submarine in greater danger with three enemy warships hunting her above. *Upright* survived the ordeal only to find it had all been in vain. The torpedoes had exploded as they struck the towline and the floating dock reached port safely.

The final two strikes for the month of July 1941 both came on the 28th when *Upholder* and *Utmost* saw success. Lieutenant Commander Wanklyn was the first. As he patrolled off Marittimo he attacked two Italian cruisers – the *Guiseppe Garibaldi* and the *Raimondo Montecuccoli* – both with a destroyer escort. His salvo of four torpedoes hit and damaged the *Guiseppe Garibaldi* but he was obliged to withdraw to avoid the counter-attack that followed. As a result he was not able to reload and finish the job. Lieutenant Commander Cayley in *Utmost* was on patrol in the Gulf of Santa Eufemia when he attacked and sank the 1,466-ton *Federico*, as one of the two torpedoes fired found its mark.

On 20 July the enemy struck back with the loss of *Union*. Lieutenant Galloway was on patrol south-west of Pantellaria when he closed to attack a small convoy of two salvage vessels and a supply ship under escort by the Italian torpedo boat *Circe* commanded by *Capitano di Fregato* Carlo Unger di Lowenberg. *Capitano* Lowenberg sighted the tracks of the two torpedoes fired by *Union* and attacked down those self-same tracks. Standing on the bridge of the *Circe* he saw the periscope of a submarine and he is reported to have said:

But the periscope was not outside the water. I sighted it under us very well at a few metres because the water was limpid, and naturally I went there quickly to ram it. But it was already too deep and so I scattered the bombs. An escorting aircraft dropped other bombs.[14]

There was sufficient oil to convince the *Capitano* that the submarine had been damaged and he continued with his escorting duties to Trapani. *Union* had been sunk with the loss of thirty-two lives.

Further losses were inflicted with both *P32* and *P33* being lost during the month of August. *P33*, under Lieutenant Whiteway-Wilkinson, was lost, believed to have been mined having sailed from Malta on 6 August to patrol north-west of Tripoli and failing to return. The cause of the loss has never been confirmed.

The loss of *P32* has created some controversy, having struck a mine off Tripoli and sinking with just two survivors, Coxswain Petty Officer Kirk and the Commanding Officer, Lieutenant Commander D. Abdy, RN. In view of these circumstances, the author feels it only right to print Lieutenant Commander Abdy's report of 30 March 1943, in which he sets out the circumstances of the loss:

Sir,
1.   I regret to report the circumstances relating to the sinking of H.M. Submarine *P.32* under my command on 18th August, 1941 and the subsequent escape by Petty Officer Kirk and myself.
2.   On 12th August, 1941 P.32 left Malta for patrol off Tripoli, east of Longitude 13 deg. 15' East. The passage was uneventful except that during the night of 13th/14th August an air raid over Tripoli was clearly visible from about 40 miles away. During the forenoon of the 14th I sighted Ras Tajura and closed the coast and proceeded to patrol to the eastward keeping just outside the 20-fathom line.
3.   During the afternoon of the 14th I sighted a small westbound convoy consisting of one escort destroyer (*Orsa* or *Ostro*), a merchant ship 1000 tons, 2 schooners

57

approximately 200 tons. I took avoiding action so as not to compromise my position so very early in the patrol; also I had been instructed that eastbound convoys were far more valuable than westbound convoys and the latter should only be attacked after due consideration. Later I received a signal ordering *P.32* to patrol in position 33 deg. 11' N 13 deg 15' E. This was executed by the morning of the 15th August.

4.   Asdic contact at 0820/18 with *Unique* is confirmed (V.A.M.s 1948B/28/8/1941). I had also attempted to gain contact with *P.33* but without result. From 0900 to 1330 I heard continual underwater explosions which I thought to be an enemy convoy approaching.

5.   At about 1530 *P.32* was brought to periscope depth and I observed a convoy of 4 medium-sized merchant ships proceeding in line ahead unescorted except by one aircraft on a course approximately 070 deg. I at once decided to attack the rear ship which appeared to be a tanker of about 6000 tons. Although I was in torpedo-firing range I still had time to close and press home my attack on the rear ship. *P.32* was taken to 50 feet and speed increased to 9 knots and this speed was maintained for 3 – 4 minutes. On sighting I had ordered the tubes to be 'blown up' but I cannot remember if the tube space had reported them as 'blown up' by the time I gave the order to regain periscope depth.

6.   At about 1540 *P.32* was therefore proceeding with some bow caps open at 9 knots regaining periscope depth when a loud explosion occurred at 34 feet and *P.32* took on a large angle bow down and out of control hit the bottom at 200 feet where she remained. *Unique* was on the surface at this time closing her new position so would probably not have heard the detonation although I learned later that the noise had been heard in Tripoli. I am unable to explain the cause of this explosion, the Italian Naval *Capitano* Di Vascello who interrogated me later said that *P.32* had not been bombed by aircraft but asked me a number of times if I had been laying mines; each time I

replied I had not and I consequently gained the impression that he had no knowledge of a mine in the position where *P.32* had been sunk which I estimate to be 008 ½ deg. 6.5 miles from Tripoli main light. I was fully aware that minefield Q.B. 11 was in close proximity and from chart M 209 the least depth in this minefield is 68 metres (223 feet). *P.32* sank in 200 feet (60.9 metres) of water according to the depth gauges which may have been put out of adjustment by the explosion; even so I consider that as my estimated position and the position given in Captain (S) Ten's letter No. 1117/5 dated 2nd September, 1941 are both outside the danger area of Q.B. 11 I did not blow myself up on this minefield.

7.   I have the impression that the explosion appeared to come from inside the submarine but I have no proof at all. It is noted that at about the period when *P.32* was sunk instances of torpedo air vessels exploding had occurred.

8.   The Control Room – crew space watertight door became shut during the final plunge. This may have been due to the door jumping off its holding-open clip and closing with the impact of *P.32* hitting the bottom which was very considerable. The submarine became flooded up to this bulkhead and I heard the ratings who were cut off shouting and thumping on the bulkhead for the door to be opened. This was impossible and their cries subsided after a short time but it shows that some time elapsed approximately 3 minutes before the whole fore part of the submarine was completely flooded up.

9.   On hitting the bottom the main motors which were still at full speed stopped, the port main motor blowing its fuses and fruitless efforts were made to raise *P.32* which was lying with about a 15 degree angle down and a 7 degree list to port. I attempted to raise the stern by blowing the after main ballast but this caused the list to increase and I consequently flooded again. No. 2 main battery by this time had started to give off chlorine gas rather badly and I decided to attempt to abandon submarine by D.S.E.A. using the engine-room hatch. Most unfortunate the jar

containing the acid which was stowed in the lavatory for destroying the Confidential Books and Signal Publications was broken when the submarine hit the bottom so there was no method for destroying them except burning. I did not order this to be carried out owing to the danger of an explosion but I had them thrown down the periscope's wells which were partially flooded with water. By this time the lights were nearly all practically out and the hull leaking in many places.

10.   I mustered what remained of the crew in the engine room wearing D.S.E.A. sets. Two ratings were without them and I decided to send them up in the bubble if possible. The Chief E.R.A. passed the remark to me that there might be some difficulty in opening the engine room hatch. This, I put down to at the time, would be because of the list on the submarine. Petty Officer Kirk has subsequently told me that he is of the opinion the engine-room hatch was clipped from the outside and further states that I gave orders after *P.32* had been bombed in June 1941 off Ferrol, Spain, that both the forward D.S.E.A. hatch and the engine-room hatch were to be clipped from the outside before leaving for patrol. I do not recollect this order.

11.   I then ordered the First Lieutenant, Lieutenant R.W. Morris, R.N., to read out the orders for working a D.S.E.A. set and personally made sure that every man knew what to do. Realising the congestion in the engine room I then called for 2 volunteers to attempt to escape with me using the conning tower as an escape chamber. Petty Officer Kirk, the Coxswain and E.R.A. Martin both volunteered and, having told the First Lieutenant to start flooding up as soon as we had left the engine room, we manned the conning tower in the order E.R.A. Martin at the top, Petty Officer Kirk and myself. I closed the lower hatch and gave the order to start breathing through the set, at the same time warning the two ratings not to forget to open the exhaust cocks on the sets when the time came. As soon as we were breathing comfortably I opened the flood valve to the conning tower and commenced flooding up slowly.

After a short time Kirk signed to me that he was having trouble to clear his ears. I stopped flooding but he signed to me to carry on. I opened the flood valve again and before very long when the water was high enough I signed to the two ratings to open their exhaust cocks. Martin at this time was struggling rather a lot but was soon able to open the upper conning tower hatch and he left the submarine. Petty Office Kirk followed and I followed last. When I reached the surface Petty Officer Kirk reported to me that when he had arrived on the surface he had found E.R.A. Martin lying with his face submerged in the water. Kirk attempted to hold his head up, but Martin's extra weight caused him to sink so he had to let him go and E.R.A. Martin was drowned.

12.   An aircraft now appeared flying low. We both waved and I presumed we had been seen for the aircraft set course for the shore which was plainly visible. We remained in the vicinity for some time waiting for the rest of the crew from the engine room to appear, but nobody escaped. We then started to swim for the shore and after being in the water for about one-and-a-half hours an Italian M.A.S. *530* appeared and picked us up. Once on board I got the Commanding Officer to take me back to the position of *P.32*. On arrival in this position I saw [a] considerable amount of oil floating on the water and [a] few air bubbles but no sign of the remainder of my crew. I then asked the Commanding Officer of the M.A.S. *530* if he had any listening device and he ordered a portable device to be placed over the side (separate report had been rendered) but the operator reported he could not hear anything. Course was then set for Tripoli where Petty Officer Kirk and I were landed at about 18.30.

I have the honour to be,
Sir,
Your obedient Servant,
D. Abdy.
Lieutenant Commander, R.N.[15]

Captain (S) First Submarine Flotilla, on forwarding the report commented:

> On balance it would have been better for the Commanding Officer to have remained with the body of his crew and made the escape with them from the engine room.[16]

But he *did* add that Lieutenant Commander Abdy may have had very good reason for the action he took and went on to say he was very diffident to criticise the actions of a man imprisoned in a submarine at 200 feet.

The month was not all doom and gloom, there being some successes that caused the enemy substantial losses. Lieutenant Hezlet in *Unique* was on patrol in the approaches to Tripoli just outside the recently swept safe channel when he identified a troop convoy of four liners. As they approached the entrance to the swept channel, they could not zigzag and that enabled *Unique* to approach at depth and avoid detection by the escorting destroyers and aircraft. He fired a full salvo of torpedoes at the liners and three hit and sank the 11,300-ton *Esperia*. The number of survivors in the water hindered the possibility of the enemy mounting a concentrated counter-attack so the submarine withdrew unscathed. Unfortunately, later in the day, she was spotted and bombed by a flying boat. Two heavy detonations were felt and the submarine was damaged, causing her to create a tell-tale oil slick on the surface that was likely to lead any hostile unit directly to her position. She withdrew to Malta.

Upholder had sailed from Malta on 15 August with Lieutenant Commander Wanklyn anxious to return to the scene of his recent triumphs off the eastern coast of Sicily. He did not have long to wait as on the 20th he was to have his next success. He was patrolling off Cape St Vito when he sighted the 852-ton *Enotria* carrying oil to the troops in North Africa. He closed, torpedoed and sank the vessel. This was a lucky area for *Upholder* as two days later a convoy of three southbound tankers fully laden and under escort from three destroyers, was sighted. A full salvo of torpedoes was fired and resulted in the 3,990-ton tanker *Lussin* being sunk. The inevitable counter-attack was mounted but although sixty-one depth charges were dropped no significant damage was sustained.

Lieutenant Commander Tomkinson in *Urge* was the next to see success having sailed from Malta on 25 August to perform a clockwise patrol Malta-Marittimo-Naples-Messina-Palermo-Malta. He had only been at sea two days and was at his first point when he attacked a convoy of five escorted merchant ships. He fired a salvo at the largest and leading vessel and hit it, damaging the fully laden 4,971-ton tanker *Aquitania*, necessitating her being towed into Trapani. The haphazard counter-attack that followed caused no major damage to the submarine; in fact *Urge* was probably put in danger more by her own torpedoes. On firing the salvo, only three of the four ran true; the torpedo in number 3 tube only travelled half-way out of the tube. It continued to 'run' in that position forcing the submarine to surface, thus displaying this angry, smoking torpedo to the naval escort just 3,000 yards away. Fortunately the torpedo fell out of the tube on surfacing and the submarine dived immediately to avoid any gun action.

Two days later, having arrived in the Bay of Naples, Lieutenant Tomkinson sighted three troop ships as they emerged from Naples itself. With their naval escort busily taking up their positions, *Urge* torpedoed and damaged the 23,600-ton liner *Duilio*, forcing her to return to Naples. He was not able to intercept the other two liners, *Neptunia* and *Oceania*. These two liners were to have charmed lives on this trip. Having escaped the clutches of *Urge* on 29 August, they were sighted the next day by *Ursula* but were beyond her reach. The following day they were again sighted, this time by *Upholder*, but the salvo of four torpedoes she fired was unsuccessful and the liners made it to Tripoli.

Meanwhile Lieutenant Commander Woodward in *Unbeaten* was on patrol in the southern approaches to the Straits of Messina. On 30 August he stood off and watched two schooners go about their business of anti-submarine patrol. These vessels were observed throughout the day and it was established the larger four-masted schooner spent most of the time stopped. *Unbeaten* closed to 700 yards and fired two torpedoes – both found the target and the 373-ton schooner *Alfa* blew up and sank.

September 1941 started with the introduction of a new Submarine Flotilla. Admiralty instructed that all submarines operating out of Malta would be designated the Tenth Submarine Flotilla under the Command of Captain George Walter Gillow Simpson.

Intelligence was received that a large convoy of liners had sailed from Italy en route to Tripoli with a large number of reinforcements for the Afrika Korps. Captain Simpson dispatched from Malta *Unbeaten, Upholder, Upright* and *Ursula* with the intention of intercepting the convoy as it approached Tripoli. All but *Upright* were equipped with the new Mark VIII torpedoes. On 18 September Lieutenant Commander Woodward in *Unbeaten* sighted the convoy which included the liners *Neptunia, Oceania* and *Vulcania*, but was unable to attack. An enemy sighting report was sent and *Unbeaten* turned to follow the convoy in the hope of picking off any ship disabled by the main attack. *Upholder* made the first strike and fired four torpedoes spread over the three liners that resulted in hits on *Neptunia*, 19,475 tons and *Oceania*, 19,507 tons. He then withdrew southward to reload his torpedoes. Some thirty minutes later Lieutenant Commander Wanklyn returned to the scene to find one liner stopped and being attended by a destroyer, and one other liner continuing her course but at a much reduced speed. Two hours later *Unbeaten* and *Upholder* sighted another liner stopped with a destroyer in attendance. *Upholder* fired first gaining two further hits and the liner sank within eight minutes.

Ursula (Lieutenant Hezlet) had received reports of the attack and anticipated one vessel was still running for Tripoli. This was confirmed when he sighted escorting vessels from Tripoli waiting to rendezvous with the convoy. *Ursula* positioned herself to mount an attack and on sighting *Vulcania* fired four torpedoes, gaining just one hit. The speed of *Vulcania* was underestimated as she was on maximum speed running for cover. *Vulcania* was sighted, apparently listing and in danger of sinking, but it was the escorting destroyers transferring large numbers of troops from one side of the liner that created this misconception; *Vulcania* subsequently arrived safely in Tripoli. The cost to the enemy was the loss of two large troop carriers together with 400 troops out of a total of 6,900, having perished before they could face Allied ground troops in North Africa. All four submarines were then recalled to Malta. This attack resulted in several awards being made to the submarine commanders. Lieutenant Commander Wanklyn was awarded the Victoria Cross, the first to be awarded to a Second World War submariner and the only one awarded to 'U' class personnel.

On 25 September all submarines of the Tenth Submarine Flotilla were deployed along the northern coast of Sicily and on the approaches to Taranto and Naples. The intention was to intercept any enemy naval units that sailed in opposition to *OPERATION HALBERD* – a major supply convoy for Malta. None of the submarines sighted any Italian battleships but during that time *Ursula* and *Utmost* sighted one cruiser with seven destroyers and three cruisers with eight destroyers respectively, but neither was able to attack. The only success was achieved by *Upright* and Lieutenant Wraith who sighted the Italian torpedo-boat *Albatros* as she carried out an anti-submarine sweep to the north-west of Sicily. He closed and fired two torpedoes, hitting and sinking the *Albatros*, thereby achieving sweet revenge for the British submarine *Phoenix* sunk the previous year by the same torpedo boat.

These successes were all the more commendable with the flat calm sea conditions that prevailed in the Mediterranean during the summer months. Unfortunately the Lords of the Admiralty saw these successes as a good opportunity to give the folks back at home some reason to be more optimistic by publishing them in national newspapers. This was much to the chagrin of the C.-in-C. Mediterranean, who once again expressed his objections and insisted that such publicity was detrimental to submarine operations and increased the risk to submariners' lives.

During October, Admiral Max Horton, Admiral (Submarines) visited the First Submarine Flotilla in Alexandria and the Tenth Flotilla in Malta. In his letter to the Lords of the Admiralty he reported that morale amongst submariners was good whilst expressing concern that in view of the operating conditions in the Mediterranean they should have a set term of operation. He also went a long way to settling the problem of publicity for the submarine operations. Whilst the C.-in-C. maintained his opposition in general to submarine operations being the subject of wide publicity, he had to concede the need for such publicity. As a result of the visit the C.-in-C. reluctantly agreed to the appointment of a Senior Naval Officer to the Mediterranean Fleet whose primary task was to write up Fleet stories and assist in the coordination of publicity generally.

Two more submarines joined the Tenth Submarine Flotilla in October 1941: *Ultimatum* commanded by Lieutenant P.R. Harrison, RN, and *Uproar* under the command of Lieutenant Kershaw. Captain (S) Tenth Submarine Flotilla, being aware of the large number of British submarines at sea, instructed that no submarine was to be attacked at night for fear of misidentification that could lead to the loss of a friendly boat. This led to some frustration for the submarine commanders as over the next few weeks they were to encounter several U-boats, both Italian and German, which were allowed to pass unmolested.

22 October was a good day for Lieutenant Commander Tomkinson and *Urge* as they patrolled off Kuriat Island. At 06.30 they sighted a southbound, laden merchant ship being escorted by five schooners. *Urge* closed and fired three torpedoes. The merchant ship's crew sighted the torpedo tracks and stopped ship and thus avoided being hit but it was sufficient incentive for the crew to lower the boats and abandon ship. This resulted in the final torpedo being fired into the ship and the 1,407-ton *Maria Pompei* sank. Later in the day *Urge* observed the 5,996-ton merchant ship *Marigola* at anchor off Kuriat. Her steering had been damaged by an earlier attack from Blenheim aircraft. One torpedo sank her but due to the shallow water she remained partly above the water. She was still lying in the same position when, on 1 November, *Utmost* came across her. Not realising she was lying on the bottom, Lieutenant Commander Cayley engaged her by gunfire with fifty out of fifty-four rounds finding the target before he withdrew leaving the *Marigola* a blazing inferno.

November 1941 was not the most successful month as there were just two successful attacks, both against Italian naval units. On the 9th, Lieutenant Commander Wanklyn in *Upholder* closed the remnants of a convoy savaged by British surface forces in the

Ionian Sea, to see three destroyers passing amongst six damaged ships. He attacked the Italian destroyer *Libeccio*, 1,449 tons, which was sunk by just one torpedo. This was the only destroyer to be sunk by *Upholder* during her service in the Mediterranean. The second strike did not come until the 21st when *Utmost*, under Lieutenant Commander Cayley, attacked an Italian naval unit consisting of two cruisers and three destroyers approaching Messina. Of the full salvo of torpedoes fired, one hit and damaged the Italian cruiser *Luigi Di Duca Degli Abruzzi* but she was able to limp into Taranto for repair.

During the next few weeks Italian naval units were to be regularly sighted, totalling five battleships, six cruisers and thirty-five destroyers, but on the majority of occasions no attack was possible. That was to change on 14 December when *Urge* and Lieutenant Commander Tomkinson sighted the battleships *Littorio* and *Vittorio Veneto* in the southern approaches to Messina. A full salvo of torpedoes was fired, of which three hit and damaged the *Vittorio Veneto*.

The only other success of the month went to Lieutenant Wraith in *Upright* when patrolling off Taranto. This time it was the merchant ships that were to suffer. On the 13th a convoy of two merchant ships with one destroyer as escort was seen to leave Taranto heading south. Lieutenant Wraith closed and fired a full salvo of torpedoes resulting in the loss of two 6,835-ton merchant ships, as the *Fabio Filzi* and *Carlo del Greco* were both hit and sunk.

The year ended with the strength of the Tenth Submarine Flotilla being further increased as *P36*, *P39* and *Una* arrived in Gibraltar en route to Malta. These were joined the following month by *P38*.

Upholder had the honour of making the first strike of 1942 on 4 January as she patrolled the northern coastline of Sicily, off Cape Gallo. At 05.35 she sighted the 5,222-ton merchant ship *Sirio*, closed and fired two torpedoes from numbers 1 and 3 tubes. Number 1 torpedo ran hot inside the tube causing the submarine to loose trim. Number 3 torpedo ran deep and exploded directly underneath the submarine. Fortunately the sea at this point was more than 500 fathoms deep and no damage was caused.

Lieutenant Commander Wanklyn persisted in his attack and fired the remaining two torpedoes, one hitting the *Sirio* but, although damaged, she was seen to continue on her way. *Upholder* surfaced to engage her by gunfire but the accurate firing of *Sirio*'s Breda automatic guns drove the submarine down. It was not possible to pursue the attack.

Lieutenant Commander Wanklyn and *Upholder* were not finished and the following day attacked the Italian submarine *Ammiraglio Saint Bon* that had been damaged and was unable to submerge. *Upholder* fired her last torpedo and the Italian submarine was sunk. Three survivors, who had been on the bridge at the time of the attack, were rescued – the officer of the watch Lieutenant Como, and the two lookouts, Petty Officer Valentino Chico and Torpedoman Ernest Fiore. It was established that *Ammiraglio Saint Bon* had only left the builder's yard four months previously and had not carried out a serious war patrol. She carried a crew of eight officers and fifty-four crew.

One week later, on 12 January, *Unbeaten* and Lieutenant Commander Woodward sank a second submarine. The German U-boat *U374*, under the command of *Oberleutnant* Unno van Fischel, was en route to Messina for repair after she had been damaged by depth charge off Tobruk whilst attacking a British convoy. The *U374* sank after being hit by two torpedoes. There was just one survivor, Seaman Johannes Ploch, who had been lookout at the time when he was blown clear into the sea to be picked up by *Unbeaten* and brought back to Malta for interrogation.

There were two other successes during January 1942 with Lieutenant S.L.C. Maydon, RN, and *Umbra*, and Lieutenant Harrison and *Ultimatum* sinking two merchant ships. *Umbra* was on patrol off Sousse on the Tunisian coast on the dark and moonless night of the 17th when she torpedoed and sank the 301-ton salvage ship *Rampino*. She was a useful target, as the Axis forces were heavily dependent on salvage operations to replace their losses. *Umbra* returned to the scene some time later and spotted one survivor on a raft; the submarine stopped and picked up Fireman Romolo Garibaldi. He remained with the submarine for the rest of the patrol acting as cook's mate and extra fore-endsman when it was necessary to reload torpedoes. The final attack of the month came on the 25th when *Ultimatum*, patrolling the southern approaches to Messina Straits, attacked and sank the fully laden 3,320-ton supply vessel *Dalmatia*. Lieutenant Maydon and *Umbra* opened the account for February 1942 when on the third day she torpedoed and sank the 6,142-ton *Napoli* in the Gulf of Hammamet as she lay at anchor off Mahedia. On the instructions of Captain (S) Tenth Submarine Flotilla, they remained in the area in the hope that a destroyer might come to the assistance of *Napoli*. None was seen and when they returned to the scene Lieutenant Maydon saw her lying on the sea bed, but still above the surface, badly listing, with a few men working on board. Information suggested that she may have had British prisoners on board which removed any chance of gun action, and as she was not worthy of a further torpedo *Umbra* withdrew leaving her to her fate.

The next action was regrettable as Lieutenant D.S.R. Martin, RN, in *Una* attacked and sank the 8,106-ton tanker *Lucania* in the Gulf of Taranto. At that time the *Lucania* was sailing under immunity with oil supplies for a repatriation ship that was returning civilians to Mombasa. Lieutenant Martin was unaware of the immunity order. He had not read the appropriate Admiralty signal when it had been presented to him by Sub-Lieutenant R.L. Jay, RN. On returning to Malta he was diagnosed as suffering from a high fever and hospitalised. On recovering Lieutenant Martin was returned to the United Kingdom to explain his actions.

This was not a lucky day for the 'U' class as it also saw the loss of Lieutenant M.H. Gardner, RN, from *Uproar*. At 06.15 on 12 February, they were patrolling on the surface off Marsa Zuaga with the Commanding Officer, Lieutenant Kershaw, Lieutenant Gardner (officer of the watch), Sub Lieutenant R. Bucknall and Acting Leading Seaman Lowe all on the bridge. An order to blow number 1 main ballast tank was given but for some reason the main vent was also opened and the submarine started to dive steeply. Lieutenant Kershaw and Leading Seaman Lowe were washed down the conning tower but were able to secure the conning tower hatch. The other two officers were both washed overboard. The submarine's descent was checked at seventy feet, she recovered her trim and resurfaced to find Sub Lieutenant Bucknall swimming in the water. He was brought on board but a full search of the area over the next four hours failed to find any sign of Lieutenant Gardner.

P36, under the command of Lieutenant H.N. Edmunds, RN, sailed from Malta to patrol the southern approaches of the Messina Straits and on 15 February she attacked an Italian naval unit of two cruisers and one destroyer. The attack resulted in the destroyer *Carabiniere* being hit and damaged. The next time she was seen was in the dry dock at Messina with forty feet of her bows having been blown off. *P36* again intercepted a naval unit the following day when two cruisers – *Gorizia* and *Trento* – with an escort of eight destroyers were seen but, on this occasion, the attack was not successful. As a result of these two attacks the crew of *P36* was obliged to endure considerable discomfort, as the two counter-attacks that followed totalled 440 depth charges.

Another sad loss during the month was that of *P38* with Lieutenant R.J. Hemingway, RN, in command. He was on the first patrol out of Malta off the island of Lampedusa on 19 February when he attacked and sank the 4,116-ton supply ship *Ariosto*. The very next day her luck ran out when she encountered the Italian destroyer *Antoniotto Usodimare* and the torpedo boat *Circe* acting as escorts to a supply convoy. The Commanding Officer of the *Circe* described the attack thus:

> As I pass over the position indicated by the sonar and the telltale bubbles, I let go a depth-charge pattern set to 75 metres. I increase to full speed to avoid damage to *Circe*. As I am clearing the area the pattern exploded. Soon afterwards the submarine is blown to the surface on my port quarter, stern down and bow pointing towards the convoy. No one leaves the submarine. I alter to starboard to close, but meanwhile *Antoniotto Usodimare* has opened fire with her main armament and machine guns. Some of her rounds are over, so I am forced to alter course abruptly. In the middle of my turn, I watch the air escort machine gunning the submarine, a second aircraft drops bombs. Suddenly the

submarine breaks surface on Red 150 degrees. Her bows rear into the air, she is leaping and diving, a few minutes later she is at 40 degrees bow down angle with her propellers turning into the air and her after hydroplanes at hard to rise. She had made her last effort to reach the surface."[17]

P38 was lost with all hands.

It was left to Lieutenant Commander Wanklyn and *Upholder* to redress the balance when on the 27th, as they patrolled off Djerba Island in the Gulf of Gabes, they located the 5,584-ton merchant ship *Tembien* approaching Tripoli with a destroyer in attendance. *Upholder* closed, attacked with three torpedoes and sank her as two torpedoes of the salvo found their target.

March 1942 was to see the enemy lose three submarines in three separate actions. The first was on the 14th when Lieutenant Harrison in *Ultimatum* on patrol off the southern Calabrian coast, torpedoed and sank the 1,461-ton Italian submarine *Ammiraglio Millo*. *Ultimatum* was able to surface and recover fourteen Italian survivors before being disturbed by passing aircraft and obliged to dive. She immediately returned to Malta to drop off the Italians before resuming patrol. The next strike was to Lieutenant Commander Woodward in *Unbeaten*. Just before dawn on the 17th he dived as normal and shortly afterwards a periscope check revealed the Italian submarine *Guglielmotti* (896 tons) on the surface making for Messina. The subsequent torpedo attack sank the submarine and, again, as *Unbeaten* approached survivors in the water, she was disturbed by enemy aircraft intervention and withdrew. The following day Lieutenant Commander Wanklyn and *Upholder* struck the final blow when they intercepted and sank the 810-ton Italian submarine *Trichero* as she approached Brindisi.

Upholder returned to the Brindisi area on the 19th to find a diesel trawler and three fishing smacks. Wanklyn surfaced close to the trawler and invited the crew to abandon ship before he chased one of the smaller craft, engaging it by gunfire, but after firing fifteen rounds and gaining only one hit he aborted this attack. Wanklyn's attention returned to the trawler, which he found to be abandoned. It was engaged by gunfire; seven rounds were fired scoring six hits and the trawler settled with three large holes on the water line.

There were other successes during the month starting with *Unbeaten* and Lieutenant J.D. Martin, RN, (in command due to the absence of Lieutenant Commander Woodward), when they struck on the very first day of the month. Whilst patrolling off Mahedia on the Tunisian coastline he intercepted, torpedoed and sank the 5,147-ton tanker *PLM 20*. Lieutenant J.B. Kershaw in *Uproar* followed this whilst on patrol off the island of Lampion. On the 5th, the *Marin Sanudo*, a 5,081-ton supply ship, was sighted under escort from two torpedo boats, but they were unable to prevent *Uproar*'s attack, which resulted in the *Marin Sanudo* being hit and sunk. Lieutenant Norman was on his first patrol in command of *Una* off Mahedia when he invited the crew of the 250-ton Italian schooner *Maria Immacolata* to abandon ship, as it was believed to be gun-running into Tripoli. Once abandoned she was sunk by gunfire. The final strike against enemy commercial resources came on 16 March when Lieutenant Martin in *Unbeaten* had moved his patrol position to an area off Cape Spartivento. He sighted the 6,339-ton merchant vessel *Pisani* being escorted by three destroyers with three aircraft in attendance. After allowing the wing destroyer to pass just 150 yards ahead of him he fired a full salvo of torpedoes; two found the target and the submarine quickly withdrew to avoid any counter-attack. When no counter-attack was experienced he returned to periscope depth and saw two of the destroyers stationary picking up survivors and the third hot-footing it back to Messina.

April 1942 was a month of contrasts; there were some successes countered by several losses. The first day of April 1942 saw the first success of the month; Lieutenant Commander Tomkinson and *Urge* were on patrol in the northern approaches to the Straits of Messina when he saw a flying boat searching along the convoy route. This was the sign of a profitable morning to follow and the submarine promptly went deep and awaited the telltale HE of an oncoming convoy. What did materialise was the HE of a heavy cruiser accompanied by two destroyers. Lieutenant Tomkinson brought *Urge* to periscope depth, fired a full salvo of torpedoes and sank the Italian cruiser *Giovanni delle Bande Nere* (5,070 tons). This was followed by a sharp counter-attack before both escorting destroyers returned to the position of the stricken cruiser to pick up survivors. *Una* and Lieutenant Norman also on patrol in the same area, followed this on 5 April, when the fully laden southbound 5,335-ton supply ship *Ninetto G* was sighted, closed, torpedoed and sunk.

These two successes were counteracted during that first week of April by the loss of *P36* as she lay alongside in Lazaretto Creek. On 1 April she was tied up alongside the depot ship HMS *Talbot* during an enemy air raid; all watertight doors were closed with only one officer and two ratings on duty aboard. A bomb exploded on the catamaran alongside the submarine blowing in the port side of the control room. *P36* rolled over and sank into the deep water of the Creek. None of the crewmembers was lost. *P36* was to lie there until 1958 when she was salvaged under the supervision of Mr P.F. Flett, OBE, towed out to sea and scuttled in deep water.

The bad news was to continue throughout the month. On 12 April *Ultimatum* was patrolling off the heel of Italy, south of the Gulf of Taranto, when she hit a mine. The explosion blew the submarine to the surface causing substantial damage, not least putting all torpedo tubes out of action. She returned to Malta for repair.

Worse was to follow. On 14 April *Upholder* was located off Tripoli by the Italian torpedo boat *Pegaso*, depth-charged and lost with all crew.

The C.-in-C. Mediterranean, in his submission on the loss of *Upholder* wrote: 'Her brilliant career was an inspiration, not only to the Mediterranean Fleet but to the people of Malta as well.'[18]

This loss also caused the Lords of the Admiralty to make an unprecedented announcement paying special tribute to *Upholder* and Lieutenant Commander Wanklyn. The full text of this announcement read:

It is seldom proper for Their Lordships to draw distinction between different services rendered in the course of naval duty, but they take this opportunity of singling out those of H.M.S. *Upholder*, under the command of Lieutenant Commander Wanklyn, for special mention. She was long employed against enemy communications in the Central Mediterranean and she became noted for the uniformly high quality of her services in the arduous and dangerous duty. Such was the standard of skill and daring, that the ship and her officers and men became an inspiration not only to their own flotilla but to the fleet of which it was a part, and Malta, where for so long H.M.S. *Upholder* was based. The ship and her company are gone, but the example and the inspiration remain. In the twenty-four successful patrols which this submarine had carried out in these waters she had built up a long record of success against the enemy, and of 36 attacks made, no fewer than 21 were successful. The *Upholder* sank 3 U-boats, 2 destroyers, 1 armed trawler, [and] 15 enemy transports and ships.[19]

Lieutenant Maydon and *Umbra* were to report success that month as they patrolled off Kerkenah. On 19 April they sighted the 4,219-ton supply ship *Assunta de Gregori*. Two torpedoes were fired, both found the target and the supply ship was dispatched to the seabed. Only two depth charges were dropped before the escorting destroyer returned to the stricken vessel to recover survivors from the water.

The final loss in April was that of *Urge* (Lieutenant Commander Tomkinson). *Urge* sailed from Malta on 27 April on passage to Alexandria as part of the evacuation of the Tenth Submarine Flotilla. She was never to arrive and as the enemy never claimed her loss it is presumed she struck a mine. There were no survivors. George Simpson, Captain (S) Tenth Submarine Flotilla wrote of her Commanding Officer:

Lieutenant Commander Tomkinson was an outstandingly able leader, whose strict disciplinary methods were mellowed by a great sense of humour, charm and under-standing. The chief difference between Tomkinson and

74

Wanklyn was that the former suffered fools less gladly. The determination, forethought and excellent eye of both officers produced results of an equally high order of merit.[20]

Vice Admiral Malta's May 1942 review contained the following statement:

> The loss of four submarines by air attack while in harbour [this included *P36*] and the difficulties of giving crews of boats back from patrol any proper rest, eventually caused the Tenth Submarine Flotilla to be temporarily withdrawn to Alexandria.[21]

With each patrol ending in Malta and the damaged submarines returning there for repair, it may have appeared that Malta was considered a safe haven. This was far from true because as British forces patrolled the approaches to the enemy naval bases the enemy reciprocated the arrangement off Malta. The Luftwaffe regularly caused damage and concern throughout the life of the Tenth Submarine Flotilla's stay in Malta. Seven air attacks were recorded against submarines as they arrived or left Malta and a further eleven caused damage to submarines alongside in harbour that included the sinking of *P36*.

This attention created an atmosphere of tension around Malta and on one occasion an unidentified submarine confronted *Upholder* as she left harbour. Three times the submarine was challenged with no reply being forthcoming. Fortunately Lieutenant Commander Wanklyn recognised the silhouette as being similar to a 'T' class submarine and curbed his natural tendencies to attack. The submarine turned out to be *Truant*.

Problems whilst approaching Malta were not always of the enemy's making. On 18 February 1942 Lieutenant Collett was bringing *Unique* back to Malta from an unsuccessful patrol when it ran aground off Rinella Point. Collett radioed for assistance but was unable to raise anyone, making it necessary for alternative action to be taken. Lieutenant Silver leapt ashore onto the rocks to find assistance. He climbed through the barbed-wire fence of the radio station to be confronted by an army sentry. Dressed for patrol in his dirty submarine sweater and old grey flannel trousers, unshaven and unwashed, Silver was escorted to the Army Officers' Mess only to be informed that they were unable to provide any transport. In order to gain the assistance needed, Lieutenant Silver ran from Rinella Point to Dockyard Creek, crossed Grand Harbour to Valetta in a dghaisa, over Valetta to Floriana and on to Sliema Creek where he found a second dghaisa to take him to Lazaretto Creek. Assistance to clear the rocks was provided by the tug *Robust*, ensuring that no more damage occurred than had already been inflicted. This grounding damaged the keel and bows and the torpedo tubes were found to be out of alignment.

It was not always the submarines' crews' greatest wish to leave Malta – even to return home. *Unique*'s departure to return to the United Kingdom to refit was delayed by a crew member who broke into the pistol locker and discharged a revolver into the control room in an effort to prevent the boat sailing, as he preferred to stay in Malta with his girlfriend. He was returned home by other means, court-martialled but allowed to continue his naval career. He was described as being deranged at the time of the incident.

On 4 May Captain (S) Tenth Submarine Flotilla and his staff flew to Alexandria leaving *Umbra* (Lieutenant Maydon) to be the final submarine to leave. After being delayed by engine trouble, she finally left Malta on 10 May 1942.

During the month of June the strength of the 'U' class submarines in the Mediterranean was to increase by four when *Unison*, *United*, *Unruffled* and *Utmost* joined the fray. Having settled in at Alexandria, the Tenth Submarine Flotilla (in conjunction with submarines from the First Flotilla) was to concentrate efforts in support of a major supply convoy destined for Malta from the Eastern Mediterranean in *OPERATION VIGOROUS*. This was the major action for the month of June 1942. During previous convoys submarines had been deployed in the close approaches of Messina and Taranto. Admiral Sir Henry Harwood, recently appointed C.-in-C. Mediterranean, believed that this was not a good strategic move as the value received from these patrols was some early sighting reports and an occasional attack on the enemy units as they returned to base, their damage done. On this occasion the submarines were deployed in a line across the Ionian Sea, north of the convoy route, in an attempt to intercept any enemy heavy surface units en route to intercept the convoy.

Ultimatum, Umbra, Una and *Uproar* all sailed from Alexandria on 6 June to join five submarines from the First Submarine Flotilla and form a defensive line to the north of the convoy route. On 14 June the Italian battle fleet sailed from Taranto and Messina to intercept the convoy. This consisted of two battleships and five cruisers with innumerable destroyers in attendance. On 13 June *Unison*, (Lieutenant A.C. Halliday, RN, commanding) intercepted two cruisers and four destroyers outside Cagliari as they sailed to rendezvous at Messina. Unfortunately his attack was not successful and the enemy ships made their rendezvous undamaged.

Lieutenant Maydon in *Umbra* was in his allotted patrol position on the 15th when he sighted the Taranto-based units – two battleships, three cruisers and nine destroyers. As he closed to attack he found himself in the centre of the battle fleet which was being attacked by British and American aircraft. Lieutenant Maydon in his patrol report wrote:

> *P35* [*Umbra*] was in the unenviable position of being in the centre of a fantastic circus of wildly careering capital ships, cruisers and destroyers, of bomb splashes, none of which, fortunately, came close, of tracer shells streaks and anti-aircraft bursts.[22]

The initial air attack damaged one cruiser but a second air attack damaged the battleship *Littorio* and she was seen heading off in a haze of smoke but not before *Umbra* had fired her torpedoes – one of which hit the battleship. The strike on *Littorio* was confirmed when she was seen in dry dock at Taranto for some time after this attack. About one hour later *Umbra* sighted the Italian cruiser *Trento* burning with two destroyers circling her laying smoke. As the submarine closed to attack, the destroyers became suspicious and forced her to go deep. On returning to

77

periscope depth some time later, Lieutenant Maydon found the *Trento* stopped and on fire. Two torpedoes were fired; both found the target and the *Trento* sank with the escorting destroyers seen picking up survivors. The demise of the *Trento* was also witnessed by *Ultimatum*, which had been forced deep before she could mount any attacks.

Summertime in the Mediterranean with long days and the sea flat and smooth, just like a mirror, made submarine warfare very difficult and the possibilities of a successful attack limited. The summer of 1942 was not an idle time as it was a period of movement for the submarine commands. The Tenth Submarine Flotilla had recently transferred to Alexandria from Malta due to enemy air supremacy over Malta. However, as the enemy land forces closed in on Alexandria, it was necessary for both the Tenth and First Submarine Flotillas to withdraw to Haifa, with the Eighth Submarine Flotilla setting up base in Beirut. In Haifa the submarine personnel were housed in a military transit camp that had been previously occupied by Allied troops. The facilities for the personnel on the base were good with plenty of opportunity for relaxation. Haifa itself offered many shore-going attractions but these were out of the normal submariners' price range. There were added bonuses with the Haifa base as the Palestine Police Force offered generous hospitality to submarine crews as they enjoyed five-day rest breaks. The police entertained the submariners in Jerusalem, Nazareth and Nablus, meeting the cost of transport from their own canteen funds. To the submariners, just out of war-torn Malta, these breaks were most welcome and gave them the opportunity to relax and take part in different activities like camel- and donkey races, followed by moonlight sheep-roasts provided by their Arab hosts.

Unfortunately this respite was temporary as on 22 July Captain (S) Tenth Submarine Flotilla returned to Malta and re-opened the base. July also saw the submarine strength supplemented by the arrival of *Unbending*. In his letter dated 10 August 1942, Captain (S) Tenth Submarine Flotilla wrote:

> It is good to be back in Malta, and much progress in the
> base had taken place, all under-rock offices and sleeping

quarters, sick bay, dental surgery, operations room etc., being finished with only the workshop to complete. The cinema has also been once more installed and improved bathrooms near the new mess decks. Naturally there is strict rationing ashore; no restaurants are open and about 25 per cent of the populace is fed from communal kitchens – this seems to be much appreciated and most efficiently run. It was noticeable that most English families were visibly thinner, but the Maltese were not. The labourer, however, does not do so much work in a day as he did a year ago.[23]

August 1942 opened with Lieutenant A.C.G. Mars, RN, on his first patrol in *Unbroken* off Lipari sland. On 13 August he sighted an Italian main naval unit consisting of the 7,405-ton 6-inch cruiser *Muzzio Attendolo*, and the 10,890-ton 8-inch cruiser *Balzano* with their usual escort of eight destroyers. A full salvo of torpedoes was fired and both cruisers were hit and damaged. There was a prolonged but ineffective counter-attack and the submarine was undamaged. Later aerial reconnaissance showed *Muzzio Attendolo* in Messina with sixty feet of her bows missing. There was no sign of the *Balzano* as she had been transferred to another port for repair.

On 17 August Lieutenant T.E. Barlow, RN, in *United*, was instructed to investigate the scene of a successful RAF attack on a merchant ship off Lampion island. The following day he sighted the 8,325-ton Italian merchant ship *Rosolino Pilo* stopped and down by the stern. Just one torpedo was sufficient to sink her but there were repercussions from this action. The *Rosolino Pilo* blew up with such ferocity that the submarine's pressure hull was pierced and all navigational and communication facilities were wrecked. Lieutenant Barlow's description of the event appears in his patrol report:

The explosion of the torpedo was followed instantaneously by another of gigantic proportions as the whole merchant ship exploded. As the Commanding Officer left the bridge, a violent hot blast reached the submarine and debris was already clattering onto the casing and before it was possible to dive a report from the motor room was received of water coming in.[24]

The damage was such that *United* returned immediately to Malta for repair. Captain (S) Tenth Submarine Flotilla was sufficiently impressed by the crew's reaction that he made the following comment:

Submarine work has always been distinguished for producing unexpected situations, which have always been met with equivalent resource on the part of the submariner. The experience of *P.44* [*United*] lives up to tradition and was dealt with by the same resource, which has ever been the submariners' gift.[25]

Just two more attacks were to enjoy success during the month of August. On the 19th, as Lieutenant Halliday patrolled off Levkas in *Unison*, the Italian tanker *Pozarica*, 1,891 tons, was sighted. A full salvo of torpedoes was fired, damaging the vessel to such an extent that it was necessary to beach her. Again this was the submarine's first patrol since joining the Tenth Submarine Flotilla. The success of these two new boys augured well for the coming autumn and winter months when operations would be pursued more vigorously. The final attack was made by *Umbra* with Lieutenant Maydon having resumed command. She was patrolling off the north-west coast of Crete when two merchant ships with a destroyer escort were sighted. One hit out of the three torpedoes fired was sufficient to dispatch the 5,465-ton supply ship *Manfredo Camperio*.

The summer months had seen very little pickings for the submarines and it was hoped that as the autumn months arrived things would improve. Lieutenant J.S. Stevens, RN, in *Unruffled* on his third Mediterranean war patrol, certainly made a good start with three sinkings in just two days. 21 September was a very busy day for Lieutenant Stevens. Early in the middle watch *Unruffled* closed the Italian three-masted schooner *Aquila*, 305 tons, surfaced and engaged her with gunfire. After the first round had found the target, the crew of *Aquila* was seen to abandon ship. The engagement was continued with eight of the next twelve rounds hitting the target, which burst into flames and sank with a small escorting vessel subsequently picking up survivors from the sea. The middle watch had not finished before they had sighted their second target of the day. The 3,890-ton Vichy-French merchant ship *Liberia* was sighted fully illuminated but as she was steaming at night in a prohibited area she was regarded as a legitimate target. One of the two torpedoes dispatched hit the *Liberia* and she sank within fifteen minutes.

Not satisfied with this success *Unruffled* remained in the same area for the following day to be rewarded with yet another target in the silent hours of the middle watch. This was the 1,110-ton Italian merchant vessel *Leonardo Palomba*, again southbound heading towards Tripoli with her cargo of petrol. On this occasion Lieutenant Stevens had to be more patient. His initial attack of two torpedoes both failed to find the target so he surfaced and engaged the vessel by gunfire. This time he was not to be so lucky as after just four rounds the *Leonardo Palomba* returned fire with her machine gun firing tracer bullets. The submarine dived to safety only to resume the attack an hour later when a further three torpedoes were fired. One hit the target amidships and the merchantman burst into flames and sank.

These successes for *Unruffled* were built on by *United* and *Umbra* and made September a reasonably successful month. *United* (Lieutenant Barlow) was the first to strike on 17 September as she patrolled off Ras Misurata. She sighted the 333-ton salvage vessel *Rostro* in company with the 158-ton Italian schooner *Giovanna*, both southbound entering the Gulf of Sirte. Two torpedoes were fired at *Rostro* causing damage that necessitated both vessels to find a safe haven and anchor. This was not to be such a safe haven as *United* trailed them to their anchorage, surfaced, engaged them by gunfire and secured several hits but did not see any damage. The submarine fired one torpedo at each of the vessels, sinking them both.

The final strike of the month went to *Umbra* and Lieutenant Maydon as she patrolled off the island of Zante in the Ionian Sea.

On 27 September she sighted a convoy of two merchant ships being escorted by four destroyers with air cover. It was obvious that the Axis forces regarded this as an important convoy and *Umbra* closed to attack. A full salvo of four torpedoes was fired with one finding the target, hitting and damaging the 6,343-ton merchant ship *Francesco Barbaro*. She was seen to be stopped and slightly down by the stern but the destroyer escort mounted a counter-attack of such ferocity that *Umbra* was obliged to withdraw. Having survived this counter-attack, Lieutenant Maydon returned to the scene and fired two more torpedoes – securing a further hit with the sinking of *Francesco Barbaro*. This was confirmed by recce some seven hours later. This was a major blow to the Afrika Korps as the *Francesco Barbaro* had been carrying a cargo of twenty-one tanks, 151 military vehicles, 1,217 tons of ammunition, 547 tons of oil and 2,334 tons of general stores.

The longer nights and the choppier seas were to lead to greater success in October 1942 with nine vessels sunk and two others damaged. The number of submarines was also increased with *Ursula* returning after refit in the United Kingdom to be joined by *Unseen*, *Unrivalled* and *Unshaken*. The number would have been greater but unfortunately *Unique* was lost on passage from the United Kingdom to Gibraltar.

The successes were to start with the very first day of the month when *United* (Lieutenant Barlow), sighted the 1,148-ton Italian merchant ship *Ravenna* beached at Locri Beach near Messina with a salvage vessel and schooner in attendance. The *Ravenna* had been attacked and damaged by Wellington aircraft of the RAF. One torpedo was fired and the schooner alongside the *Ravenna* was sunk. The *Ravenna* was seen to have settled further down into the water and a further torpedo was fired but missed the target. The submarine withdrew after Lieutenant Barlow had decided that another torpedo was not worthwhile. He returned to the scene three days later and found the stricken *Ravenna* with both forward holds blown open and number one hold blown open on both sides down to water level. She was later towed into Messina and salvaged.

Lieutenant E.T. Stanley, RN, and *Unbending* had sailed from

Malta on 5 October on his first Mediterranean war patrol to cruise to the east of the island of Djerba on the eastern approaches to Tripoli, arriving in position on the 7th. The next day the 349-ton coaster *Lupa* was sighted and attacked by firing two torpedoes, both of which failed to find the target. *Unbending*, not to be denied, surfaced and engaged the *Lupa* by gunfire but just two or three rounds out of forty fired found the target. Whilst they caused no serious damage to the vessel, they were enough to encourage the crew to stop engines and abandon ship. The *Lupa* was then boarded to find she was carrying a large amount of wine and food. She was sunk by demolition charge with the boarding party withdrawing in such haste they forgot to collect a crate of dead chickens they had set aside to confiscate.

The next day *Unbending*, having remained in the same patrol area, was to strike again. During the afternoon Lieutenant Stanley sighted a convoy of six schooners (two of which appeared to be performing anti-submarine activities) and so he decided to bide his time and await dusk. At 19.00 he surfaced, engaged the nearest schooner by gunfire and while none of four rounds fired hit the target, the crew was seen to abandon ship. The schooner was boarded and after it was established she carried fodder she was sunk by fire. *Unbending* remained in the area which had brought so much good luck, to be rewarded yet again just three hours later when the 1,851-ton *Alga* with her cargo of petrol hove into view. She was subjected to a torpedo attack with just one finding the target, resulting in both the ship and the sea around her bursting into flames as the petrol ignited. The *Alga* sank amid a mass of flames. On arrival back at Malta at the completion of the patrol the gunlayer's performance was subject to comment from Captain (S) Tenth Submarine Flotilla when he wrote:

> The Gunlayer who had the distinction of only securing two hits out of 44 rounds fired without opposition who in practice has proved entirely satisfactory. It is evident that he is temperamentally unsuitable for a Gunlayer in action. Failure to hit the target is undoubtedly due to the Gunlayer losing his head.[26]

Whilst *Unbending* remained on patrol, intelligence was received that enemy shipping movements in the Tyrrhenian Sea indicated that a convoy was being assembled and was expected to head for Tripoli. On the 18ᵗʰ this intelligence was confirmed with the sighting of the convoy consisting of three merchant ships and one tanker all being escorted by seven destroyers, southbound off Cape St Vito, Sicily. On receipt of this information Captain (S) Tenth Submarine Flotilla ordered all submarines to intercept the convoy along the route it was expected to take, bearing in mind recent attacks on shipping bound for Tripoli.

It fell to *Unbending* and Lieutenant Stanley to strike the first blow when at 11.15 on the 19ᵗʰ his torpedo attack resulted in the sinking of the 4,459-ton merchant ship *Beppe* – a ship that had survived being damaged by *Ursula* exactly one year previously. This attack also resulted in the sinking of the Italian destroyer *Giovanni de Verazzano*, 2,000 tons. The convoy had not seen the last of British submarines because at 15.10 Lieutenant Mars and *Unbroken* made their attack. A salvo of four torpedoes was fired 'fanned', in an attempt to cover the majority of the convoy. This resulted in the 5,397-ton Italian vessel *Titania* being hit and damaged. On this occasion the enemy escorts hit back hard, twenty depth charges being dropped, with two patterns of four nearly proving fatal. Damage was caused to the submarine's batteries causing a serious battery fire, which could not be extinguished, making the air in the submarine heavy with fumes and gas. Fortunately there was no salt water evident and so chlorine gas was avoided. Amongst all this activity and tension one must look for calmness in the crew and Able Seaman John Jones eased the tension. He wrote out a short note and handed it to Lieutenant Mars, it read:

> Jones, John A.B. D/JX 254129. Request to go back to General Service.[27]

Away from the major convoys, other submarines continued to pick off their individual targets throughout the month. On 10 October *Unison* (Lieutenant Halliday) was patrolling off the Greek coast near Navarin when he sighted and attacked the

4,653-ton *Enrichetta*. All three torpedoes fired found the target, which sank within moments of being hit. When the submarine returned to periscope depth Lieutenant Halliday confirmed that the *Enrichetta* had sunk and saw survivors clinging to pieces of wreckage in the sea. Two survivors were seen just yards from the periscope clinging on and shaking their fists at the periscope. With the approach of a destroyer to collect the survivors, *Unison* made a discreet withdrawal. On 11 October Lieutenant Stevens in *Unruffled* was in the Neapolitan area when he sighted the 1,397-ton Italian merchant vessel *Una* southbound out of Naples. Four torpedoes were fired but none found the target. *Una* had seen the torpedo tracks so slowed engines and allowed the torpedoes to pass ahead of her. She immediately turned about with the intention of heading back to the safety of the port but this manoeuvre allowed *Unruffled* a second bite of the cherry and on this occasion she did not fail. At a range of 1,400 yards Lieutenant Stevens fired the one remaining loaded torpedo and hit the *Una* just forward of the funnel. She was obviously carrying a highly inflammable cargo as she immediately burst into flames and after several small explosions sank within the hour. Two days later, having been re-deployed to Cape Gallo on the northern coast of Sicily, *Unruffled* attacked the Italian steamer *Loreto*, 1,055 tons. One hit out of two torpedoes was sufficient to sink the steamer within twelve minutes of being attacked.

The final attack for October 1942 was on a vessel previously damaged by aircraft of the RAF and which had been beached off Khoms with her cargo of military motor transports. *Umbra* (Lieutenant Maydon) had been dispatched from Malta to deal this vessel a final blow. On approaching the scene on the 23rd, Lieutenant Maydon saw the 8,670-ton *Amsterdam* beached and in the process of unloading her cargo whilst under the protection of an armed trawler and two anti-submarine schooners. The subsequent torpedo attack caused further damage to the *Amsterdam* rendering her beyond repair, and also sank the 182-ton tug *Pronte*, which was in attendance. The submarine quickly withdrew as she was being machine-gunned and bombed by aircraft but no damage was inflicted.

November 1942 was to see the first positive step in the defeat of the Afrika Korps with *OPERATION TORCH*, the landing of Allied forces on the coast of north-west Africa. The 'U' class submarines played a small part in this assault with *P48*, *Una*, *Unshaken* and *Ursula* all involved in the landings. They initially landed beach reception parties on the respective beaches and maintained a presence to act as outer beacons for the incoming assault troops. *Umbra*, *United*, *Unruffled* and *Utmost* sailed from Malta to patrol off the Italian coastline in an attempt to intercept any Italian main naval units intended to counter the assault. These patrolling submarines were restricted to one isolated success when on 6 November off Cape Gallo *Unruffled* sighted the Italian cruiser *Attilio Regolo* under escort from six destroyers. Lieutenant Stevens closed, attacked with a full salvo of torpedoes and seriously damaged the cruiser. This necessitated her being towed into Palermo resulting in her being put out of action for some considerable time.

Notes

1. National Archives Kew Reference: ADM 199/415.
2. National Archives Kew Reference: ADM 234/381.
3. National Archives Kew Reference: ADM 199/1819.
4. National Archives Kew Reference: ADM 199/1819.
5. National Archives Kew Reference: ADM 199/1817.
6. *Forces Sweethearts* by Joanna Lumley.
7. National Archives Kew Reference: ADM 199/1881.
8. National Archives Kew Reference: ADM 199/1817.
9. National Archives Kew Reference: ADM 199/414.
10. National Archives Kew Reference: ADM 199/414.
11. National Archives Kew Reference: ADM 199/414.
12. National Archives Kew Reference: ADM 199/415.
13. National Archives Kew Reference: ADM 199/415.
14. Italian newspaper *Corriere Della Sera* dated 12 August 1941.
15. National Archives Kew Reference: ADM 199/1115.
16. National Archives Kew Reference: ADM 199/1115.
17. *The Fighting Tenth* by John Wingate, DSC, RN Rtd.
18. National Archives Kew Reference: ADM 199/1817.
19. *Periscope Patrol* by John Frayn Turner.
20. National Archives Kew Reference: ADM 199/1819.
21. National Archives Kew Reference: ADM 199/424.
22. National Archives Kew Reference: ADM 199/1813.

23. National Archives Kew Reference: ADM 199/1917.
24. National Archives Kew Reference: ADM 199/1820.
25. National Archives Kew Reference: ADM 199/1820.
26. National Archives Kew Reference: ADM 199/1222.
27. National Archives Kew Reference: ADM 199/1225.

IV

THE MEDITERRANEAN:
OPERATION TORCH TO THE ITALIAN ARMISTICE

November 1942 to September 1943

Signal.
From: Flag Officer, Submarines
To: Captain (S) One
*   Captain (S) Ten*
We watch with pride the splendid continuing successes of your submarines rendered so specially meritorious by reason of the difficult weather conditions.[1]

After the success of *OPERATION TORCH* is was imperative that the British submarines maintained their vigil on the approaches to Tripoli and other North African ports to intercept all maritime communications. The 'U' class continued their contribution to these actions. However, the immediate aftermath of *OPERATION TORCH* was one fraught with danger for the patrolling submarines; both *Ursula* and *Unshaken* were surprised as large liners en route back from the landings passed unannounced through their patrol areas. One of these encounters interrupted *Ursula* as she manoeuvred to attack the U-boat *U73*. This was particularly galling as it was the third encounter with U-boats in two days and had appeared to be the best opportunity for success. As a result of complaints from the submarine commanders, Captain (S) Eighth Submarine Flotilla admitted that although he had warned submarine commanders to expect friendly shipping without warning he had been unaware that they would be routed through the submarine line. He stated that it was rare for British ships to be routed through Allied submarine patrol areas without previous knowledge. The run of bad luck continued when, on 12 November, as Lieutenant Maydon with *Umbra* was patrolling the Gulf of Eufemia, he sighted three Italian battle-ships in the company of twelve destroyers. A full salvo of four torpedoes was fired without success – probably due to an over-estimation of speed.

The first success for some time fell to Lieutenant Maydon in *Umbra* when, on patrol off the western coast of Italy, he sighted the 15,209-ton Italian merchant ship *Piemonte* with one small torpedo boat as escort and accompanied by one aircraft. One of two torpedoes fired hit and damaged the *Piemonte*, which spurred the escorts into action. This resulted in a counter-attack consisting of two bombs from the aircraft and twenty depth-charges from the torpedo boat, but no damage was reported to the submarine. The *Piemonte* was beached to be re-floated later and repaired.

The next success was reported on 21 November with *United*, under the command of Lieutenant J.C.Y. Roxburgh, RN, deployed off the port of Burat el Sun. During the forenoon he sighted a U-boat travelling towards the port at speed. A full salvo of torpedoes was fired without success and the U-boat entered the port safely to be seen later in the day leaving the port, but *United* was not able reach a position to mount an attack. Frustrated by this lack of success Lieutenant Roxburgh took *United* into the port and engaged a moored schooner by gunfire. After twelve hits the schooner was seen to sink. He then turned his attention to a small coaster tied up alongside but after a few rounds the gun jammed and the submarine broke off the engage-ment and retired to sea. This action caused the port authorities to introduce an anti-submarine patrol, and *United* was re-deployed to patrol off Cape Misurata. It was there on the 23rd that they sighted a convoy of six small craft, and closed to engage them by gunfire, but again the gun jammed and the submarine dived to withdraw.

The problem of the gun jamming was not restricted to *United*. It also created a problem for Lieutenant Stevens in *Unruffled* who sighted and attacked a small tug in the Gulf of Sirte on 21

November. The first round misfired but was cleared successfully by re-cocking. After the first round had discharged, the breech had to be hammered open and shut each time. This caused such a delay in re-loading that just two rounds were fired each minute which allowed the tug to make harbour in safety.

25 November was a black day for 'U' class operations. *Utmost*, whilst on patrol off Cape Marittimo, Sicily, was located by the Italian torpedo boat *Groppo* after an unsuccessful attempted torpedo attack on the Italian cruiser *Barletta*. *Groppo* located *Utmost*, attacked by depth charge and sank the submarine. On this same day *Unshaken* was on patrol in the Gulf of Lions and experiencing severe weather conditions when the Commanding Officer, Lieutenant Oxborrow, was lost overboard from the bridge. Yeoman of Signals S.B. Bennett and Able Seaman C. Thorn, manning the bridge at the time, were also lost. After surfacing to make better time towards their allocated patrol area, the submarine lurched and water poured down the conning tower into the control room. Fearing the submarine would founder, the lower hatch was closed and a check was carried out that revealed number 6 main vent was open. The only explanation for this was that when the submarine lurched everyone had to grab hold to prevent falling and someone had inadvertently grabbed the number 6 main vent lever which had opened the main vent accidentally. The conning tower was pumped out and after some delay the submarine re-surfaced but there was no sign of the Commanding Officer or any of his colleagues. A full search of the area was made but to no avail. *Unshaken* was ordered to return to Gibraltar and on 29 November rendezvoused with HMS *Sapphire* to allow Lieutenant J. Whitton, RN, to assume command.

December 1942 was greeted with success as Lieutenant R.B. Lakin, RN, in *Ursula* was on patrol in the Gulf of Genoa, off Savona. On the first night in bright moonlight he sighted the 100-ton anti-submarine schooner *Togo*. The submarine surfaced and engaged the schooner by gunfire, but after just nine rounds had been fired and three had found the target, the gun jammed. However, those three hits were enough to encourage the crew of the schooner to abandon ship which when boarded was found to be carrying twelve depth charges. An explosive charge was set alongside these and the submarine withdrew to enjoy the sight of the schooner being destroyed by an explosion of magnificent proportions.

This was not to be the last success for *Ursula* as just two days later she encountered the Vichy-French steamer *Sainte Marguerite*, 1,855 tons, sailing off Oneglia. The submarine engaged the steamer by gunfire and after nine rounds the gun again jammed. By this time the ship, which had been returning fire from an after-gun, had stopped and Lieutenant Lakin, fearing it to be a 'Q' ship, fired one torpedo which passed under the steamer but was sufficient to encourage the crew to abandon ship by small boat. *Ursula* went alongside the boat and established that whilst it was a Vichy French vessel flying Vichy-French colours it was, in fact, manned by a crew of young Germans. At first they asked to be taken prisoner then later decided against this and pushed off from the submarine and headed for the French coast. The steamer was boarded and searched with all documents and fresh supplies, together with various mementoes, being confiscated. The steamer was then sunk with twenty-five pounds of Amatol explosive placed against the forward bulkhead.

On 7 December the mementoes taken from the *Sainte Marguerite* were put to use. *Ursula* was off Ibiza when they sighted a schooner. As the submarine surfaced and closed she hoisted the Nazi ensign taken from the *Sainte Marguerite*. As the light was fading the 6-inch Aldis lamp was used to illuminate the ensign. The schooner was persuaded to heave to, launch a boat and accept a boarding party. This time *Ursula*'s crew was not so lucky as the schooner had a cargo of rough salt bound for Majorca and had no food on board. The schooner's skipper did offer a bottle of foul-tasting wine before they parted the best of friends with a good deal of Heil-ing.

Ursula's success was joined by *Umbra* and Lieutenant Maydon whilst off Mahedia in the Gulf of Hammamet on 2 December when they sighted the 1,097-ton Italian ship *Sacro Cuore*. They engaged the vessel by gunfire, shooting holes along the entire water line and after just eleven rounds saw the ship being abandoned, so they ceased firing. The submarine then set about recovering the survivors and found that one boat contained nine members of the Luftwaffe and about a dozen German army personnel. The army personnel had been flying from Tripoli en route to Italy when their aircraft had crashed, due to a lack of fuel, and the crew of the *Sacro Cuore* had rescued them. The prisoners were taken directly to Malta where much to their amazement they were all given new boots. They did not believe that expensive leather boots would still be available in Malta. This proved to be a good propaganda exercise and helped ease the interrogation of the prisoners from whom much good information was gleaned.

Lieutenant Turner in *Unrivalled* was patrolling in the Gulf of Tunis on 3 December when he sighted the 81-ton Italian schooner *Cesira Curreri* after a day when he had mounted two torpedo attacks with no success. He surfaced and engaged the schooner by gunfire. One or two hits were made and the crew abandoned ship to swim for shore – not waiting to lower a boat. The submarine withdrew leaving the schooner damaged and abandoned.

Umbra returned to the fray (after landing her prisoners in Malta) on 9 December off Hammamet when the 1,699-ton German steamer *Svelberg* was sighted under escort from three aircraft. Three torpedoes were fired; two struck the *Svelberg* and she sank after exploding in spectacular fashion, indicating that she had been carrying explosives or ammunition. The explosion was such that Lieutenant Maydon claimed one of the aircraft had been brought down. Captain George Simpson in a reaction to this claim said:

> *P35* feels inclined to claim one aircraft from the explosion though the torpedoing of an aircraft at 1000 feet seems more like the story of a rear gunner.[2]

Umbra continued her patrol in the Gulf of Hammamet when on 11 December she was dispatched to investigate a rubber dinghy sighted adrift. She closed the dinghy and found it to contain two German airmen who were so anxious to be rescued they overturned the vessel. One of the men was too weak to climb onto the fore casing so it was necessary for Lieutenant Bruce Collins to dive into the water to rescue him. These two airmen had been part of a crew of four flying in a Ju88 with about thirty other aircraft from Tripoli to Trapani when they had been attacked by Beaufighters and shot down. The other two members of the crew had been killed in the action.

This patrol went from success to success when on 11 December, patrolling off Sousse, *Umbra* located yet another target. Just one torpedo was sufficient to sink the 2,875-ton German merchant ship *Macedonia* loaded with motor transport and cased aircraft. She was left damaged and sitting on the bottom when the submarine was obliged to withdraw due to the attentions of a torpedo boat that had arrived on the scene. The *Macedonia* was salved, only to be sunk at a later date by *Unseen*.

The successful run by *Unruffled* and Lieutenant Stevens was continued on 14 December when two merchant ships were sighted off the Skerki Bank en route for Tunisia under escort from two torpedo boats. *Unruffled* dispatched three torpedoes; one hit the 6,666-ton *Castelverde* causing her to stop. A depth-charge counter-attack forced the submarine deep but on returning to periscope depth some thirty minutes later the final torpedo was fired and the *Castelverde* immediately sank. *Unruffled* then watched as the 4,959-ton *Onestas* blew up as *Sahib* hit her from the opposite side of the convoy.

This was to see the end of Allied submarine successes for a time. The next reported sighting was on Christmas Day and was to be to the detriment of the submarine crews. Lieutenant Turner in *Unrivalled* approached a large schooner off Mahedia in company with two smaller craft. The submarine surfaced on a bright moonlit night, closed and engaged the schooner by gunfire, but the target replied with accurate Oerlikon fire that raked the submarine, forcing her to withdraw. Unfortunately, as the submarine's gun crew was withdrawing over the conning tower, Able Seaman Jack Sim was hit in the stomach and later died without ever regaining consciousness. He was buried at sea following a funeral service in the fore ends. Worse was to follow when *P48*, patrolling sixteen miles north-west of Zembra Island, was located by the Italian torpedo boat *Audace*, depth-charged and sunk with the loss of four officers and thirty crew – surely the cruellest Christmas for the 'U' class crews.

Boxing Day, 26 December, was a far better day. First *Unbroken*, under the command of Lieutenant B.J.B. Andrew, RN, sighted the 2,835-ton *Djebel Dira* in the Bay of Naples under escort by an armed merchant cruiser. A full salvo was fired and the *Djebel Dira* was hit and damaged. After avoiding the usual depth-charge counter-attack Lieutenant Andrew came to periscope depth and saw the *Djebel Dira* stationary with fifty feet of her bows missing and a schooner standing by to rescue her crew. As she was so badly damaged and stood a good chance of sinking he decided not to waste any further torpedoes. In fact, the *Djebel Dira* was towed back to Naples and repaired.

At the same time *Unrivalled* was patrolling in the area of Kuriat when she attacked the 69-ton Italian schooner *Margherita*. The attack had just commenced when the submarine was forced to dive by the approach of an aircraft but later returned to the surface and resumed the attack by gunfire. Two or three hits resulted in many small explosions from the small-arms ammunition the schooner was carrying. After these explosions the *Margherita* sank. This brisk successful action helped raise the crew's spirits after the loss of Able Seaman Sim on the previous day.

Further success was to fall to *Ursula*, which had opened the month's campaign when, on 28 December, she sank the 4,140-ton German merchant ship *Gran*. This merchant ship was north of Marittimo heading for North Africa full of troops and under escort from two destroyers when a salvo of three torpedoes hit and sank her. After a short ineffectual counter-attack the escorting vessels broke off and were seen busy rescuing survivors from the water.

Ursula was again in action on 30 December but this time with a different result. As she patrolled off Cape San Vito on the Sicilian coast she sighted a convoy of three ships being escorted by four destroyers. She commenced her attack only to be pushed deep by one of the escorts and as she came back to periscope depth, saw the target ship zigzag and head straight for her. Before *Ursula* could get to a safe depth she was rammed by the merchant ship causing such substantial damage that she immediately returned to Malta before being dispatched to the United Kingdom for repair.

The final day of the year saw *Unrivalled* add to her success. She attacked the 345-ton Italian ship *Maddalena* by torpedo. It was her intention to attack with two torpedoes, but on firing the first the submarine dipped; before she could be righted to continue the attack the torpedo was heard to hit and sink the *Maddalena* together with her load of wheat heading for Tripoli.

Lieutenant Maydon on the last Mediterranean patrol for *Umbra* opened the account for 1943. On 9 January he sighted the Italian merchant ship *Emilio Morandi*, 1,523 tons, hugging the coastline between Mahedia and Kuriat under escort from four tank-landing craft. His initial attack of two torpedoes, fired separately, was unsuccessful but as the target was only making 5 knots, he maintained contact and carried out a further attack after dusk. On this occasion he fired just one torpedo at a range of 600 yards, hitting and sinking the *Emilio Morandi*.

Umbra was to have further success on the morning of 12 January when two Italian caiques were seen leaving the harbour of Hammamet. The submarine surfaced and engaged both vessels by gunfire but they quickly turned and headed for the beach. One made it and was safely beached but the crew of the second, *Nuovo Domenico*, panicked and attempted to abandon ship. They lowered the boats but both of them upturned and the crew had to swim for shore. Twenty-four rounds were expended obtaining five hits on the *Nuovo Domenico* and she caught fire and drifted onto the beach in flames. The scene was checked two days later to find both vessels still on the beach – of no further use to the enemy.

Flushed with success, Lieutenant Maydon intercepted an unescorted ship off Kalibia on 15 January. He surfaced and engaged her by gunfire but the target vessel quickly returned fire. After just two rounds from her gun *Umbra* was straddled by enemy gunfire; with this Lieutenant Maydon broke off the action and dived for cover.

The same day saw *United* (Lieutenant Roxburgh) patrolling off

95

Marittimo when he attacked a large merchant vessel under escort from two Italian destroyers. A full salvo of torpedoes was fired at the merchantman, all of which missed the intended target, but luck was on the side of *United* as the same torpedoes hit and sank the escorting destroyer *Bombardiere*, 1,646 tons. The crew of the submarine was not to consider this lucky during the next few hours as they were subjected to a concerted hunt and counter-attack by the second destroyer and a number of 'E' boats that joined the search. The counter-attack lasted for some thirteen hours and the Commanding Officer commented:

> Had it not been for the skilful and unruffled demeanour of Able Seaman Donald Duckers, H.S.D., the submarine may well have found herself in difficulties. He proved invaluable to the Commanding Officer during the rather trying period and he is deserving of the highest praise.[3]

The patrol area was so active that for more than thirty-six hours Lieutenant Roxburgh was unable to surface other than for just one minute to allow the atmospheric pressure to be released and ensure the crew's survival. In his patrol report Lieutenant Roxburgh explained:

> Surfaced at 18.36 (18 January) after being submerged for thirty-six-and-half hours during which time the hatch was open for a minute at 22.24 on 17th thereby releasing the pressure in the boat but not allowing any fresh air to enter the boat. Oxygen from the Oxy bottles was released hourly after the first two hours dived but unfortunately, owing to a grave oversight, there was no PROTOSORB on board to get rid of the carbon dioxide. By the time *P.44* surfaced, practically the whole crew and officers were showing considerable distress through carbon dioxide poisoning. On surfacing, the Commanding Officer, whose mental powers were much reduced, was feeling far from aggressive, and he spent the first five minutes on the bridge being extremely ill, as did the Officer of the Watch up there with him and a large number of the crew below.

It was providential that there were none of the enemy near when *P.44* did eventually surface.[4]

The next day *United* was to intercept yet another convoy of ten vessels but the experiences of the previous day had had a devastating effect on efficiency. The torpedo tubes had not been reloaded and the submarine was obliged to go deep to allow the convoy to pass unmolested.

17 January was a successful day with both *Unrivalled* and *Unseen* finding and destroying targets. Lieutenant Turner and *Unrivalled* engaged the 91-ton armed tug *Genova* by gunfire off Sousse. After several hits were recorded the tug was damaged and beached but the intervention of the shore batteries obliged *Unrivalled* to withdraw seawards. At this time Lieutenant Crawford in *Unseen* was off Djerba Island when he torpedoed and sank the Italian merchant ship *Zenobia Martini*, 1,455 tons. There was a short, sharp counter-attack from the escorting destroyer before it withdrew and was seen busily picking up survivors from the sea. Lieutenant Crawford followed this with further success the following day, when, off Zuara, he intercepted, torpedoed and sank the 1,598-ton Italian merchant ship *Sportivo*.

Lieutenant Mars in *Unbroken* then took up the cudgel when on 19 January, whilst on patrol off Ras Turgueness, he struck a mighty blow against the Axis forces. At 16.30 he sighted the 6,107-ton Italian merchant ship *Edda* under escort from two torpedo boats and carrying an estimated 5,000 men to reinforce the Afrika Korps. The *Edda* was closed, torpedoed and sunk within twenty-five minutes, resulting in a desultory counter-attack before the escorts were obliged to return to attempt the rescue of survivors.

The following two days belonged to Lieutenant Turner and *Unrivalled* in the area around Mahedia and Kuriat. On 20 January he attacked two 150-ton auxiliary minesweepers – one towing the other. He hit and sank one and the resultant explosion caused the second to founder before it could be beached. Thus he had destroyed the auxiliary minesweepers Nos. 31 and 36 in the one attack. The next day was the turn of two Italian schooners, again, one towing the other. These were engaged by gunfire and the towing vessel, the 140-ton *Margherita*, was hit and sunk. The second vessel, the 120-ton *Ardito*, was then boarded and after removing some 'loot' she was sunk by demolition charge.

Lieutenant Turner was to continue his good fortune on the days to follow. On 23 January he sighted the 37-ton schooner *Michelino* at anchor off Sousse. He engaged her by gunfire and had caused some damage before the shore batteries intervened, driving the submarine out to sea. The next day Lieutenant Turner was to spot four Beaufighters shooting up a small ketch and forcing the crew to abandon ship. The aircraft withdrew but the ketch did not sink. *Unrivalled* closed, boarded and sank the ketch by demolition charge. On return to Malta Captain (S) Tenth Submarine Flotilla commented:

> This patrol was much to *P.45*'s liking. It is considered that the Commanding Officer showed commendable enterprise in the use of his gun in a class of submarine, which is not conveniently designed for the use of this weapon.[5]

Lieutenant Stanley in *Unbending* was to see further success on 23 January as they patrolled the southern approaches to Messina. The Italian liner *Viminale*, 8,500 tons, was being towed into Messina for repairs and *Unbending*, not to miss any chance, fired three torpedoes and reported two hits. Lieutenant Stanley believed they had both been on *Viminale*, but as she did not sink, he thought he had only caused additional damage to the liner. In fact one of the tugs, the 337-ton *Luni*, had also been hit and had sunk. The subsequent counter-attack by depth charge was prompt and accurate causing such major damage to the submarine's batteries that she was recalled to Malta.

The concluding days of January 1943 belonged to *Unruffled* and Lieutenant Stevens. On 23 January off Hammamet they engaged the 89-ton Italian schooner *Amabile Carolina* by gunfire, recording ten hits on the target before the shore batteries forced the submarine to dive. Not to be denied, Lieutenant Stevens put one torpedo into the *Amabile Carolina* and saw her disintegrate in smoke and flames before sinking. On the 24th *Unruffled* found the 361-ton Italian tanker *Teodolinda* at anchor close to Hammamet, and fired two torpedoes. The first failed to find the target, passing underneath the vessel – the second certainly did not miss. The *Teodolinda* sank in front of the eyes of the onlookers who had gathered on the shore. The 46-ton Italian schooner *Redentore* was the next to fall to *Unruffled* when she was spotted on 26 January, engaged by gunfire and, after nine rounds, was abandoned by her crew. The submarine closed and boarded the ship and finding her awash to deck level left her to sink of her own accord.

The month was closed by *Unruffled* when Lieutenant Stevens used his reasoning and experience to intercept a German vessel en route to North Africa. He had received conflicting reports in respect of a medium-sized merchant vessel en route for North Africa, estimating the destination to be either Sousse or Sfax. He had also heard reports of heavy air-raid activity on the port of Sfax and decided to head for the approaches to Sousse. This decision was proved right when at 10.00 on 31 January *Unruffled* sighted the German merchant ship *Lisbon*, 1,800 tons, coast-crawling as she headed for Sousse. Lieutenant Stevens was unable to close to an optimum attacking position, but in order not to miss the opportunity he fired a full salvo of four torpedoes from a range of 8,200 yards. One of these hit the *Lisbon* and she stopped giving off black smoke before there was a large explosion – the *Lisbon* subsequently sinking just one hour after the attack. On their return to Malta Captain (S) Tenth Submarine Flotilla commented:

> The interception on 31st January was the result of sound reasoning and determined action, and was particularly satisfying as 2,000-ton vessels are the largest on the coast and are scarce at that. *P.46*'s new name *Unruffled* is well suited to her Commanding Officer.[6]

On the very first day of February 1943, *Una* (Lieutenant Martin) attacked two schooners at anchor off Naboel by gunfire, scoring several hits on both vessels before the intervention of an anti-tank gun from the shore forced her to dive to evade damage. She was just a little late and as the bridge was cleared for diving one small shell burst and splinters hit Able Seaman Donohoe in the buttocks causing some discomfort. *Una* found she was unable to reach a safe depth as there was insufficient water. She surfaced and ran for cover during which she was hit on two more occasions before she moved clear. *Una* returned to Malta to land Able Seaman Donohoe where the vessel's damage proved to be insignificant and she sailed the same day to continue her patrol, the last before she was returned to the United Kingdom.

The remainder of *Una*'s patrol was to be off Messina where she was to cause more damage to Axis forces. On 10 February, whilst off Cape Stelletti, she torpedoed and sank the 4,260-ton Italian merchant ship *Cosala*, which was last seen stuck stern first in shallow water with her bows sticking out of the water. *Una* followed this with a final success on 15 February when she found the 3,360-ton *Petrarca* damaged and beached north of Crotone. *Una* evaded the anti-submarine patrol of a brigantine and schooner and fired three torpedoes into the stricken ship which was loaded with ammunition. This hit was followed immediately by several small explosions and some twenty minutes later by one large explosion. This was the final act of the campaign for *Una* and subsequent aerial reconnaissance showed the *Petrarca* to be sunk with only the masts and funnel showing above the water.

4 February was to see further success when Lieutenant Crawford in *Unseen* sighted the 1,085-ton merchant ship *Le Tre Maria Sorelle* off Alice Point under tow. Two torpedoes were sufficient to send her to the seabed.

At this time the Eighth Army was advancing eastwards across North Africa effectively reducing the availability of submarine targets with the consequence that submarine patrols in that area were curtailed. Whilst targets were reduced and more difficult to locate it did not stop submarine commanders attacking at every available opportunity. On 8 February Lieutenant A.R. Daniell, RN, and *Unison* were in the Gulf of Hammamet when he came upon three small boats in the forenoon. The encounter was well reported by Lieutenant Daniell in his patrol report when he wrote:

Surfaced and engaged three motor barges by gunfire. First attacked the near barge, the crew of which had already abandoned ship and were pulling strongly for the beach. Within one minute on surfacing all three barges had stopped and on receiving attention from the gun were abandoned; one caught fire and sank rapidly, one rolled over and lay on the bottom with her side out of the water and the third was still afloat having been hit and damaged later to be beached. As the submarine had been on the surface for 15 minutes bombarding these barges we dived and withdrew.[7]

This attack accounted for the 64-ton *Carlo P*, the 58-ton *Luigi Verni* and the 56-ton *Angela*.

Three days later *Unison* was to have her final success of this patrol when she sank an unidentified 350-ton merchant vessel, obviously fully laden, in the Gulf of Hammamet, off Sfax. The merchantman was engaged by gunfire and hit as the crew abandoned ship with some alacrity when she caught fire. The reason soon became obvious and Lieutenant Daniell described the scene in his report as:

His fuel was alight and in the glare of the fire the swastika was seen flying at the stern. The vessel blew up with a terrific explosion just one hour after the submarine surfaced.[8]

Between the attacks from *Unison*, Lieutenant E.T. Stanley in *Unbending* was also to have a hand in the disruption of enemy shipping. On 9 February off Monopoli he sighted the 2,515-ton merchant ship *Eritrea* travelling unescorted. Three torpedoes were fired; one found the target and the submarine was able to stand by and watch the crew abandon ship. Although she did not appear to be sinking, just twenty-three minutes later she finally went under.

The following day, not satisfied with his earlier success, Lieutenant Stanley went searching off the coast of Montenegro where he found two northbound ships. After allowing the first one to pass he fired two torpedoes at the larger second vessel. Both missed, exploding on the rocks beyond and the submarine was taken deep for a few minutes. On returning to periscope depth he could find no trace of either ship but a search of the shoreline found the 855-ton passenger ship *Carlo Margottini* hidden in Noce Bay. *Unbending* entered the bay and fired two further torpedoes – one hit and broke the back of the *Carlo Margottini*. She was last seen beached and apparently beyond repair.

16 February was a good day for Lieutenant Turner and his submarine *Unrivalled*. The previous day he had unsuccessfully attacked a heavily laden lighter under tow when the intervention of shore batteries caused him to withdraw before he could complete his attack. Today was to be different when he sighted the four-masted Italian schooner *Sparviero*, 498 tons, anchored off Rocella Ionica. The one torpedo fired found the target, breaking the back of *Sparviero* and she was last seen sunken in shallow water. This was followed later the same day when, still off Rocella Ionica, he sighted the 2,215-ton Italian merchant ship *Pasubia*. The destroyer escort was carrying out the usual procedure of indiscriminate dropping of depth charges. On this occasion *Unrivalled* was unfortunate when, as she was passing under the escort, a depth charge fell very close, putting the Asdic out of action. Not deterred, Lieutenant Turner continued his attack and sank the *Pasubia*, with one torpedo from four finding the target.

The final acts for the month were to fall to *Unruffled* and Lieutenant Stevens. On the 18th he was patrolling off the village of Naboel when he came across two schooners, one being the 75-ton *L'Angelo Raffaelo*. He fired three torpedoes at these schooners, none of which found the target but the crews, on seeing the torpedoes, abandoned ship leaving both schooners to the mercy of the oncoming gale that drove both to the shore and wrecked them. On 21 February Lieutenant Stevens mounted the final attack of the month when he torpedoed and sank the 2,115-ton German merchant ship *Baalbek*.

The 'U' class account for March was opened on the fourth day when *Unseen* (Lieutenant Crawford) was on patrol north of Sousse. She sighted the 2,875-ton *Macedonia*, which had been previously damaged by *Umbra* in December 1942. Her cargo was being salvaged by a floating crane before one torpedo struck and sank her, putting her beyond salvaging. It also had the effect of persuading the floating crane to abandon any thought of continuing the salvage operation, and she dashed back to the safety of Sousse harbour.

On 14 March *Unbending* was standing-by off Cape Spartivento to pick up a landing party that had landed the previous night on a sabotage mission. As he checked the area the Commanding Officer, Lieutenant Stanley, sighted a convoy of three southbound merchant ships with an escort of two E-boats accompanied by two aircraft. *Unbending* closed the convoy and fired a full salvo of four torpedoes. Two hit and sank the main target, the 2,163-ton Italian ship *Citta di Bergamo*, another missed the main target but, fortuitously, hit and sank the smaller *Cosenza*, 1,471 tons. The submarine was then subjected to a negligible depth-charge counter-attack before withdrawing from the area. She was later to perform a rescue mission. Flight Sergeant M.E. Redden, the sole survivor of a Baltimore aircraft shot down by two Me210s, was afloat in the Mediterranean when he was picked up by *Unbending*, suffering from nothing more serious than bruising and shock.

During the afternoon watch of 23 March, Lieutenant Daniell in *Unison* sighted a convoy sailing along the southern Italian coastline off Cape Spartivento. It included the 1,833-ton tanker *Zeila* and was under escort from one destroyer, four anti-submarine vessels and what appeared to be a heavy air escort. This obviously was an important cargo of fuel destined for North Africa – a worthy target. *Unison* closed, attacked and sank the *Zeila* by torpedo.

Unrivalled (Lieutenant Turner) made the final attack of March as they patrolled the Sicilian coast. On 29 March they sighted two German sub-chasers at anchor in Picarenci Bay, near Palermo. The 1,374-ton *UJ2201*, (formerly the *Bois Rose*) and *UJ2204* (formerly the *Boreal*) were both torpedoed and sank where they lay. This attack led to a counter-attack of some fifty-one depth charges that was again inefficient and ineffective as no damage was inflicted on *Unrivalled*.

During the previous two months, officers commanding 'U' class submarines on patrol in the Mediterranean reported that on three separate occasions they were subjected to rifle- or machine-gun fire as they closed the coastline. Shore batteries, including anti-tank guns, engaged them on a further four occasions. One submarine, *Unseen*, was challenged by a patrolling E-boat but she managed to dive and avoid any contact and on this occasion no attack was experienced. On other occasions the submarines were not so lucky and withstood prolonged depth-charge attacks – one consisted of more than 130 charges. Fortunately these attacks were not accurate and the only damage inflicted on any submarine was accidental and caused by the precautionary depth charge fired as *Unrivalled* made her approach to sink the *Pasubia*.

April 1943 saw considerable loss of enemy shipping with the 'U' class submarines sinking ten vessels and damaging a further three. The first vessel to be lost was the 230-ton Italian schooner *Triglav* on the very first day of the month. Lieutenant Turner in *Unrivalled* located her off Cape St Vito, torpedoed and hit her, causing a large explosion, following which the vessel disintegrated and sank.

Lieutenant Mars was coming to the end of his last patrol in command of *Unbroken* when on the afternoon of 4 April, whilst deep, he heard the HE of several ships above. He immediately went to periscope depth and saw a large tanker under escort from several torpedo boats. A full salvo of four torpedoes was fired; one hit was heard and the 9,545-ton tanker *Regina* was damaged sufficiently to force her to be beached nearby. This was followed by a sharp counter-attack lasting just eighteen minutes and consisting of twenty-five depth charges that caused superficial damage to the submarine's bridge structure.

Unshaken (Lieutenant Whitton) was in the Gulf of Hammamet when on 7 April he spotted a two-masted schooner hauled up the beach at Nabeul but obviously still operable as her sails were set. Accordingly she was deemed a legitimate target so *Unshaken* engaged her by gunfire and gained six hits from the ten rounds fired that caused her to catch fire. The submarine then withdrew to sea leaving her ablaze. The following day Lieutenant Whitton was to have greater success as he patrolled off Sousse. The 1,245-ton Italian merchant ship *Foggia* was to cross his path and in doing so was torpedoed and sunk.

Lieutenant J.P. Fyfe, RN, was off the southern coast of France on the first Mediterranean patrol for *Unruly* when, on 12 April, he sighted the German merchant vessel *St. Lucien*, 1,256 tons, off Port Vendres. The ship, previously known as the Danish vessel *Aalborg*, was closed and, after firing two torpedoes, two hits were heard and the *St. Lucien* sank. Another submarine to find success on her first Mediterranean patrol was *Ultor* under the command of Lieutenant G.E. Hunt, RN. He was on patrol in the Gulf of Genoa on 14 April when he found the 2,125-ton Vichy-French merchant ship *Penerf* bound for Antibes and operating under German control. A full salvo of torpedoes was fired and with three hits recorded the *Penerf* was dispatched to the deep; the crew safely abandoned her and headed for the coast in two lifeboats.

On 18 April *Unseen* (Lieutenant Crawford) was patrolling off Cape Gallo, west of Palermo, in a glassy calm sea, when three ships in convoy were sighted. Having selected the nearest vessel as the target, *Unseen* closed to a range of 800 yards, fired a full salvo of torpedoes and recorded one hit. This one hit sank the 600-ton German anti-submarine boat *UJ2205* (previously known as the French ship *Le Jacques Coeur*). The attack was heard by *Unison* which was patrolling the neighbouring area. The crew of *Unseen* welcomed this success for, just two days earlier, they had been subjected to a bomb attack and suffered the effects, but fortunately no damage had been incurred. With the sea so calm, it created a mirage, putting submarines in danger of being located by patrolling aircraft. There were occasions when the threat was from friendly forces, not enemy aircraft, as Lieutenant Daniell in *Unison* was to experience when on 15 April they were located on the surface by a patrolling Wellington aircraft. Fortunately the aircraft was identified as 'friendly' and the submarine remained on the surface which resulted in the radio operator intercepting the sighting report by the Wellington bomber – the submarine dived before any attack could be mounted.

The next day, 19 April, was the turn of Lieutenant Turner in *Unrivalled* to inflict loss on the enemy. On patrol off Ustica Island he attacked and sank the 850-ton German supply ship *KT7* as she lay stopped after being damaged by Allied aircraft. One torpedo hit was sufficient to complete the job. *Unison*, patrolling the adjacent area, experienced the results of this attack as they heard the explosion when the torpedo hit and later saw the resultant column of smoke in the distance. Later the same day Lieutenant Turner was to enjoy further success when, off Cape St Vito, he torpedoed and sank the 1,642-ton Italian tanker *Bivona*.

Having heard and seen the results of two previous successful submarine attacks Lieutenant Daniell and *Unison* were to gain their own success. Patrolling south-west of Marittimo en route for Malta on 21 April at the end of a frustrating patrol, he sighted the brand-new 6,406-ton Italian ship *Marco Foscarini*. Two of the four torpedoes fired found the target and the *Marco Foscarini* sank.

The next two successes for the month fell to Lieutenant B.J.B. Andrew, RN, on his first patrol in *Unbroken*. Having failed to hit a passing U-boat with a full salvo of torpedoes that he saw explode on the shore beyond the target, he was to gain success on 22 April off Cape Gallo. They sighted the 380-ton Italian schooner *Milano* at anchor fully laden with crates. Just one torpedo was sufficient to see the *Milano* disintegrate and sink with only the poop sticking out of the shallow water, the crew struggling to cling to any bit of wreckage available. On 26 April *Unbroken* was to continue her success off Palermo when she attacked and damaged the 4,638-ton Italian steamer *Giacomo C.* Just one hit was sufficient to force the steamer to be beached but she was repaired later and put back into service.

Lieutenant Whitton in *Unshaken* was to close the month when operating off Marsala on 28 April. During the previous night they had been the subject of an attack by a 'friendly' destroyer that had opened up with pom-pom and machine gun. The submarine was forced to dive to avoid damage. During the forenoon Whitton sighted a number of small troop carriers being escorted by one torpedo boat. He fired three torpedoes scoring one hit. That one hit sank the 652-ton Italian torpedo boat *Climene*. Although successful the attack was commented upon by Captain (S) Tenth Submarine Flotilla when, forwarding the patrol report, he wrote:

In spite of this successful attack it is my opinion that these shallow draught destroyers should not normally be attacked. Orders to this Flotilla are being issued accordingly.[9]

Unshaken finished this particular patrol in unusual fashion. As she approached Malta in fog she encountered a large convoy at the end of the searched channel. Having asked the escorting destroyers if he could be of assistance, Lieutenant Whitton led the convoy safely into Malta while the destroyers chased off to find any stragglers. Again Captain (S) Tenth Submarine Flotilla was none-too-pleased as enemy submarines seeking easy targets regularly patrolled the approaches to Malta. He commented:

> My feeling of slight anxiety over the fact that Unshaken was in the midst of six merchant ships and eight destroyers in thick fog were unwarranted.[10]

Early May was a busy period for Unrivalled and her Commanding Officer Lieutenant Turner. On 6 May off Cape Vaticano he fired three torpedoes at the 223-ton topsail schooner Albina. Unfortunately the torpedo tracks were spotted by the schooner, which manoeuvred and avoided them. The very next day the Albina was intercepted again and yet again the torpedo attack was unsuccessful. On this occasion both torpedoes appeared to malfunction and collided with each other. Not to be denied a second time, Unrivalled surfaced and engaged the Albina by gunfire and after recording seven or eight hits the crew abandoned ship allowing her to drift onto the shore badly damaged. Two days later it was the turn of the 763-ton Italian naval auxiliary vessel Santa Maria to cross the path of Unrivalled. She was not as lucky as Albina had been, as two torpedoes found the target and Santa Maria sank, with her crew left swimming in the sea.

Lieutenant Fyfe in Unruly was to carry on the good work. On 16 May he torpedoed and damaged the 3,200-ton Italian ship Tommaseo off Catania. Four torpedoes were fired, one finding the target, but the Tommaseo was only damaged and the submarine was forced deep by a counter-attack from the escorting destroyer.

On returning to periscope depth Lieutenant Fyfe saw the *Tommaseo* stopped, damaged, and down by the stern. As he manoeuvred to deliver the *coup de grâce* his approach was interrupted and the submarine was bombed by escorting aircraft that had located it at periscope depth due to the glassy calm sea conditions. Thus *Unruly* was obliged to withdraw and leave the *Tommaseo* afloat, albeit badly damaged. This bad luck was to hold out for the full patrol as Fyfe later failed on two occasions to mount a successful attack on two U-boats on 21 May. On the first occasion he was unable to establish the course and speed of the U-boat due to poor visibility and on the second a full salvo of torpedoes failed to find their target and the U-boat proceeded unmolested.

Unbroken (Lieutenant Andrew) was on her thirteenth patrol but it was not to prove unlucky for them. On 19 May they were patrolling in the Gulf of Eufemia when they came upon a floating crane, normally used in the salvage of cargo from stricken shipping. It was on tow from the Italian tug *Enrica* of 269 tons and escorted by one seaplane. The *Enrica* was torpedoed and sunk with the submarine withdrawing as the seaplane landed to pick up survivors. Just two days later, still in the Gulf of Eufemia, a convoy of three merchant ships under escort from two destroyers with air cover was sighted. The convoy was closed and a full salvo of four torpedoes was fired which resulted in the 5,140-ton Italian merchant ship *Bologna* being hit and sunk. Again the submarine withdrew without any serious counter-attack, as the escorting destroyers were seen stopped picking up survivors from the sea.

June 1943 was to be another successful month as the enemy lost a further eight merchant ships to the 'U' class submarines with the added bonus of one destroyer being damaged. Lieutenant Stevens in *Unruffled* struck the first blow on 3 June off Cape Suvero when he torpedoed and sank the important 9,805-ton German tanker *Henri Desprez*. The escorting torpedo boat made a counter-attack of fifteen depth charges but the submarine sustained no damage.

14 June was another bad day for the enemy as they lost two vessels totalling almost 10,000 tons. The first submarine to strike

was *United* and Lieutenant Roxburgh when the German liner *Ringulv* (previously the 5,153-ton French ship *Sainte Marguerite*) was sighted off the south Calabrian coast under escort and with aerial cover. A full salvo was fired and two hits were obtained and as the submarine went deep the crew was able to hear the sounds of the liner sinking. A patrolling aircraft, overhead at the time, saw the explosion at first hand and was able to confirm the sinking of the liner. The second strike of the day went to Lieutenant Fyfe in *Unruly* off Cape Vaticano when he sighted the 4,485-ton Italian merchantman *Valentino Coda* being escorted by one destroyer. The weather was foul, making the sighting of any submarine difficult so, taking advantage of the conditions, *Unruly* ran in on the surface, fired her salvo of torpedoes and sank the *Valentino Coda*. This attack was commented upon by Captain (S) Tenth Submarine Flotilla when he wrote:

This was a remarkably well conducted surface attack and reflects great credit on Lieutenant Fyfe's judgement.[11]

The following day, 15 June, belonged to Lieutenant Hunt and *Ultor* on patrol off the northern coast of Sicily. The 137-ton cable-laying vessel *Tullio* was sighted off the island of Salina and from her actions it appeared she was being used as an auxiliary minesweeper. Lieutenant Hunt attacked and sank the *Tullio* by torpedo. He followed this up later in the day with an attack on an unidentified Orsa-class destroyer causing her to be damaged.

Another day, another loss, as the very next day *Unison* and Lieutenant Daniell sighted the 2,998-ton Italian tanker *Terni* (previously known as the French ship *Azrou*) under escort from a destroyer and a torpedo boat. As the submarine closed, Lieutenant Daniell was amazed that neither vessel made any attempt to zigzag, making the attack that much easier. *Unison* closed and sank the *Azrou* with two of four torpedoes finding the target. The encounter is well described by Lieutenant Daniell in his patrol report when he wrote:

After firing, the submarine was taken to 120 feet and turned to the north-east. One torpedo was heard to hit after the running time for 700 yards. This explosion was closely followed by a heavier one before what was judged to be another hit. This was succeeded by a terrific concussion that severely shook the submarine (and her inmates) breaking about 30 lamps and bringing down from the pressure hull a rain of rust and cork-paint. It is considered that this explosion was caused by the target blowing up, for the depth charges which followed 5 minutes later sound, in comparison, like distant hull-tapping.[12]

Lieutenant Roxburgh and *United* followed up his success of 14 June by a further sinking on 20 June just fifteen miles south of Cape Spartivento. During the afternoon watch Lieutenant Roxburgh sighted the 3,514-ton Italian liner *Olbia*. On closing her the Commanding Officer described her as a very nice, modern-looking liner with a raked bow but could see no escort. *United* closed and fired a full salvo of torpedoes, obtaining three hits. *United* returned to periscope depth to find the *Olbia* stopped, burning furiously, listing to starboard and enveloped in smoke from aft of the bridge. A large hole had been blown out of the stern on the waterline and flames were seen coming from under the bridge and from further aft. Every member of the submarine's crew had the chance to look through the periscope at the stricken vessel before the *Olbia* exploded and sank in less than an hour.

The final days of June belonged to *Unshaken* and her Commanding Officer Lieutenant Whitton as they patrolled the eastern coastline of Sicily. On 22 June he attacked the 69-ton schooner *Giovanni G* off Cape Murro di Porco with both torpedoes fired finding the target, which disintegrated with the masts and sails being flung over 100 feet into the air before the schooner sank. This was the 1,000th torpedo fired by the Tenth Submarine Flotilla and resulted in another outstanding success. The following day gave Lieutenant Whitton further joy when, off Syracuse, he fired his final two torpedoes and sank the 1,425-ton merchant ship *Pomo* (formerly the Yugoslav vessel *Niko Matkovich*). The *Pomo* was in company with another ship and being escorted by two destroyers when she was hit as they left

110

the harbour of Syracuse. The submarine withdrew as the destroyers and accompanying ships were seen picking up survivors.

July was to see the implementation of *OPERATION HUSKY*, the Allied landings in Sicily, and submarines of the Tenth Submarine Flotilla being deployed in support to intercept the Italian fleet should they put to sea. All the submarines were operating under strict instructions to reserve their first salvo of torpedoes to attack warships or merchant ships over 4,000 tons. The second salvo was to be reserved for warships of cruiser or above. On the completion of these supporting patrols when submarine commanders had watched U-boats pass unmolested due to these restrictions, Captain (S) Tenth Submarine Flotilla was to make the comment that he thought these restrictions defrauded the submarines of valuable targets.

The only successful submarine attack carried out by a 'U' class prior to *OPERATION HUSKY* was on 12 July by Lieutenant Hunt and *Ultor*. On 8 July off Cape Milazzo, north of Messina, they sighted the 6,200-ton *Valfiorita* on her maiden voyage to Taranto being escorted by one destroyer. She was well outside any restriction on attack. Lieutenant Hunt attacked and three out of four torpedoes found the target; the *Valfiorita* burst into flames and sank.

This patrol sector was being shared with *Unruly* and Lieutenant Fyfe. On 12 July he sighted two German U-boats southbound but withheld fire due to the restrictions placed upon him with regard to *OPERATION HUSKY*. This was more frustrating as just two hours after watching these U-boats pass, the restrictions on attack were lifted. However, he did not have long to wait as shortly afterwards the Italian submarine *Acciaio*, 630 tons, was found going southbound and coast-crawling approaching Cape Vaticano. A full salvo of torpedoes was fired and the *Acciaio* was dispatched to the bottom.

A second Italian submarine soon followed the *Accaiao* when on 15 July the 2,200-ton *Remo* crossed the path of Lieutenant Roxburgh in *United* as she patrolled in the Gulf of Taranto. A full salvo of torpedoes sank the *Remo* much to the chagrin of her Commanding Officer, *Tenente* di Vascella Salvatore, who lost his ship on his twenty-ninth birthday. He was taken prisoner along with the Navigating Officer Midshipman Carlo Montemagno and Seaman Electrician Dario Cortopassi, and delivered to Malta for interrogation by the appropriate officials.

With the torpedo restrictions lifted, *Unshaken*, under the command of Lieutenant Whitton, was north of Crotone on 14 July when they sighted two anti-submarine schooners. These schooners had been patrolling every day and had become a source of great annoyance to all submarine commanders. *Unshaken* closed and fired two torpedoes which hit and sank the 105-ton schooner *Cesena*. Lieutenant Whitton in his patrol report wrote:

> The first torpedo completely disintegrated the target. The second schooner picked up a large number of up to thirty survivors but not before four large explosions, quite close, were experienced. These may have been bombs but it was generally considered that they were depth charges from the sunken schooner.[13]

On 17 July *Unrivalled* (Lieutenant Turner) sailed from Malta to patrol the northern approaches to the Straits of Messina. The first day of action was the 23rd off Cape Vaticano when he sighted an unescorted tug. Three torpedoes were fired but all failed to find the target due to the submarine drawing attention to herself. An error during the torpedo firing drill caused her to break the surface allowing the tug to locate the torpedo tracks and manoeuvre to avoid being hit. *Unrivalled* then surfaced to engage the tug by gunfire but no hits were obtained and when the gun finally jammed the action was called off and the submarine withdrew. Thus three torpedoes were fired and thirty rounds of ammunition were expended which resulted in no sinking or damage. No wonder Captain (S) Tenth Submarine Flotilla commented:

> So far the patrol had been a chapter of accidents.[14]

Later the same day Lieutenant Turner sighted a German U-boat. This was a late sighting that only gave one slight opportunity to attack. *Unrivalled* turned to a firing course and fired the remaining one torpedo at a range of 4,000 yards, which missed the target.

The following day they sank the 68-ton Italian schooner *Impero* north-west of Stromboli by gunfire and demolition charge after searching the vessel and taking possession of the charts, ship's papers and other souvenirs. The crew and passengers, consisting of twenty Italian Navy Reserve Officers, together with men fleeing Trapani, were rescued by using the schooner's own lifeboat. After taking two officers and two petty officers prisoner, the remaining survivors were given medical and food supplies and left to pull the twenty miles to the coast. What looked like a resounding success was somewhat soured when it was later established that the schooner had been carrying the monthly pay for the Italian minesweeper crews amounting to 1.5 million lira – a souvenir missed by the boarding party. Just one day later, off Cape Vaticano, *Unrivalled* attacked by gunfire and damaged both the 80-ton Italian tug *Iseo* and the schooner she had under tow. Both vessels were hit several times before they were beached and *Unrivalled* was obliged to withdraw to avoid the attention of the shore batteries. They returned the following day intent on finishing the job but as they approached they sighted the 102-ton Italian schooner *San Francisco di Paola* in the area. She was engaged by gunfire and hit three times out of six rounds; all were on the water line. She quickly turned towards the shore and the protection of the shore batteries, which forced the submarine to withdraw before any further damage could be inflicted. It was noticeable that during this gun action one of the prisoners taken from *Impero*, *Capitano Commissario* Gallia Sebastiano, was seen to be assisting the ammunition supply party. Lieutenant Turner in his patrol report commented that the *Capitano*'s major concern was not for his countrymen in the schooner but for himself and the length of time the submarine was spending on the surface under the guns of the shore batteries.

Unrivalled, arriving at Bizerta on completion of the patrol, joined *Unsparing* (which had arrived just two days earlier) to be the first submarines to use the new base. Lieutenant Turner described the port thus:

113

The city of Bizerta has ceased to exist from the point of shore leave facilities but transport can be arranged to take libertymen to and from Tunis. Tunis is almost unscathed except for the harbour and docks. Prices are high. Libertymen should be warned against some of the wine. Beer can be obtained but beer tickets, which are issued at Bizerta, should be taken.[15]

From an operational point of view he also reported the problems of approaching Bizerta and advised that a pilot be used to avoid collision with the many wrecks in the harbour. He also pointed out the problem of obtaining diesel fuel as he believed the grade of oil available was poor and so neither submarine refuelled whilst there.

Usurper and Lieutenant D.R.O. Mott, RN, had sailed from Algiers and on 27 July was off Ajaccio, Corsica. During the afternoon watch Mott sighted two steamers and one barge under escort from one destroyer leaving the port of Ajaccio, and closed with the intention of attacking both steamers. Two torpedoes were fired and the 2,536-ton *Chateau Yquem* was sunk. The intention to attack the second steamer with the other two torpedoes had to be abandoned when the submarine lost depth during the first firing. 'Q' tank was flooded and the submarine dropped to 150 feet and settled. A counter-attack was made by the escorting destroyer and although one pattern fell close to the submarine, no damage was reported. Lieutenant Mott was to write later:

I spent the rest of the evening regretting that I had not first fired at the destroyer although she was probably the less important target.[16]

On 30 July 1943, *Unbroken* sailed from Malta to return to the United Kingdom after a successful time in the Mediterranean. The Admiralty comments on her service in the Mediterranean were:

The skill with which she was handled throughout this long period (March '42 – July '43), in most hazardous waters, and her many successes against the enemy, reflect the highest credit on the two Commanding Officers, Lieutenant A.C.G. Mars, D.S.O., D.S.C., and Lieutenant B.J.B. Andrew, D.S.C., and her ship's company.[17]

August 1943 opened with two 'friendly' incidents that involved unnecessary injuries and the loss of one life. On 2 August *Unison* was leaving Bizerta en route to Malta when an American merchant ship fired on her. Unfortunately the gunfire was so accurate that the bridge of the submarine was hit, causing the death of the Officer of the Watch, Lieutenant J.P. King, RNR. The Commanding Officer, Lieutenant Daniell, was injured necessitating the amputation of two toes. Leading Signalman James Halliday seriously damaged his right leg falling into the control room from the conning tower and the Coxswain, Petty Officer George Oliver Day, slightly hurt his leg. The injured were treated in Bizerta and Lieutenant King was buried at sea, off Bizerta.

The second incident also occurred at Bizerta when the Navigating Officer of *Unsparing*, Lieutenant A. Watson RNVR, was swimming over the side of the submarine. He slipped on the gun platform and fell, striking his throat. The result of the fall was a swelling at the base of his neck and his throat was blocked making it difficult to breathe. He was rushed to the No. 56 United States Army Hospital and had a successful operation for a ruptured larynx. He was detained in the hospital beyond the sailing time for *Unsparing* and Lieutenant Spratt, an officer taking passage from England to Malta, took over the duties of Navigating Officer.

These unfortunate incidents were counteracted by an early success for *Unruffled* and Lieutenant Stevens. They were off Brindisi on 3 August when they sighted the 3,355-ton Italian merchant ship *Citta di Catania* heading into port fully laden with troops. The submarine manoeuvred into an attacking position and fired a full salvo of torpedoes, three of which found the target, and the ship vanished in smoke and flame before sinking within three minutes of being struck. There was no counter-attack as the escorting ships were too busy attending to the survivors who were clinging to the debris of the *Citta di Catania* or swimming in the water.

Brindisi was to be the target for the next attack – not the port, but the ship of that name. On 6 August *Uproar*, under the command of Lieutenant L.E. Herrick, RN, was patrolling off Bari using her newly fitted radar system when they picked up three vessels leaving the port. *Uproar* closed and identified the 1,977-ton Italian passenger ship *Brindisi* leaving Bari under escort from two small patrol vessels. The target was closed and dispatched with one of three torpedoes hitting her. The submarine withdrew to sea whilst the escorting vessels were busy attending to the stricken ship. This patrol was cut short when a member of the crew was found to be suffering from a poisonous hand that did not respond to treatment.

Bari was to remain a happy hunting ground and a few days later, on 10 August, it was the turn of Lieutenant Whitton in *Unshaken* to achieve success. Having experienced the heartbreak of jettisoning sixty-seven pounds of fresh meat owing to a defect in the refrigerator, she was to revel in that success. They sighted the 7,192-ton naval transport *Asmara* as she left the port under escort from one destroyer. The attack that followed caused sufficient damage to *Asmara* that, as she started to list, the crew abandoned her. *Unshaken* was obliged to withdraw and was subjected to a counter-attack that lasted ninety minutes and consisted of twenty depth-charges. This attack was not too accurate and the submarine reported no damage. Some time later the submarine returned to the scene and watched the *Asmara* turn turtle and sink.

No further success was recorded until the end of the month when, on 27 August, *Unruffled* (Lieutenant Stevens) attacked the 2,474-ton Italian merchantman *Citta di Spezia*, off Brindisi. A full salvo of torpedoes fired from 4,300 yards was sufficient to dispatch the *Citta di Spezia* to the depths. On the same day Bari again became the centre for success when Lieutenant Barlow and *Unseen* attacked and sank the 985-ton Italian merchant ship *Rastrella*. The *Rastrella* had been requisitioned by the Italians in 1942 and renamed, having previously been known as the Greek ship *Messaryas Nomikos*. On returning to periscope depth some thirty minutes after the attack, Lieutenant Barlow saw that the escorting destroyer had left the scene having abandoned a raft

116

with twelve survivors drifting in the sea; three of these were badly injured. Four survivors were taken prisoner and the remainder were given food and medical supplies and allowed to proceed. A flying boat was seen approaching and *Unseen* withdrew in the hope that the seaplane would assist the survivors.

Unseen was to carry on the good work the following day when, off the Albanian port of Valona, they sank the 103-ton anti-submarine schooner *Fabiola* by demolition charge. The submarine surfaced and engaged the target by gunfire but the gun jammed – a problem frequently experienced. However, the gun action was sufficient to encourage the crew of the *Fabiola* to abandon ship. She was boarded to find the Captain, *Capitano* Antonio Vidas, and the boatswain, Carlo Dazzi, still on board. Both were taken prisoner and the schooner sunk.

On 28 August Lieutenant Hunt was off Alice Point in the Gulf of Taranto in *Ultor* when he saw the 679-ton Italian torpedo boat *Lince* beached having run aground on 4 August. Her bows were well beached but her stern was still afloat and a large number of men were seen digging a ditch either side in an attempt to re-float her. Just one torpedo was enough to see her break in two and sink in fifty fathoms of water.

The last success for the month went to Lieutenant A.D. Piper, RNR, and *Unsparing*. On the very last day of the month they were off Bari when they located a convoy hugging the coastline. It consisted of one large merchant ship under escort from two destroyers and four corvettes, all to seaward and accompanied by aerial cover. Lieutenant Piper found himself outside the screen and some 4,000 yards from the target. He decided to abort his attack as he thought the torpedo tracks would be seen by the escorts and avoiding action would be taken. Captain (S) Tenth Submarine Flotilla agreed with this reasoning but added a more experienced Commanding Officer would have penetrated the screen by closing the target earlier and faster. Not to be outdone, Lieutenant Piper maintained his position and was rewarded later when he sighted the naval water carrier *Flegetonte*, 1,182 tons. Two torpedoes were enough to sink her and the submarine withdrew under an inaccurate depth-charge attack that caused no damage.

The Italian Armistice was agreed on 3 September 1943 and included the immediate transfer of the Italian fleet to Allied ports without delay. The submarines out on patrol did not receive the news of the surrender until it was transmitted on 8 September and during which time they continued to achieve a degree of success against merchant shipping.

Lieutenant Whitton in *Unshaken* was on patrol off Brindisi in the forenoon of 5 September when they sighted, torpedoed and damaged the 5,843-ton Italian tanker *Dora C* under escort from two corvettes and one destroyer. The tanker was hit by one of four torpedoes fired, and limped into the port of Brindisi.

In the early hours of the next day *Universal*, under the command of Lieutenant C. Gordon, RN, successfully attacked two schooners off Spezia. At 05.45 he attacked by gunfire the 100-ton schooner *Tre Sorelle*. After just six rounds the crew abandoned ship and a further five rounds saw the target sink. It had not been possible to board her as the action was interrupted by an approaching E-boat. Two hours later it was the turn of the 114-ton *Ugo* to be fired upon and the crew abandoned her to her fate. As *Universal* closed the *Ugo*, her intentions were again thwarted by an approaching E-boat and the schooner was sunk by a further burst of gunfire. This was particularly pleasing for the crew of *Universal*, as a few days earlier they had come close to disaster. She was on her second patrol in the Mediterranean and on 4 September fired her first salvo of torpedoes at two tankers, claiming two hits (which have not been confirmed subsequently from any source). Disaster almost occurred when the submarine nearly broke surface in front of the escorting vessels and drastic action was necessary to prevent this. Captain (S) Eighth Submarine Flotilla, Captain G.B.H. Fawkes, RN, later commented on this when he wrote criticising the training procedure; he said:

This was the first salvo that *Universal* has fired in anger, the only other salvo fired being during discharge trials. During work-up period at home, it has been ascertained that only two torpedoes were fired. I feel strongly that the working-up period at home should not be considered complete unless at least two salvos – apart from discharge trials – have been fired.[18]

This was not the end of the patrol for *Universal* and further incidents were to come her way. On 9 September she was put deep by HE approaching at speed and was kept deep for a further four hours as the Italian battle fleet left Spezia in accordance with the conditions of the Armistice. Lieutenant T.E. Barlow, on passage to Gibraltar en route for the United Kingdom in *Unison*, sighted the fleet, consisting of two Littorio- and five Condottieri-class cruisers together with seven destroyers. Lieutenant Barlow wrote:

> This was an unforgettable sight, fully enjoyed by all and a suitable climax to sixteen months in the Mediterranean.[19]

The final act of *Universal*'s patrol was to come on 11 September when they intercepted a small yacht, forty miles south of Toulon. After taking off the four Italian sailors, who were using the yacht to escape from Toulon, it was sunk by ramming. One of the survivors, Signalman Giusti Gustavo, later wrote to Lieutenant Coates-Walker who was serving on *Universal* at the time. He wrote:

> My Dear Mr. Walker,
>
> I am writing this short letter in the hope that you are keeping in the best of health as I am at present. In case you do not know who this letter is from I am the Italian sailor whose life you saved in the middle of the Mediterranean last September.
>
> I wish to take this opportunity of expressing my sincere and heartfelt thanks to you, the man who saved my life. I would like very much to show how grateful I am to you by giving you a present but in *[my]* present position I regret to say it is impossible, but I wish you to know that I shall never forget you until I die. The humanly act which you performed in saving my life will always remain imprinted on my brain. Here at Brindisi I am working for the British

Navy as an interpreter. A job I like very much knowing that the job I am doing helps in a small way to hasten the end of the war I do it with the utmost care and attention. Having progressed considerably in the speaking of English since last seeing you *[I]* am now, even if I say it myself, a very capable interpreter.

Will you kindly convey my regards and best wishes to the rest of the crew in your ship. To you and to the rest of the ship's company I wish all the very best of luck.

I shall finish this letter again expressing my appreciation of what you did for me and hoping one day I might have the opportunity of seeing you and speaking to you and also that you will write to me in reply to this letter.

Yours very sincerely,

Signaler Giusti Gustavo.[20]

A further development of the Italian Armistice was the interception at sea of Italian submarines. The first was on 9 September (just one day after the Armistice news had been received) when *Unshaken* and Lieutenant Whitton encountered the Italian submarine *Ciri Menotti*. A shot was fired over her and she was ordered to stop but she refused to do so and returned fire by machine gun. The *Ciri Menotti* was eventually stopped and boarded and her Commanding Officer, *Tenente di Vassalo* Giovanni Manunta, explained that he intended heading for Brindisi but, after receiving a boarding party, *Tenente* Manunta reluctantly agreed to head for Malta. To ensure his compliance, a boarding party lead by Lieutenant D. Swanston, RN, the spare Commanding Officer on board *Unshaken* as supernumerary, together with three other ratings, were put aboard for the passage. As further insurance one Italian officer and three ratings were transferred to *Unshaken*.

The second submarine to be intercepted was the *Corridoni* under the command of *Tenente de Vassalo* Aquini. On this occasion it was the *Dolfijn* manned by personnel of the Royal Netherlands Navy under the command of Lieutenant Commander H. Van Oostrom Soede. The *Corridoni* had escaped from La Maddalena and was short of fuel. She was instructed to call at Porto Ferrajo, Elba and proceed to Bone. She was allowed to proceed unescorted and was detained at Elba and never completed her journey.

Two days later as *Unshaken* escorted the *Ciri Menotti* into Malta, the Polish-manned submarine *Sokol* (under the command of Lieutenant Commander George Koziolkowski), whilst standing off Brindisi, intercepted two Italian submarines, both of which had recently sailed from Pola. The first, *Vittore Pisani*, had a boarding party put aboard and was instructed to head for Taranto, being the nearest Allied port. The second, *Otario*, was instructed to follow *Vittore Pisani* making her own way as there were no crew members or small arms available for such a venture. Both arrived at the designated port without any further incident.

On 19 September Lieutenant Turner in *Unrivalled* closed a trawler off Bari flying the Italian naval ensign. He instructed the trawler to convey Sub Lieutenant J. Evans, RN, with his minder Able Seaman D. Lower into Bari to contact the Port Admiral. To ensure the safe return of Sub Lieutenant Evans the commander of the trawler was detained on board the submarine. Sub-Lieutenant Evans did, in fact, return safely and brought with him an Italian Naval Officer with the brief to advise Lieutenant Turner to enter Bari and berth *Unrivalled* alongside. Lieutenant Turner reluctantly accepted this advice and entered the harbour to hold a conference with the Port Admiral. This meeting is well described by Lieutenant Turner himself as:

Contrammiraglio Tommaso Panunzio, *Commandante de Marina* Bari, was a pathetic figure. Extremely distressed at the plight of his country, his service and the shocking state of discipline in the armed forces. Himself a submarine officer, he said he had learned his profession with the British Submarine Service. He was genuinely pleased that the war with Britain, which he never wanted, was ended but was concerned at the internal war he is certain will take place in a disrupted Italy. He was apologetic, courteous and a gentleman. He was extremely nervous and his fingers shook as he used both hands to drink a cup of tea offered to him while in conference with me. He promised eight

121

ships would sail at 18.00 and hoped to give me nine. On leaving the submarine, a car drove up in haste and a Petty Officer, also nervous, reported to him. I could see many men were running about excitedly in the streets. There was an air raid warning in progress and the Admiral told me the German forces were reported to be arriving. This proved to be untrue but I had no intention of being caught alongside and told the Admiral to sail his ships, as many as possible, immediately and that I would wait outside that harbour for them.[21]

Unrivalled patrolled outside the harbour with all guns manned but as there was no sign of any German entry into the town it was decided to re-enter the harbour. As the submarine closed the harbour the first of six ships was seen to be leaving so Sub-Lieutenant Evans and Telegraphist J. Byrne were transferred to the 5,536-ton *Lucrino* to act as Convoy Commander, and the escort to Malta commenced.

The *Unrivalled* was later joined by *Unruly* to assist with the normal problems of convoy work. Problems of transferring supplies from one vessel to another and the ever-present problem of stragglers were all to be dealt with by these two submarines. To add to these problems, during the forenoon of 12 September a German bomber dived out of the sun and bombed the convoy with one large bomb that dropped well clear. Lieutenant Turner commented on this air attack by saying:

This incident had excellent results. It demonstrated the flaws in our preparedness for such events and this was corrected. Its effect on the ships of the convoy was electrical. They made large alterations of course to begin with but were quick to reform when it was evident the danger was past and many "extra revolutions" of speed were found. Ships normally straggling astern leapt into life. More lookouts and binoculars were seen on their bridges. AA gun crews closed up with steel helmets in the Commodore's ship – on the whole the bomb was a blessing and did no harm at all.'[22]

The convoy arrived safely in Malta on 14 September and Captain G.C. Phillips, RN, Captain (S) Tenth Submarine Flotilla commented:

> Lieutenant Turner received a written testimonial from the Senior Italian merchant ship Captain for his conduct of the convoy. It is considered that this operation showed commendable enterprise on the part of Lieutenant Turner and that the part played by Sub-Lieutenant Evans contributed in no small measure to the successful delivery of this unusual submarine 'bag'.[23]

The reason for the Polish-manned submarine *Sokol* being off Brindisi when they intercepted the Italian submarines was that Lieutenant Commander Koziolkowski had been ordered to contact the Naval Authorities there. He first attempted this by signalling the shore signal station but these efforts were ignored. He then closed a patrolling torpedo-boat but on seeing the submarine it scuttled back into port. Having been frustrated by these constant rebuffs Lieutenant Commander Koziolkowski was pleased when the hospital ship *Saturnia* hove to at his behest. The ship's captain visited the submarine before an Italian minesweeper came out to rendezvous with the *Saturnia* and confirmed there were no German troops in Brindisi. The *Saturnia* was instructed to proceed to Taranto unescorted. Lieutenant G.G. Taylor, RN, the Royal Navy Liaison Officer, together with his escort of two ratings, was dispatched into Brindisi aboard the minesweeper. He found that considerable confusion reigned inside the port; the harbour was crowded with shipping mostly damaged or full of refugees and he arranged for seven merchant ships to leave Brindisi for Taranto, six of which were to leave that very night.

Lieutenant Taylor also found the Italian cruiser *Scipio Africanus*, together with two destroyers and eight corvettes, still in Brindisi in contravention of the Armistice agreement. The Port Admiral insisted that they could not sail in accordance with the agreement as they remained in Brindisi on a special mission. It was established that the Italian King, Marshall Badoglio, and the whole

Italian Government were in Brindisi and the warships were standing by to evacuate them. *Sokol* remained on patrol outside the port and Lieutenant Commander Koziolkowski held a personal meeting with the Italian Admiral. Afterwards he wrote in his patrol report:

> He appeared to be in trouble, which I believe was quite true, having the harbour overcrowded with shipping and more ships expected to come, including the *Vulcania*, and two naval training ships, *Cr. Columbo* and *Am. Vespucci*. I was shown the daily report of ships in the harbour and out of eighteen in number only three were not marked damaged or unseaworthy. I remarked to have watched them on the previous days to come under their own power, all being new modern ships, which remark quite embarrassed the Admiral. I believe the master[s] claimed their ships to be damaged because they did not like the prospect of being sent far away from home and especially to proceed without minesweepers like the first convoy sent to Taranto on the 12th. Besides sending ships to Taranto was not a solution and the Admiral agreed to prepare the next convoy in two to three days time which might go to Malta. The reason for the delay was that all ships were bringing hundreds of evacuees and as there was no possible accommodation for them, they were being kept for the time being on board. Both the Admiral and the submarine *Pisani* were unbelievably astonished to find a submarine under Polish colours in the Adriatic. The Admiral was full of hospitality, offering *Sokol* a berth on the cruiser. As the recall signal was received with orders to leave the area that night, I did not enter the harbour. The reception of the shore party in the town was extremely enthusiastic, including the hugging and kissing by women offering champagne, expressing welcome to the Allies and hate for Fascism – it appeared that there was not any single Fascist in Brindisi![24]

Notes

1. National Archives Kew Reference: ADM 199/415.
2. National Archives Kew Reference: ADM 199/1813.
3. National Archives Kew Reference: ADM 199/1820.
4. National Archives Kew Reference: ADM 199/1820.
5. National Archives Kew Reference: ADM 199/1821.
6. National Archives Kew Reference: ADM 199/1225.
7. National Archives Kew Reference: ADM 199/1822.
8. National Archives Kew Reference: ADM 199/1822.
9. National Archives Kew Reference: ADM 199/1823.
10. National Archives Kew Reference: ADM 199/1823.
11. National Archives Kew Reference: ADM 199/1824.
12. National Archives Kew Reference: ADM 199/1822.
13. National Archives Kew Reference: ADM 199/1823.
14. National Archives Kew Reference: ADM 199/1821.
15. National Archives Kew Reference: ADM 199/1821.
16. National Archives Kew Reference: ADM 199/1818.
17. National Archives Kew Reference: ADM 199/1826.
18. National Archives Kew Reference: ADM 199/1823.
19. National Archives Kew Reference: ADM 173/18354.
20. Lieutenant Ronald Coates-Walker, RNVR Rtd.
21. National Archives Kew Reference: ADM 199/1821.
22. National Archives Kew Reference: ADM 199/1821.
23. National Archives Kew Reference: ADM 199/1821.
24. National Archives Kew Reference: ADM 173/1854.

V

THE MEDITERRANEAN
AND BEYOND

Italian capitulation through to VJ Day

*I am happy to report that the state of the British and Polish
submarines in the Mediterranean generally is highly satisfactory
and well up to the standards of the Submarine Service.*

Admiral Max Horton[1]

With the capitulation of the Italian forces, German shipping was
obliged to find alternative bases with the consequence that
submarine patrols were concentrated on the southern coast of
France, Corsica and along the Bay of Genoa. Success was to come
on 21 September 1943 with *Unseen* (Lieutenant Barlow) off
Spezia when two merchant ships were sighted escorted by
E-boats. Lieutenant Barlow waited until the two target vessels
were overlapping, fired a full salvo of torpedoes and was able to
report the sinking of the 2,600-ton *Kreta* (previously known as
the French ship *Ile de Beaute*) and the 3,894-ton auxiliary
minelayer *Brandenburg* (previously the French ship *Kita*).

The following day was to belong to Lieutenant Herrick and
Uproar for, as they patrolled off Porte Ferrajo on the Isle of Elba,
they sighted and sank the 731-ton naval auxiliary *Andrea
Sgarallino*. They were to have more success later in the patrol
when on the 27th they sighted the 9,945-ton tanker *Champagne*,
damaged and beached just south of Bastia. Just one torpedo was
sufficient to hit and further damage the tanker as she settled
further down in the water. The *Champagne* had been beached due
to an earlier attack carried out by *Ultor* and Lieutenant Hunt on

126

24 September when they had sighted her leaving Bastia, loaded with motor lorries, and under a heavy escort. On this occasion they had scored two hits forcing the merchant ship to be beached half a mile south of Bastia. They returned to the scene the following day in the hope of finishing the job with their last torpedo. Unfortunately it missed the target but fortune was to shine on *Ultor* as this torpedo found a Siebel ferry in attendance, sinking it before the submarine had to withdraw due to the attentions of the patrolling E-boats.

Ultimatum and Lieutenant Kett made the final thrust in this area for the month of September. On the last day of the month they were patrolling off Toulon when they spotted four large, self-propelled, 500-ton ammunition barges under escort from seven French chasseurs. Lieutenant Kett closed the convoy and attacked by torpedo, hitting and sinking one of the barges. The subsequent explosion was so ferocious that it damaged the submarine with 'H' sea flood valve flooding 'H' tank, causing the submarine to plunge to a depth of 160 feet before hitting the seabed. This collision caused damage to the propeller and Asdic dome. The damaged submarine lay on the seabed for seven-and-a-half hours whilst the escorting vessels above searched in vain. Silent running was ordered and was only broken by fits of coughing from crewmembers suffering from heavy coughs and colds.

As the pattern of the campaign changed, the main thrust of the submarine patrols was slowly diverted to the Aegean Sea and the German activities amongst the Greek Islands. On 27 September Lieutenant A.D. Piper, RNR, in *Unsparing*, was off Cape Malea on the southern coast of Greece when he intercepted the 28-ton caique *No. 238*. As he opened fire on the caique the crew abandoned ship, the vessel was boarded and demolition charges placed. Unfortunately these failed to detonate and the caique was sunk by gunfire.

October 1943 opened with *Unshaken* and Lieutenant Whitton patrolling off the Island of Elba and on the second day he intercepted a convoy of troop-carrying 'F' lighters. He surfaced and engaged them by gunfire, strafing one lighter and causing many casualties, but the gun jammed after just twenty-five rounds. The lighter returned fire with her Oerlikon guns causing slight damage to the aerial set-up, and forced the submarine to dive for cover.

On 3 October Lieutenant Mott, patrolling the Gulf of Genoa in *Usurper*, sighted the German anti-submarine vessel *UJ2208* which he attacked with torpedoes but without success. The subsequent counter-attack by *UJ2208* was so accurate that the *Usurper* was lost along with her entire crew.

Lieutenant Piper and *Unsparing* opened their October campaign with a dramatic rescue some 125 miles south-west of the coast of Crete. On the 7th they sighted what appeared to be an abandoned open boat but on closer inspection they found two German soldiers both close to death from starvation. The two men belonged to the 6 *Festungs* Battalion 999, 21st Company. They were in such a poor physical condition that they were very happy to be taken prisoner. They explained that on 29 September they had left the island of Kaso as part of a group in fifteen small boats under tow from a motor boat bound for the neighbouring island of Scarpento. At that time they had three men on board but during the night of 30 September the wind got up and the boats were cut adrift and the third member of their crew dived over the side and swam off. The two remaining soldiers were adrift in a small boat with no food or water. They rowed for some time in what they believed to be the direction of Scarpento but after a while became exhausted and allowed themselves to be carried by the wind, hoping it would bring them to land. When they were found they were 145 miles from Kaso in the opposite direction to Scarpento. Both men were treated for their various ailments and survived the ordeal.

This was the start of a busy month for Lieutenant Piper and *Unsparing* for the very next day they encountered the caique *Alep*. One star shell fired to assist in identification in the dark was sufficient to encourage the crew to abandon ship. The caique was closed and on closer inspection was found to be en route from Limassol to Haifa to deliver 1,470 cases of Cyprus brandy to the NAAFI there. Once this had been verified the crew were encouraged to return to their craft and Lieutenant Piper sent over a pack of 200 cigarettes as compensation for their inconvenience. The skipper of *Alep* returned the compliment and sent over three bottles of excellent Cyprus brandy and both vessels went on their way.

9 October was to see *Unsparing* intercept the schooner *Abdullah* and as the submarine opened fire the crew abandoned ship. This resulted in no hits on the schooner so Sub Lieutenant H. Straw, RNVR, and a skeleton crew were put aboard and the *Abdullah* was taken under tow to Beirut.

Unsparing was to end the month as it had begun. On 29 October as they were patrolling south-west of Anaphi they attacked a convoy of two escorted merchant ships. They torpedoed and sank the 1,160-ton troop carrier *Ingeborg* with two from four torpedoes finding the target. The submarine went deep and on returning to the scene some five hours later witnessed a scene of utter devastation. There were lifeboats, rafts of all description and bodies strewn amongst the wreckage. The German auxiliary patrol boat *AS49* (previously known as the 60-ton *Nioi*) was crammed with survivors and was stopped attempting to rescue more from the water when the one torpedo fired found the target and she disintegrated on impact. Before the submarine finally withdrew from the scene they inspected the floating lifeboats but found no sign of life. The last thing they saw was an Arado seaplane taxiing towards Stampalia with survivors clinging to the wings and floats.

The following day *Unsparing* was not so lucky. Whilst off Amorgos they made a surface attack on a caique which turned out to be a troop carrier. As they surfaced and closed and the gun crew went to action stations, the caique opened fire with machine guns and cannon. The Gunnery Officer, Sub-Lieutenant Straw ordered the decks to be cleared in preparation for the submarine to dive. Before this could be achieved a shell hit the base of the conning tower, blowing a hole one-foot square in the bridge casing. This hit resulted in the death of Able Seaman Wilson who was lost over the side and also caused injuries to the Gunnery Officer and Petty Officer Parry. Petty Officer Parry had shrapnel damage to his face with several pieces entering his right eye. These injuries gave such cause for concern that Lieutenant Piper decided to curtail the patrol and return to Beirut for the Petty Officer to receive medical attention. The body of Able Seaman Wilson was never recovered from the sea.

Whilst these patrols amongst the Greek islands were being pursued by submarines of the First Submarine Flotilla, submarines from the Eighth and Tenth Submarine Flotillas were still giving attention to the southern coastline of France. On 14 October *Unseen* and Lieutenant Crawford were on patrol off Toulon when they sighted the U-boat *U616* but before any attack could be mounted the U-boat's lookouts spotted the *Unseen* and she turned away and dived to safety. The crew of *U616* was to have the same type of luck the following day, this time at the hands of Lieutenant Boyd in *Untiring*. On this occasion her torpedoes were actually fired but the lookouts spotted the tracks and the U-boat turned to safety. These two incidents highlighted the concentration and efficiency of the crew of *U616*.

There were three further successes during October and the first went to Lieutenant Hunt and *Ultor* as they patrolled the Gulf of Genoa. On the 19th they sighted the 3,723-ton German passenger ship *Aversa* under escort from several surface vessels. Lieutenant Hunt closed the target, torpedoed and sank her. He was able to watch as the *Aversa*, hit by two torpedoes, reared up vertically until eighty feet of her bows were out of the water, then sink within four minutes.

On the 22nd *Unseen* and Lieutenant M.L.C. Crawford, patrolling in the Gulf of Genoa, off Imperia, fired a salvo of torpedoes at two 150-ton 'F' lighters; one, *F541*, was sunk. The second lighter made off towards land pursued by *Unseen* but the fourth torpedo failed to find its target.

On 30 October *Ultimatum* (Lieutenant Kett) was on patrol off Toulon when they sighted the *U431* under the command of *Oberleutnant* Dietrich Schoneboom. *Ultimatum* fired three torpedoes and heard what sounded like a hit, and contact with *U431* was lost. Obviously the submarine claimed the sinking, but this was overruled by the Admiralty U-boat Assessment Committee who awarded the loss to an aircraft of 179 Squadron.

The month of November 1943 was a very quiet time for the 'U' class submarines. On 6 November Lieutenant Turner in *Unrivalled* rescued two British flyers from their dinghy afloat in the

Aegean Sea. They were the pilot and observer of a Beaufighter aircraft shot down earlier in the day during an attack on enemy shipping. Both were in good spirits. On the 16th *Universal*, off Toulon, sighted a U-boat but before any attack could be mounted the U-boat lookouts had seen her and had dived to safety. The only success of the month was to fall to Lieutenant Gordon and *Universal*, still patrolling off Toulon, when on the 22nd he torpedoed and sank a 600-ton lighter that exploded on impact and sank almost immediately.

December 1943 was to see major changes for the Tenth Submarine Flotilla. Captain G.C. Phillips, Captain (S) Tenth Submarine Flotilla left Malta to set up a new base at La Maddalena to facilitate easy access to the southern coastline of France. The base became operational on 5 December with the first submarine, *Uproar*, arriving on the 17th. Captain Phillips gave his assessment of the base in his Monthly General Letter dated 10 January 1944 when he wrote:

> The Submarine Barracks was previously occupied by the Tenth Submarine Flotilla of the *Regia Marina*. Accommodation for officers is good, except that no wardroom was provided. A wooden hut has been erected for this purpose and was painted out by a team of submarine officers. It provided for a very reasonable ante-room and messroom. Ratings accommodation, as I understand is usual in Italian Barracks, is below the standard which we normally provide, but alterations and additions have affected a marked improvement in this respect. The Italian repair ship *Paccinotte* is being used as the flotilla workshop. She is manned by a mixed compliment of Italian Naval and civilian technicians who, under close supervision from the flotilla staff, are producing good results. The submarine pens are undamaged and provide excellent berthing for U-class submarines. They are adjacent to *Paccinotte* and are five minutes walk from the Barracks.[2]

Prior to arriving at La Maddalena, *Uproar* under the command of Lieutenant Herrick, enjoyed success whilst on patrol along the

French coastline between Nice and Cannes. On 6 December, off Cape Drammont, they sighted the 11,718-ton German liner *Vergilio* (previously known as the Yugoslav ship *Dubrovnik*), under escort from just one destroyer. A full salvo of torpedoes was fired; one found the target and the *Vergilio* was sunk. The submarine was subjected to a short and ineffective counter-attack before the escorting destroyer was obliged to call off the encounter and go to the aid of the stricken liner. This was the last ship over 10,000 tons to be sunk by Allied submarines in the Mediterranean.

More success was to be enjoyed by Lieutenant Boyd in *Untiring* when on 14 December they discovered the German minelayer *Netztender 44* laying mines off Monaco. The minelayer was followed as she entered the harbour and from 500 yards out Lieutenant Boyd fired one torpedo through the harbour gate hitting the *Netztender 44*. She still had a quantity of mines on board and the resultant explosion uprooted trees along the seafront and caused considerable damage to the International Geographical Building, together with other seafront properties.

Untiring had not yet finished causing damage to enemy shipping but before she could make any further attacks she herself was subjected to a torpedo attack. On 17 December she was patrolling on the surface off Cape Moli when she was sighted by a destroyer and attacked by torpedo. Fortunately none found the target; all passed well ahead and the submarine dived to safety. Later that day *Untiring* was to gain success when they came across a small convoy under escort from two anti-submarine vessels. *Untiring* torpedoed and sank the tug *Faron* causing damage to the second vessel, which was then beached. Just one hour later *Untiring* returned to the scene, fired one torpedo and hit the vessel, which blew up with all the ammunition she carried, and sank. Lieutenant Boyd described the final moments of the attack in his patrol report thus:

> When last seen the escorts had given up the unequal struggle, tucked their heads into the beach and presented rounded sterns to the storm; they looked curiously like dejected cattle on a wet and windy day. Having lost both

132

their charges, they remained where they were, pointing (appropriately enough) towards the town of Finale.[3]

The next day, 18 December, was to see further successes for the British submarines. In the forenoon Lieutenant Gordon in *Universal* was patrolling along the northern Italian coastline between Rapallo and Spezia when he sighted two merchant ships being escorted along the coast on the 100-fathom line. He closed and fired a full salvo; two torpedoes hit and sank the 2,497-ton *Le Foce*. Lieutenant Hunt in *Ultor* followed this later in the day when he torpedoed and sank one of two 250-ton French barges intercepted off Toulon.

The Aegean Sea was still the priority of the First Submarine Flotilla and Lieutenant Fyfe in *Unruly* was dispatched to patrol the area. On 2 December he was patrolling south of Levitha when he engaged a two-masted 50-ton caique by gunfire. Of fifty-eight rounds expended just twelve hit the target, sinking the caique as the crew of two escaped by small boat. This was to be the only success of this patrol. A further gun engagement, expending the remaining thirty-four rounds was made on another caique but no damage to the target was reported. Torpedoes fired at caiques in the port of Panormos, Mikonos, missed the targets and exploded when they hit the rocky shoreline. Captain D.C. Ingram, RN, Captain (S) First Submarine Flotilla, commented on the attack by questioning the wisdom of a torpedo attack on such small targets. The only other attack was a torpedo attack on the German minelayer *Drache* loaded with troops, but again the torpedoes failed to find the target.

The final action of 1943 was to the detriment of the British submarines, and *Unseen* in particular. She was on her final patrol in the Mediterranean off the southern coast of France when, on 21 December, a patrolling anti-submarine vessel located her. The first pattern of depth charges exploded very close to the submarine, the effect being described by Lieutenant Crawford in his patrol report as:

The whole submarine seemed to jump and quiver with a whipping effect.[4]

This attack lasted just eight minutes and during that time the engine-room hatch lifted slightly letting seawater into the engine room, 'Q' tank flooded and 'H' gauge glass was smashed along with a large amount of crockery. It was also discovered that a leak had occurred to the telemotor supply for numbers 2 and 4 torpedo bow caps. The submarine was taken deep to 200 feet and slipped away southward to safety. When they surfaced some three hours later there was no sign of the attacking vessel. Lieutenant Crawford decided to stay off shore on the following day to effect minor repairs to enable him to remain on patrol but no further incidents were experienced.

Untiring (Lieutenant Boyd) opened the year of 1944 when on 6 January he torpedoed two 'F' lighters off Spezia, sinking one of 350 tons. Lieutenant Boyd was also to close the month on 31 January off Cape Camarat by firing at and sinking two 500-ton coasters being escorted by several small, armed surface vessels.

In early January Lieutenant Fyfe was patrolling in the Aegean Sea in *Unruly* but was not to gain any success during his first encounter with the enemy. On 7 January he was patrolling the eastern approaches to the Doro Channel when he encountered the German tanker *Bacchus* under escort from two destroyers. He was not in a position to attack and in order to gain such a position it was necessary for the submarine to close on the surface. As he attempted to do so he was seen by one of the escorting destroyers and forced deep, enabling the *Bacchus* to make good her escape. The Polish submarine *Dzik* attacked *Bacchus* later the same day but the attack failed and she was able to continue her passage oblivious of any threat.

Lieutenant Fyfe was not finished and continued his patrol in an aggressive manner. On 10 January he sank a 100-ton caique by gunfire off Cape Doro and followed this up later in the day by sinking a 40-ton caique, again by gunfire, in Vitali Bay on the island of Andros. The next day he closed the port of Panormos and sank three further caiques of 40-, 100- and 150 tons respectively by gunfire. This attack was described by Lieutenant Fyfe in his patrol report:

A keen interest was displayed by the locals, with the exception of one old man fishing from about 300 yards away, who evidently considered his evening meal to be of vastly greater importance. A hard race for a point of vantage, between a nun and a well-proportioned young woman was also observed. The latter won in a canter![5]

15 January 1944 saw them sink a small 20-ton caique off the island of Tinos, again by gunfire.

On his way back to Beirut, Lieutenant Fyfe expended the remainder of his ammunition by bombarding the lighthouse at Kandelusia but only three hits were made and little damage was done. On returning to Beirut Captain D.C. Ingram, Captain (S) First Submarine Flotilla commented:

The sinking of these caiques is always stimulating to the ship's company and keeps up the interest and excitement. I consider Lieutenant Fyfe showed great enterprise in effecting these sinkings, which in some measure made up for the disappointment in being thwarted in his attack on the morning of 7th January.[6]

Lieutenant A.D. Piper in *Unsparing* was also on patrol in the eastern area of the Aegean during this month. On 15 January he attacked several caiques by gunfire in the harbour of Port Plati on the island of Samos. The action led to three caiques sunk and two others damaged, with only nineteen rounds of ammunition expended. The submarine was then obliged to withdraw due to the attentions of shore-based machine-gun fire. This was a welcome break for the crew of *Unsparing* as on three consecutive days earlier in the patrol they had sighted caiques but for one reason or another had not been in a position to make a positive attack. The only other success for the patrol was during her return passage to Beirut when they bombarded the lighthouse at Kandelusia. This was just two days after *Unruly* had visited the lighthouse but on this occasion the bombardment was more successful with several hits being recorded, one of which demolished the lantern, and Lieutenant Piper commented:

135

This light would not be much use for quite a while.[7]

To ensure the lighthouse stayed out of commission Lieutenant Kett in *Ultimatum* continued the attention by bombarding it during the night of 5 March and scoring seven hits out of the ten rounds expended.

While the submarines of the First Submarine Flotilla were patrolling the Aegean, the Tenth was keeping up the pressure along the southern coast of France. Lieutenant Chapman in *Upstart* had a near miss on 21 January whilst patrolling off Cape Camarat. The submarine came from deep to periscope depth to attack a camouflaged tanker under escort from a destroyer. Due to an error in the drill, the submarine broke the surface. Fortunately they were able to rectify the mistake quickly but it was too late to gain a good attacking position and four torpedoes were fired, more in hope than anticipation – all four missing the target.

Lieutenant Chapman was not to let this deter him and during the following days made a real nuisance of himself along the coastline. On 23 January he bombarded a suspected seaplane station at the head of the Gulf of Napoule obtaining twenty-two hits from twenty-five shots before the gun jammed and the submarine withdrew. On 27 January he bombarded another suspected seaplane station, this time near St Raphael in the Gulf of Frejus scoring fifty hits out of fifty-two shots before all the ammunition was expended and the submarine withdrew seawards.

Upstart and Lieutenant Chapman returned to the area on his next patrol and on 15 February they were off Toulon when they sighted the 1,796-ton German ship *Nieder Sachsen* laying mines off Cape Cepet, accompanied by two 'R' boats. One of three torpedoes fired hit the vessel and she was seen to sink, with the survivors crowding onto the decks of the two escorting vessels. On the same day Lieutenant Hunt in *Ultor* was further along the coast off St Raphael when he engaged and sank a modern 50-ton schooner by gunfire.

At this time the northern Aegean Sea was being patrolled by *Unsparing* (Lieutenant Piper). On 19 February they were patrolling the Gulf of Salonika on a dark and cloudy night when they encountered a convoy of two ships, including the 3,754-ton tanker *Peter*, with two armed escorts. As a result of a misunderstanding of orders just one torpedo was fired but, fortunately, it found and damaged the *Peter*. The submarine was taken to 150 feet and shut off for depth-charging and they were not disappointed as just ten minutes after the *Peter* was hit, the counter-attack commenced. This was especially accurate and the submarine was damaged; in particular the 'Q' tank vent was blown open, sending the submarine down to 325 feet, and this depth was held only by increasing speed. The damage put every compass out of action. Navigation for the remainder of the patrol relied upon a 1914-18 army field compass belonging to the Torpedo Officer. The *Peter* was originally abandoned after one of the holds was flooded but the crew were persuaded to return when it appeared that she was not going to sink, and she was eventually beached at the port of Volo some nine hours later.

Lieutenant Piper was to continue carrying the fight to enemy shipping and on 22 February he sank, by gunfire, the 10-ton caique *Evengelistria* off Volo, taking prisoner the three Greek crew members. He followed this on 25 February with two more successes off Cape Drepano. First he sank the 50-ton caique *SY547*, initially engaging her by gunfire, but after the crew abandoned her she was boarded and sunk by demolition. Later in the day he encountered another caique, this time of 100 tons, and carrying petrol. He engaged her by gunfire and the caique was hit, burst into flames and sank.

It is necessary to return to Toulon for the final action of the month with Lieutenant Herrick and *Uproar*. They celebrated the extra day of Leap Year on 29 February by torpedoing and sinking the 3,152-ton German-controlled steamer *Artesian* (formally known as *Chietti*); all four torpedoes found their target.

By now locating targets was becoming very difficult and March 1944 saw just three successful attacks which resulted in enemy shipping losing two vessels. The first, on 13 March, fell to Lieutenant Hunt in *Ultor* patrolling off Monemvasia when he torpedoed a stationary 'F' lighter in the Bay of Paleo, sinking her with just one torpedo. Six days later, on 20 March, it was to *Unswerving* and Lieutenant M.D. Tattersall, RNVR, that the opportunity of a second strike fell. They were patrolling some thirty miles north of Suda Bay, Crete when they encountered an 80-ton caique. After expending four rounds, two found the target and it burst into flames followed by a spectacular explosion as the caique, carrying ammunition, sank without trace. There is no record of any survivors. During the afternoon of Sunday 26 March Lieutenant Herrick in *Uproar* was to close the harbour at Oneglia and engage, by gunfire, the 5,011-ton German tanker *Matara*. The tanker was damaged in the superstructure by sixteen hits out of twenty-eight rounds expended before the submarine was obliged to withdraw to sea to escape the attentions of the shore batteries.

Lieutenant Hunt and *Ultor* were patrolling in the western Aegean Sea determined that April 1944 was not to be as bare as the previous month. He set about this task on 3 April by closing Port St Nikolo on Kythera and engaged shipping within the port by gunfire and expended fifty-three rounds of ammunition. The result of this bombardment was two 80-ton caiques and one 30-ton caique sunk in the water and a further 50-ton caique destroyed as it stood on the stocks – as were the stocks them-selves. This bombardment was witnessed by the local residents and they stood and applauded Lieutenant Hunt's efforts.

The next day, as they were on passage to a new patrol area, they encountered a 40-ton caique and engaged it by gunfire. Five rounds were sufficient to cause the caique to explode and sink. The crew of three was safely taken off in a small dinghy and left to make their way to shore. This was adequate recompense for a failure earlier in the day when the gun had jammed forcing the engagement on a 60-ton caique to be aborted without success.

Just two days later, on 6 April, *Ultor* was off Port Kiparissi when they engaged a 50-ton caique by gunfire. The target was hit, caught fire and sank. Later in the day a further two caiques were sighted. The submarine surfaced and engaged by gunfire. After being hit the crew of the larger 40-ton caique abandoned ship with some alacrity and not without cause as shortly afterwards the vessel was totally demolished by a most impressive explosion as the cargo of ammunition detonated. The smaller caique was left unmolested to allow her to collect the survivors swimming in the water.

The very next day off Monemvasia they saw a large 200-ton caique at anchor flying the Nazi flag and with German-uniformed sailors manning the vessel. Just one torpedo was sufficient to sink the target. This was the final attack of the patrol and on return to Malta Captain (S) First Submarine Flotilla commented:

> This was a most valuable contribution to the cause. It is some time since a submarine could be spared for this type of offensive action as recently all effort has been directed towards the interception of shipping on the open sea routes. I consider that *ULTOR* carried out this patrol in a most enterprising and energetic manner, making the fullest use of the opportunities presented.[8]

Ultimatum (Lieutenant W.H. Kett) was also on patrol in the Aegean Sea at this time. On 5 April he was in Suda Bay when he sank a 40-ton caique by gunfire, then was obliged to withdraw to escape the attentions of the shore batteries. The following day off Anti Kithera he sank a 30-ton caique by gunfire that was carrying oil drums on the deck and under German control.

As *Ultimatum* and *Ultor* returned to base the area was left to Lieutenant D. Swanston, RN, in *Unruly*. On 19 April they encountered a two-masted, 30-ton caique south of Psara which was quickly dispatched with just four rounds of ammunition. Later the same day it was the turn of the caique *Agios Ionna* to receive the attention of *Unruly*. As the submarine surfaced the crew abandoned the caique and it was then closed, boarded and sunk by demolition charge.

On 21 April *Unruly* intercepted the 36-ton caique *Kal93* north of Khios and after a very short gun action the caique was abandoned. As a result the gun action ceased and the caique boarded. The vessel was improperly showing the Red Cross flag and markings. She was, in fact, carrying drums of oil and a search revealed a German ensign secreted under the master's pillow. This was considered sufficient to justify sinking the vessel and this was done by demolition charge after allowing the crew to make good their escape.

The southern coast of France was not being neglected and on 11 April *Untiring* (Lieutenant Boyd) was patrolling along the coastline of the French Riviera when she detected a convoy approaching from the south. The 2,500-ton tanker *Cerere* was under escort from two destroyers and two UJ-boats, together with aerial cover. A full salvo of four torpedoes was fired and the tanker sank in a mass of flame, smoke and burning debris. The next day found *Untiring* off Oneglia watching as the town was subjected to an Allied bombing raid. As they did so they saw the 1,190-ton German ship *Diana* leaving port in an attempt to avoid damage but the submarine denied her that safety. She was torpedoed and sunk as she was still in sight of the port.

Lieutenant Boyd and *Untiring* made the final attack of the month. 27 April found them patrolling off Toulon when they spotted two UJ-boats sweeping the approaches to the harbour. Lieutenant Boyd decided that he would not wait to be located and that attack was the best form of defence. He waited until the UJ-boats were about to complete a leg of their zigzag and fired three torpedoes at the nearest one. This resulted in the sinking of the 943-ton *UJ6705* (formerly known as *Clairvoyant*).

Untiring was to open May 1944 as they had closed the month of April. The first day found them patrolling off Port Vendres when they saw the German-controlled 2,147-ton French ship *Astree* approaching the port. A salvo of torpedoes ensured she never made it as one found and sank the target. Further along the coast at Oneglia, *Upstart* and Lieutenant Chapman occupied the minds of the enemy with their bombardment of the olive-oil refinery, reporting more than twenty hits on the large oil containers and surrounding buildings.

Lieutenant Chapman maintained this offensive throughout the patrol and on 4 May made two further gunnery attacks on shore-based targets in a repeat of his actions on a previous patrol. The first was the railway sheds at Cannes harbour causing damage before heading off to bombard a seaplane hangar south of St Raphael. During these two raids *Upstart* expended fifty-one rounds of ammunition and recorded forty-three hits.

They withdrew from St Raphael, with all ammunition expended, as several explosions of the damaged hangar were displayed clearly in the evening light. *Upstart* headed for home and Lieutenant Chapman later commented upon these attacks:

We had been given an expensive bit of kit by His Majesty. We must do the best we could with it.[9]

Upstart and Lieutenant Chapman returned to the area and on 21 May they were again off Port Vendres when they intercepted the 2,955-ton German ship *Saumur* fully laden with iron ore from Barcelona, under escort from two UJ-boats with air cover. A salvo of torpedoes saw the *Saumur* hit and the stern fall away before the whole vessel sank.

Lieutenant Hunt in *Ultor* was also patrolling the southern French coast and on 11 May he was off the Hyeres islands when he torpedoed and sank an 850-ton KT ship (*Kriegstransport*) under escort from two E-boats. His next attack was on 15 May when he fired on a laden 80-ton lighter forcing it to be beached and abandoned. Before the job could be completed the shore batteries intervened and the submarine withdrew to sea.

He returned to the area later in the month and on 30 May re-opened his account off Cape Camarat. A small convoy was encountered that consisted of a 1,000-ton salvage vessel towing a 400-ton lighter together with three 'F' lighters all under escort from three 'R' boats. *Ultor* closed, fired a salvo of torpedoes and sank the salvage vessel. The submarine went deep and after a quick reload of torpedoes returned to periscope depth to find one of the 'R' boats was alongside the stationary lighter. One further torpedo was sufficient to dispatch both the lighter and 'R' boat. The next day, the last of the month, found *Ultor* off Ciotat running on the surface when she engaged two 150-ton minesweepers by gunfire. One of the minesweepers was hit, burst into flames and blew up before sinking, but before the second vessel could be engaged the shore batteries intervened and the submarine withdrew to seaward.

The first day of May saw Lieutenant Kett in *Ultimatum* patrolling south-east of the Cape of Matapan when he sank a

30-ton caique by gunfire, taking on board the three Greek crew members. Conversations with these Greek seamen gave Lieutenant Kett all the information he needed to persuade him to attack the harbour of Koroni. They told him that the harbour and the associated repair yards were under German control and very busy.

The next day *Ultimatum* closed Koroni and established that the harbour was indeed very busy and several large caiques were on the slipways of the repair yard. Lieutenant Kett waited until the evening, closed the harbour, surfaced and commenced a gunnery action. In just eighteen minutes sixty-two rounds of ammunition were expended and severe damage was inflicted with five 125-ton caiques destroyed as they stood on the slipways under repair and two 100-ton caiques sunk as they lay anchored in the harbour. A further 100-ton caique was damaged along with several small harbour craft. This success was followed a few days later with a more sobering action. On 10 May the submarine was located by two patrolling anti-submarine vessels and subjected to an attack that lasted over three hours. The attack was sufficiently accurate to cause substantial damage to the submarine. 'H' tank was flooded through the sea vent; 'Q' tank was flooded with the outboard vent cracking open sending the submarine plunging to a depth of 400 feet, well below the recommended safety depth. The after-ballast pump, internal phone system and pump order systems were all put out of action. A further problem occurred when the main battery shorted creating a fire in the motor room. As a result of this damage *Ultimatum* cut short the patrol and returned to base.

Fortunately this did not leave the Aegean Sea free from the attentions of British submarines as Lieutenant Tattersall and *Unswerving* were on station in the Gulf of Nauplia. On 3 May they sighted a convoy that included the German ships *Gertrud* and *Suzanne* being escorted by four U-boats and numerous aircraft. Before they could get into an attacking position the submarine was sighted, illuminated by searchlight, and forced deep. On returning to periscope depth the convoy was no longer in sight. The *Gertrud* was not always to enjoy such luck as one month later, on 1 June, she was sunk off Heraklion by aircraft of the

RAF. Still smarting from the failure to mount an attack on the convoy, Lieutenant Tattersall intercepted two small caiques of 25- and 40-tons, surfaced and sank both by gunfire.

Two days later, having remained in the Gulf of Nauplia, *Unswerving* intercepted and sank two 50-ton caiques by gunfire and later in the day a further small 25-ton caique was similarly dealt with. This small caique had red crosses marked on either bow and displayed the Red Cross flag at the masthead together with the Greek flag and the German requisition pendant.

On 12 May Lieutenant C.W. Taylor, RNR, on his first Mediterranean patrol in *Vampire*, struck the first blow in the Mediterranean campaign for these newly modified submarines. They were on patrol off Monemvasia when they encountered a small 10-ton caique carrying ten drums of oil from Crete to Piraeus. The submarine surfaced, fired one round and the crew of three Greek seamen abandoned ship to be picked up by the submarine before she rammed and sank the caique, a controversial sinking of which Captain (S) First Submarine Flotilla wrote:

> The sinking of the small caique on 12th May, was contrary to Standing Orders, which bans caiques under 20 tons. There was, however, no apparent reason to suppose that she was a partisan caique and she was carrying a small quantity of oil from Crete to Piraeus.[10]

The only other action during the month of May was taken by *Unsparing*, when on 19 May, she closed the harbour at Kamara Bay, Kos, and bombarded four caiques hauled up on the shore. Two were destroyed and the others were badly damaged when gunfire from the shore caused the submarine to withdraw before her task could be completed.

Lieutenant Hunt in *Ultor* was the first to strike in June 1944. As they patrolled off Port Vendres on the southern French coast they torpedoed and sank the 2,588-ton supply vessel *Alice Robert*. This was not to be the last success for *Ultor* as later in the month they returned to the southern French coastline to inconvenience enemy shipping even more.

143

Their opening attack came on 20 June off Cannes when they torpedoed and sank an 'F' lighter. This was surpassed on 27 June when at 04.15 they sighted the 3,315-ton merchant ship *Cap Blanc* under escort from three destroyers and a corvette. *Ultor* closed and discharged a full salvo of four torpedoes, hitting the target that sank after a huge explosion. Two hours later they sighted the 5,260-ton tanker *Pallas* under tow by two tugs with a surface escort of four destroyers, two corvettes, one UJ-boat and two 'R' boats and supported by air cover from five aircraft. The sea conditions were excellent – very choppy making observation of a submarine periscope difficult, so *Ultor* trailed the tanker until 08.15 when the torpedo tubes had been reloaded with the last two torpedoes. Lieutenant Hunt then closed the target, evading the escorting vessels, and attacked the *Pallas* with both torpedoes finding the target. The submarine withdrew at depth and about one hour later she returned to periscope depth to see the tanker lying stopped with her back broken. Lieutenant Hunt allowed the crew to view the scene, the fruits of their labour, before *Pallas* finally sank at 10.00.

On returning to Maddalena these attacks by *Ultor* were commented on by Admiral Sir John Cunningham. In his report to the Admiralty he wrote:

> Great credit is due to the Commanding Officer of H.M. Submarine *ULTOR*, Lieutenant G.E. HUNT, DSC, RN, for this most satisfactory patrol during which one 'F' lighter, one 3,000 ton merchant vessel and one tanker were sunk. H.M. Submarine *ULTOR*'s actions on the morning of 27th June rank with some of the most outstanding of the war.[11]

Other successes were reported off the French coast during the month. On 10 June *Untiring* and Lieutenant Boyd torpedoed and sank the 398-ton UJ-boat *UJ6078*, (previously the French yacht *La Havraise*), off Le Ciotat. On 21 June Lieutenant Gordon in *Universal* sank the 250-ton yacht *FMA 06* by torpedo as she was carrying out hydrophone duties off the port of Toulon. The following day *Universal*, patrolling off Cassis, sighted two liners at anchor close to the breakwater. A full salvo of four torpedoes was

144

fired and both liners were hit. The first, *Sampiere Corso*, 3,823 tons, was seen to sink immediately; the second, the 4,930-ton *President Dal Piaz* was seen in flames half-submerged, lying on the sea bottom. This attack was subject to comment by Captain (S) Tenth Submarine Flotilla who wrote:

> I consider that the brilliant results achieved on this patrol were no mere matter of luck but were directly due to the determination, offensive spirit, and courage of Lieutenant Gordon.[12]

Whilst these submarines were grabbing the headlines off the French coast, the action was continuing amongst the Greek islands. On 9 June *Vivid*, under the command of Lieutenant J.C. Varley, RN, patrolling north of Heraklion, Crete, sighted the 1,545-ton *Tanais* under escort from three 'R' boats and an anti-submarine schooner. This was the only remaining vessel of a convoy attacked earlier by RAF aircraft. At 03.00 in bright moonlight *Vivid* attacked from periscope depth, hitting and sinking the *Tanais*. This was the only success for *Vivid* on her first Mediterranean patrol. The remainder of the patrol was frustrated by the attentions of escorting destroyers as she closed to attack on two separate occasions but the patrol was judged to be a success with the loss of *Tanais* confirmed.

On 21 June Lieutenant Piper in *Unsparing* was patrolling north of Cape Malea when he sighted a convoy that consisted of a Siebel ferry and a lighter being escorted by one UJ-boat. This convoy was closed and from 1,500 yards four torpedoes were dispatched. The submarine immediately went deep and on returning to periscope depth eleven minutes later Lieutenant Piper saw that the UJ-boat, *UJ2106* (previously known as the 450-ton vessel *Tenedos*), and the lighter had both sunk. The Siebel ferry was stopped picking up survivors covered in oil. *Unsparing* wasted no time, reloaded one torpedo tube and with that one torpedo she dispatched Siebel ferry *284* to the seabed.

Two days later, on 23 June, Lieutenant C.W. Taylor in *Vampire* was on patrol north of Kandelusia when they engaged the caique *Abba* by gunfire and when the bombardment proved unsuccessful she was boarded and sunk by demolition charge. The next day *Vampire* closed the harbour at Mandraki on the island of Nisseros and bombarded the caique yards. Thirty rounds of ammunition were fired resulting in the destruction of one 100-ton caique on the beach, one 200-ton caique on the stocks and damaging a further three smaller vessels.

The only other success for this month fell to Lieutenant M.D. Tattersall and *Unswerving*. On 23 June they were patrolling along the Salonika to Skiathos shipping route when they sighted two armed 100-ton caiques. The submarine surfaced and engaged them by gunfire. These vessels, manned by German personnel, usually put up a fight in such circumstances but on this occasion that was not to be. *GN61* was sunk with no trace of survivors; *GN62* was abandoned and after picking up seven German ratings she was boarded and sunk by demolition charge. Captain (S) First Submarine Flotilla wrote:

> Our submarines have learned to treat these armed caiques with great respect even when encountered singly, and *UNSWERVING* is to be congratulated on this courageous and highly successful action in which the biters were badly bitten.[13]

Vox, on her second Mediterranean patrol and under the command of Lieutenant J.M. Michell, RN, was off Cape Kamili on 3 July when they sighted two caiques flying the German flag. They were closed and engaged by gunfire. The smaller of the two, of just thirty tons, was sunk with the expenditure of seventy rounds of ammunition. The inaccuracy of the gun's crew was explained by the Commanding Officer as sickness. The sight-setter was the only regular member of the gun's crew who was still healthy – the remainder were ill with sandfly fever. The second and larger caique made for the safety of a small bay but was pursued there, engaged by gunfire, and sunk after twenty-five rounds had been expended, of which sixteen found the target. The following day *Vox* sighted the 150-ton caique *KAL 14* being escorted by three 'R' boats. With such a heavy escort, this was obviously a valuable cargo, and *Vox* made a successful torpedo attack, watching the target blow up in a huge sheet of fire as the cargo of petrol exploded.

On 10 July *Vox* was off Steno Pass when the German ship *Anita* was sighted hugging the shoreline. The submarine closed, torpedoed and hit the *Anita* forcing her to be beached, but this did not ensure the safety of the ship as she was lost during the night leaving telltale oil drums and one abandoned lifeboat.

Success continued when on 14 July Lieutenant Varley in *Vivid* discovered the 553-ton German refrigerator ship *Suzanne* at anchor in Lividia Bay, Telos with just one UJ-boat in attendance. As the submarine closed to attack, the UJ-boat weighed anchor and headed straight for the submarine; Lieutenant Varley ignored this and concentrated on the *Suzanne*. Two torpedoes were fired at close range with the first hitting and sinking the *Suzanne*, the last remaining German refrigerator ship in the Aegean.

Vivid followed this with a successful attack on a convoy of five caiques under escort. The largest caique of about 100 tons fell behind and was engaged by gunfire, but the armed escort intervened and attention was diverted to her until she withdrew under gunfire. This allowed *Vivid* to devote her attention to the original target and after four hits from fourteen rounds the caique blew up and sank. The remainder of the convoy was now well out of range and *Vivid* returned to patrolling duties.

27 July found Lieutenant Ogle and *Vigorous* patrolling along the Heraklion–Piraeus shipping channel. Early in the middle watch a well-armed caique was sighted southbound. It was engaged by gunfire and after eight hits were recorded the caique stopped and the crew was seen to abandon ship. The target, now identified as the 700-ton caique *Doxa*, was closed and it was established that there were at least ten men still on board, including members of the Afrika Korps. The prevailing weather conditions made it impossible to get alongside so the submarine stood off and sank her by gunfire.

The remaining successes for the month of July were made by submarines of the Tenth Submarine Flotilla operating from Maddalena along the southern coastline of France. On 14 July Lieutenant Gordon in *Universal* sank the 350-ton Spanish schooner *Sevillona*. Although flying the Spanish colours the schooner was operating in waters designated as a 'Sink on Sight' area off Cape Bear. The initial torpedo attack was unsuccessful so the submarine surfaced and engaged the schooner by gunfire, which encouraged the crew to abandon ship with some alacrity. Before the task could be completed the shore batteries intervened and the submarine submerged and withdrew to safety. Even though abandoned the *Sevillona* continued to make headway at about three knots. The submarine trailed her and, having reloaded her tubes, fired two further torpedoes and dispatched the *Sevillona* to the deep.

Lieutenant Hunt and *Ultor* were on their final patrol in the Mediterranean when, on 21 July, they torpedoed and sank the 916-ton coaster *Hardy*, south-west of Cape Camarat. *Ultor* returned to Maddalena on completion of Mediterranean duties before heading for the United Kingdom.

Lieutenant Michell and *Vox* opened the account for August in similar vein to July 1944. On the first of the month they were patrolling the Aegean, south of Santorini, when they sank a small 25-ton caique by gunfire, killing one and injuring the remaining three crew members. The injured men were taken on board the submarine but one died during the transfer. The remaining men were transferred to a smaller caique later in the day and allowed to proceed without hindrance.

Vox maintained her attention on caique convoys and on 3 August, off Heraklion, a three-boat convoy was sighted under escort from the 75-ton *GK61* (previously known as the *Petrel*). At this time Lieutenant Michell was not able to mount an attack but by persevering he was able to intercept the convoy the next day. On this occasion he torpedoed and sank the escorting *GK61*. On seeing the target blow up and sink, *Vox* surfaced and engaged the three caiques by gunfire; Lieutenant Michell set out his reasons in his patrol report as:

a)   I expected the crews to be in a panic after seeing their escort blown to pieces.
b)   I did not wish them to have time to scatter.
c)   To finish off three caiques at night, close range was essential, or we should run out of ammunition.[14]

Within minutes of surfacing the submarine was caught in hot crossfire from the caiques with shells bouncing off the bridge and casing and splinters hitting two of the gun's crew, though they were not seriously injured. As the submarine manoeuvred into a more advantageous position the caiques split up and ran for Candia. One was immediately engaged by gunfire, set ablaze and sunk. One of the other two lost engine power and was engaged by gunfire and sunk. The third caique was allowed to collect survivors and head for safety. During this encounter the submarine received several direct hits with one shell entering the bridge, three more penetrating the lower bridge plating and casing, and the forward jumping wire was cut through. There are no reports of any serious injury to any member of the crew.

Lieutenant R.D. Cairns, RN, in *Virtue* was to account for six further caiques in the southern Aegean. On 16 August off Cape Malea he sank three caiques with a total tonnage of sixty-five tons. Two were sunk by ramming and the third was sunk by gunfire after three rounds were expended. Seven survivors were plucked from the sea and later transferred to a small fishing boat to make their way to shore. On 19 August they caught a 60-ton caique leaving harbour on Milos heavily laden with oil drums. She was engaged by gunfire and after nine rounds she went up in a sheet of flame before sinking. Two days later, on 21 August, off Cape Spada, they rammed and sank a 50-ton caique and followed this by the sinking of a 20-ton vessel with three rounds of ammunition. *Virtue* then returned to Malta where Captain (S) First Submarine Flotilla commented:

This was a very satisfactory bag and was accomplished for the expenditure of 25 rounds of H.E.D.A. ammunition.[15]

Vampire (Lieutenant Taylor) was off Mykoni on 25 August when they encountered three caiques on two different occasions. The first, fully laden and of 50 tons, was sunk by gunfire at 10.00. The second, of 60 tons, was sunk by gunfire at 12.10, quickly followed by a 30-ton caique at 12.15, again by gunfire.

Vox would close August by sinking the caique *CHA113* by gunfire on the last day of the month and watching the survivors, four men and one woman, head for Candia in a small boat.

September 1944 was to see the demise of the Tenth Submarine Flotilla. On 8 September C.-in-C., Mediterranean instructed that the submarine base at Maddalena be closed down and the Tenth Submarine Flotilla be absorbed into the First Submarine Flotilla at Malta. At that time the Lords of the Admiralty publicly expressed their appreciation of the fine record of the Tenth Submarine Flotilla during the previous three years in the Mediterranean. This appreciation reflects the successes the flotilla achieved. During its lifetime their record shows 648,629 tons of shipping sunk, 400,480 tons of shipping damaged and ten U-boats sunk. Another indication of the planning being made was the notification to the C.-in-C., Eastern Fleet that, on the completion of the European War, it would be possible to allocate certain 'U' class submarines to his command.

Thus, activities along the coast of southern France were curtailed and the submarines from Maddalena reinforced the First Submarine Flotilla operating in the Aegean out of Malta. During this time of re-assessment, and in an attempt to reduce the time between base and patrol areas, advanced submarine bases were established on Khios and Mitylene with a facility to re-arm, refuel and replenish. This allowed submarines to be withdrawn from regular patrols and held in immediate reserve should they be required. The potential for these bases was reported upon by visiting submarine commanders. Lieutenant J.R.H. Haddow, RN, in *Visigoth*, first visited Khios and reported that the harbour was ideal for submarines to berth alongside. The inhabitants appeared to be pro-British, helpful and friendly. It was Lieutenant Ogle in *Vigorous* who reported upon Mitylene saying that the inhabitants were extremely hospitable and genuinely glad to see them. Any attempt to thank them for their hospitality was swept aside by the local people saying they had waited four years for the opportunity.

At a time when all this reorganisation was taking place there were still enemy actions to counteract and on 22 September Lieutenant Taylor and *Vampire* were off Skiathos when they sighted the 3,800-ton tanker *Peter*. This tanker was on her first voyage after being damaged earlier by *Unsparing* and was the largest vessel available to the Germans in the Aegean. Lieutenant Taylor saw a considerable number of people on the foredeck as *Peter* was engaged in transferring troops and equipment to Salonika. The submarine closed, attacked and sank the *Peter* as two of the four torpedoes found their target.

Other submarines were also active in the Aegean and the caique fleet was to suffer more losses. On 24 September three submarines found success. With the approach of darkness Lieutenant Haddow in *Visigoth* bombarded the harbour of Agios Strati, sinking one 100-ton caique and damaging several others. At 20.30 Lieutenant Michell in *Vox* sank an 80-ton caique by gunfire off Cape Kassandra, followed at 21.00 by Lieutenant Ogle in *Vigorous* sinking another 80-ton caique by gunfire.

Lieutenant Michell and *Vox* had further success the following day; having remained off Cape Kassandra, they intercepted another 80-ton caique. This they sank by gunfire after the cargo of flares and ammunition exploded, setting her on fire. This was followed up on 27 September when *Vox*, patrolling north-west of Cape Pori, intercepted a convoy of lighters and caiques. Three torpedoes were fired as one of the lighters and one caique were overlapping; one torpedo hit and sank the 200-ton lighter *SF121*. Captain (S) First Submarine Flotilla described this attack as being 'a skilfully executed and accurate attack in difficult conditions and *VOX* is to be congratulated on her well deserved success.'[16]

Vigorous had maintained a patrol position off Cape Drepano and on 26 September intercepted the 750-ton *Salomea* transporting troops and materials from Mudros to Salonika. Lieutenant Ogle fired a full salvo of four torpedoes, hit and sank the *Salomea* but not before she exploded in a huge, brilliant display that forced the submarine to dive to avoid falling debris.

On October 3 Lieutenant Tattersall and *Unswerving* were to strike one of the final blows in the Mediterranean theatre of war. It was the very last sinking by torpedo. They were off Cape Kassandra in the early part of the middle watch when they sighted the 1,810-ton tanker *Berta*, under escort from a destroyer. On a brilliant, moonlit night *Unswerving* attacked from periscope depth, hitting and sinking the tanker with her final salvo of torpedoes. *Unswerving* was then recalled to Malta.

Whilst that was the final torpedo attack there were still further gunnery actions to take place against the small caiques operating in the Aegean. Lieutenant R.D. Cairns in *Virtue* carried out these attacks on three consecutive days in early October.

9 October saw *Virtue* off Cape Stavros, Northern Crete, when they fired on the 35-ton caique *Agios Matheus* carrying tyres and spare parts for aircraft. After four hits from the seven rounds shot the caique sank. The following day they intercepted the 50-ton caique *Agia Anna* operating under German control en route for Santorini. She was sunk by gunfire. Later the 150-ton caique *Sofia* was intercepted, also en route for Santorini. She was boarded and found to be carrying sixteen motor cycles and aircraft spare parts. The submarine stood off and sank her by gunfire. The next day, 11 October, in Candia Bay, *Virtue* sank a 200-ton water tanker by gunfire together with a 40-ton caique and damaged a 20-ton motor launch before being driven off by shore batteries.

On 8 November 1944 C.-in-C., Mediterranean instructed Captain (S) First Submarine Flotilla to cease British submarine operations in the Mediterranean and ordered the flotilla to be disbanded.

With the cessation of submarine activity in the Mediterranean there was a need to re-deploy the past members of the First and Tenth Submarine Flotillas. To meet the commitment previously made to the C.-in-C., Eastern Fleet, six boats (all of which were fitted with air conditioning) were to be deployed to the Far East for anti-submarine training. *Vigorous*, *Visigoth* and *Vivid* were to join the East Indies Fleet and *Virtue*, *Voracious* and *Vox* to join the Pacific Fleet.

Whilst intended for anti-submarine training exercises this did not stop these submarines from finding a small piece of the action in Far Eastern waters. Lieutenant Michell in *Vox* was en route from Fremantle to Melbourne on 2 March 1945 when he sighted an unidentified merchant ship but before they could take any action, the merchant ship commenced firing on them and it was necessary to dive to avoid any damage.

On 22 June 1945 *Vivid* (Lieutenant Varley) was on her first Far Eastern war patrol in the Malacca Straits when they intercepted a junk. The junk was closed and after firing three rounds across her bows she was boarded and her cargo was established to be thirty tons of baled leaf tobacco. Demolition charges were placed and the junk was sunk but it took a long time to settle, possibly due to the buoyancy of the cargo. The three-man crew was taken on board the submarine as Lieutenant Varley believed their small sampan was not suitable to carry them the forty miles to safety. However, when it was discovered that one of the crew members was suffering from an advanced case of syphilis, it was decided that all the survivors should take their chances in the small sampan. They were given provisions and set off towards Sumatra.

The only other action for the 'U' class in the Far East fell to Lieutenant N.R. Wood, RN, and *Vigorous* as they patrolled off the north-eastern coast of Sumatra on his first Far Eastern war patrol. No active shipping was found but on 16 July Lieutenant Wood found a beached coaster and in his frustration fired forty-three rounds, of which twenty-three found the target. They left the coaster when it was considered to be a complete loss. Later that same day they closed the town of Olehlem on the north-east coast of Sumatra and bombarded the pier and a crane, which were hit repeatedly and badly damaged before the submarine withdrew seaward.

These were the only actions reported by the Commanding Officers of 'U' class submarines in Far Eastern waters before the Japanese surrender of 15 August 1945, and with the signing of the surrender treaty on board USS *Missouri* on 2 September, all conflict ceased.

Notes

1. National Archives Kew Reference: ADM 199/1115.
2. National Archives Kew Reference: ADM 199/1917.
3. National Archives Kew Reference: ADM 199/1818.
4. National Archives Kew Reference: ADM 199/1824.
5. National Archives Kew Reference: ADM 199/1824.
6. National Archives Kew Reference: ADM 199/1824.
7. National Archives Kew Reference: ADM 199/1818.
8. National Archives Kew Reference: ADM 199/1821.
9. Letter to author from Paul Chapman dated 11 March, 1993.

10. National Archives Kew Reference: ADM 199/1815.
11. National Archives Kew Reference: ADM 199/1821.
12. National Archives Kew Reference: ADM 199/1823.
13. National Archives Kew Reference: ADM 199/1822.
14. National Archives Kew Reference: ADM 199/1816.
15. National Archives Kew Reference: ADM 199/1816.
16. National Archives Kew Reference: ADM 199/1816.

VI

THE ALLIED NAVIES'
CONTRIBUTION

I, Boris Karnicki, commanding O.R.P. Sokol *declare war on you
Benito Mussolini.*[1]

Scant mention has been made of the Allied navies' contribution
to the war effort. This was such a significant contribution that it
deserves to be recognised. The efforts of these men from all
nations are to be applauded and it is befitting that this be recorded
in a specialised area of *The History of the British 'U' Class Submarines.*
(Author's note)

In January 1941 it was agreed to loan HMS *Urchin,* still at the
Naval Construction Yard at Barrow-in-Furness, to the Free Polish
Navy. It was renamed *Sokol* and Commander Boris Karnicki was
appointed in command. This was the first of twelve 'U' class
submarines loaned to various Allied navies during the conflict and
similar arrangements were made at the end of hostilities in respect
of the Royal Norwegian Navy and the Royal Netherlands Navy.

The first to be loaned was the first into action, as on 15 July
1941 *Sokol,* on patrol off the Ile D'Yeu in the Bay of Biscay,
attacked an escorted supply ship. Unfortunately, on this occasion
all four torpedoes fired missed the target as at the time of firing
she was obliged to take emergency avoiding action due to the
intervention of one of the escorting vessels. Whilst this first attack
was unsuccessful, *Sokol* and Boris Karnicki were to go on to better
things.

Her second contact with the enemy was a more bizarre affair.
On 19 August they were again patrolling submerged in the Bay

of Biscay when they became aware of a trawler behaving very suspiciously. This trawler kept station some 2,000 yards from the submarine and followed every change in speed and direction in an exercise that appeared to be testing some type of listening device. This was the last recorded incident before *Sokol* sailed to serve in the Mediterranean on 19 September 1941.

The agreement by the Polish authorities that allowed *Sokol* to be deployed to the Mediterranean was a cause of concern to Commander Karnicki as at that time Poland was not at war with Italy. To circumvent the problem he took matters into his own hands. After passing Gibraltar he gathered the complete complement of the submarine in the control room and announced for all to hear:

I, Boris Karnicki, commanding O.R.P. *Sokol* declare war on you Benito Mussolini.

On 2 October 1941 it was agreed to transfer *P41* (under construction at Barrow-in-Furness) to the Norwegian Navy, to be renamed *Uredd*. This was just one day after *Sokol* had arrived in Malta to join the Tenth Submarine Flotilla.

After his unsuccessful patrols in home waters, Commander Karnicki and *Sokol* were the first to strike against the enemy. On 28 October 1941 they were on patrol in the approaches to Naples, off the island of Ischia, when they torpedoed and damaged the 5,413-ton armed merchant cruiser *Citta di Palermo*. Unfortunately during this attack the submarine broke surface and was quickly located but she dived and was able to avoid any damage from the subsequent counter-attack. Three days later *Sokol* attacked by torpedo and gunfire an unidentified merchant ship that may have been damaged but no confirmation was ever received.

November 1941 was to see *Sokol* off the mainland of Greece and on 19 November Commander Karnicki decided to attempt an entry into the port of Navarin. Intelligence suggested that a convoy was being assembled there and the harbour was not protected by any anti-submarine devices. This was not so and as *Sokol* made her initial approach she was caught in anti-submarine nets. Fortunately she was able to disengage herself without doing any damage or being located by enemy lookouts. Two days later she closed the harbour again and fired torpedoes into it, reportedly damaging the Italian warship *Aviere*. It has not been possible to confirm this from German or Italian records nor has it been so in respect of a further attack reported by *Sokol* on a convoy of two merchant ships leaving Navarin later that day.

Sokol continued her patrols mainly in the Gulf of Taranto in an attempt to intercept enemy shipping en route to North Africa, but for the remainder of 1941 she had no success to report. It was not until 8 February 1942 that she was next to see success. Whilst on patrol off Ras Turgueness on the Tunisian coastline, they intercepted the 392-ton Italian schooner *Guiseppina*. They pursued the schooner until she hove to, boarded and removed her documentation before sinking her by demolition charge.

This success was not to change her luck as on 10 March she was off the island of Pantellaria when enemy aircraft attacked her. *Sokol* had sighted a merchant vessel but in a sea that was so calm the escorting aircraft spotted her and bombed her, forcing her deep, thus allowing the merchant vessel to pass unmolested.

This was the first experience of being bombed but it was not to be the last. On 17 March she was alongside in Malta during an enemy air raid when five bombs fell close by and damaged the battery cells. On 19 March, as she was being moved from Lazaretto Creek to Grand Harbour, she was attacked by two Me109 aircraft and sustained additional damage. On 31 March, with all the repair work completed, *Sokol* was preparing for patrol duties when enemy bombers again damaged her. Many battery cells were damaged and filled with chlorine gas so it was necessary for men to don gas masks and the DSEA escape equipment as they disconnected the battery and cleared the boat of gas. She was damaged again during a bombing raid on 8 April.

The final ignominy was to occur on the night of 15 April as she was being moved from Marsa to Grand Harbour. It was a particularly black night and as they entered Grand Harbour they fouled the boom and bumped heavily against rock, damaging the starboard propeller. The damage was such that she was returned to the United Kingdom, sailing from Malta on 17 April after having the damage temporarily repaired.

As *Sokol* was leaving Malta for repair, a second Allied-manned submarine commenced patrolling off the Norwegian coastline. The Norwegian-manned submarine *Uredd*, under the command of Lieutenant R.O. Roren, had commenced her first patrol on 9 March 1942 and was to remain a member of the Ninth Submarine Flotilla based at Dundee until she was lost in February 1943.

Lieutenant Roren's first contact with enemy shipping was not a success. On 10 September 1942 they were patrolling in the vicinity of Andfjord when they were troubled by the actions of several fishing boats. These boats were ever present throughout the day. Some had lookouts posted in the crow's nest and none appeared to be fishing. This led Lieutenant Roren to believe that shipping of some importance was about to depart Andfjord. This suspicion was confirmed when two main German warships were sighted, believed to be the *Admiral Scheer* and possibly the *Tirpitz*, but they were too far away to mount an attack. In this instance it was decided to transmit an enemy sighting message but this was not possible for more than two hours which made the information irrelevant and the enemy ships were not located.

Uredd had more luck on her next patrol on 18 October 1942 patrolling in the vicinity of Aradelflu. The 3,715-ton German merchant ship *Libau* was sighted and after being hit by one of two torpedoes was seen to go aground on rocks making salvage. Lieutenant Roren watched smaller ships flying the Norwegian flag pass unmolested. His reasons for this were purely national-istic and were justified in his patrol report as:

a) These ships and their trade were essential to the Norwegian people in the coastal districts.
b) Any such attack could be used as strong propaganda on the Norwegian front by quislings.[2]

The next patrol for *Uredd* commenced at Lerwick on 11 November 1942 again to patrol the Norwegian coastline. On 20 November noise was heard coming from the forward casing in front of the gun platform. Investigations showed that this was due to periscope clamps breaking loose in very heavy weather. To avoid any damage and to prevent the noise being heard by enemy forces these clamps were brought inboard. Two days later they sighted a submarine that was identified as the Russian boat *K3*. This caused a flurry of signals between the Admiralty and the Russian authorities. However, on *Uredd's* return from patrol it was established that she was out of position. The inclement weather had denied Lieutenant Roren the opportunity to calculate her position correctly. This patrol lasted twenty-two days in the terrible weather conditions normally experienced off Norway at that time of year and was subject to comment from both the submarine's Commanding Officer and Captain (S) Ninth Submarine Flotilla. Lieutenant Roren wrote in his patrol report:

> It is my considered opinion that 'U' class submarines are too small to operate effectively in the Arctic Ocean during winter, when continuous heavy weather is likely, and my experience during this patrol has strengthened my conviction.[3]

Captain L.M. Shadwell, RN, Captain (S) Ninth Submarine Flotilla, supported this when he wrote:

> 1. I agree with the Commanding Officer's opinion that 'U' class submarines are not suitable for protracted patrols in the Arctic Ocean, especially during the winter months.
> 2. On this occasion the officers and company of *UREDD* returned from patrol more in need of a rest than I have seen them on any previous occasion.[4]

After two further patrols, both of which were uneventful, *Uredd* sailed from Lerwick on 5 February 1943 to implement *OPERATION SEAGULL* but was lost before it could be implemented.

On 27 February the Lords of the Admiralty commented on Lieutenant Roren and *Uredd* thus:

> *UREDD* had rendered most valuable support to the Allied submarine fleet, performing her patrols with skill and notable success and at the time of her loss she was engaged

in a special operation entailing hazardous duties off the Norwegian coast.[5]

On 13 March 1986 the location of *Uredd* was designated as a war grave.

The next submarine to join the fleet was the Dutch-manned *Dolfijn* under the command of Lieutenant H.M.L.F.E. van Oostrom Soede. On 8 October 1942 she joined the Third Submarine Flotilla for trials before being transferred for service in the Mediterranean. After her trials and two incident-free war patrols *Dolfijn* arrived in Algiers on 23 January 1943 for service with the Eighth Submarine Flotilla.

On their second Mediterranean war patrol Lieutenant Oostrom Soede and *Dolfijn* enjoyed their first success. On 9 February 1943 they were patrolling the south Sardinian coast-line off Cape Spartivento when they sighted the 615-ton Italian submarine *Malachite*. During the forenoon watch she was seen to surface and rendezvous with two anti-submarine vessels that were to act as escorts into the port of Cagliari. A full salvo of torpedoes was fired, one of which hit the *Malachite,* and she was seen to sink stern first. Due to the presence of the escorting vessels *Dolfijn* immediately went deep and withdrew. After one blank patrol *Dolfijn* returned to the Sardinian coastline. On 29 March, off Cavoli, the 1,143-ton Italian steamer *Egle* was attacked and sunk by torpedo.

The next contact with enemy forces was on 25 May 1943 when Lieutenant Oostrom Soede went to investigate the anchorage at Santa Maria north of the Messina Straits. There he found an Italian MTB that appeared to lack armament. As they closed to attack, the submarine was hit by rapid machine-gun fire injuring Lieutenant H.J. Brakema and Seaman First Class Hennevelt, and *Dolfijn* was forced to withdraw. The submarine was diverted to Malta to discharge the injured before resuming her patrol with no further incident.

Lieutenant Oostrom Soede was not to experience further success until 4 July 1943 when he was off Civita Vecchia. At this time they were on patrol as cover for ships of the Italian main fleet that were likely to intervene in *OPERATION HUSKY*. During

160

the morning watch they sighted the 5,788-ton Italian steamer *Sabbia*. They attacked and fired two torpedoes, one of which hit and damaged the steamer. The submarine immediately went deep and on returning to periscope depth some three hours later saw the *Sabbia* being towed towards Civita Vecchia by one of the escorting vessels. The *Sabbia*, having been damaged earlier by *Ursula*, had run out of luck on this occasion as she was later seen sunk in the harbour and beyond salvage. 4 July was a lucky day for *Dolfijn* as they went on to intercept the 165-ton Italian schooner *Adalia*, board her and sink her by demolition charge.

Later, on the same patrol, they were to enjoy further success. On 13 July as they patrolled between Corsica and mainland Italy they intercepted the 137-ton Italian schooner *Stephano Galleano*. They engaged her by gunfire and after twenty-two hits out of twenty-nine rounds of ammunition the schooner hove to. As her crew had abandoned ship she was boarded and sunk by demolition charge.

These successes were followed by an incident-free patrol but success was to return in September 1943 on her ninth Mediterranean patrol off Bastia, Corsica. On 10 September they sighted a submarine – later identified as the Italian boat *Corridoni*. In view of the capitulation of Italian forces the Italian Commander, Lieutenant Aquini, was invited aboard *Dolfijn* for discussions before being allowed to proceed under his own steam. The next day they sighted the 7,980-ton Italian ship *Humanitas* leaving the port of Bastia. A full salvo of torpedoes severely damaged the stern of the *Humanitas* putting her beyond repair and she was sunk later by the Italian authorities.

Two days later, during the forenoon of 13 September 1943, off Levant *Dolfijn* encountered two 250-ton German transport barges hugging the shore. *Dolfijn* surfaced and engaged them by gunfire; the sixth round knocked out the machine gun of the nearest barge and a fire started. Attention was then switched to the second barge as by this time the crew had abandoned her. Both barges, obviously carrying petrol, burst into flames and sank.

The next six months were barren times for *Dolfijn* during which she was transferred to the First Submarine Flotilla, arriving in

Beirut on 4 January 1944. It was April and her fifteenth Mediterranean patrol before she found further success. On 17 April off Milos in the Aegean Sea they finally recovered their luck. At dawn they surfaced to engage by gunfire the 129-ton Greek caique *Agios Georgius Hydra*. The crew was seen to abandon ship and the caique sank. Later the same day they sighted the caique *Theonie* and, although of just 6 tons, she was sunk by gunfire. This was in direct contravention of Captain (S) First Submarine Flotilla's instructions on attacking caiques under 20 tons but she was flying the German flag and thus brought her within sinking criteria. This was the final Mediterranean patrol for *Dolfijn* before heading back to the United Kingdom. Captain (S) First Submarine Flotilla wrote:

> *DOLFIJN* now leaves the Mediterranean for the United Kingdom to refit. She will be very much missed in the flotilla.[6]

On completion of her refit Lieutenant J.B.M.J. Maas assumed command of *Dolfijn* and they were to patrol home waters as part of the Ninth Submarine Flotilla, but they were to see little action. They became the objects of friendly fire on 10 January 1945 as they sailed from Lerwick when they were attacked by four 'friendly' Mosquito aircraft, damaging the bridge and periscope. Lieutenant Maas described the attack in his patrol report:

> The officer of the watch reported four low-flying twin-engined aircraft flying straight at the boat from right ahead. Dived. When the submarine was passing 20 feet two bursts of machine gun or cannon fire were heard to hit the bridge. Came to periscope depth after remaining deep for ten minutes; both periscopes were found to be out of action, the forward periscope being black and producing water. The aft periscope was dry but useless since it obviously had been hit with a lot of dirt and stuff shaken down on the lenses. A resistance test of the Main Aerial indicated a full short. With this knowledge it was decided to remain deep for another half-hour. Surfaced. Set course for Lerwick.[7]

Dolfijn went on to Dundee for repairs and although she carried out other patrols no other incidents were reported and she was sold to the Royal Netherlands Navy in August 1945.

Free Polish personnel manned a second submarine, *Dzik*, commissioned on 14 November 1942 under the command of Lieutenant Commander B. Romanowski. After her work-up period and one North Sea patrol *Dzik* was dispatched to the Mediterranean and arrived in Gibraltar on 25 March 1943 to join the Eighth Submarine Flotilla. After just one patrol she was transferred to the Tenth Flotilla and arrived in Malta on 5 May 1943.

On her first patrol from Malta *Dzik* was to see her first success when at 06.30 on 24 May they sighted the 12,000-ton tanker *Carnaro* off Cape Spartivento. She was under escort from a destroyer and one other armed vessel and air cover provided by three aircraft. The submarine closed and a full salvo of torpedoes was fired, one of which hit and damaged the tanker. In the flat, calm sea the torpedo tracks were spotted by the escorting warship and a depth-charge counter-attack was mounted but it was inaccurate and no damage was done to the submarine. The discomfort of the depth charges was quickly overcome when, on returning to periscope depth, Lieutenant Commander Romanowski saw the *Carnaro* ablaze and being towed into Messina harbour. The *Carnaro* was subsequently repaired and returned to service.

In September 1943 *Dzik* was deployed off Bastia, Corsica as intelligence sources suggested that the Germans were about to evacuate the island. At 15.30 on 21 September they saw the 6,397-ton ship *Nicolaus* in the mouth of the entrance to the harbour being manoeuvred by tug. A torpedo attack sank the *Nicolaus* across the harbour entrance, trapping all shipping in Bastia and leaving them open to attack by aircraft of the RAF. The Commanding Officer described the result of the attack as seeing only the foremast and the funnel of the target vessel in the mouth of the harbour.

The next day, having moved to patrol off Bari, Lieutenant Commander Romanowski sighted a convoy of Siebel ferries under escort. The attack was well described by him in his subsequent patrol report when he wrote:

At 17.25 the O.O.W. saw a large formation of Siebel ferries coming from the direction of Bastia. I came to the periscope and saw about 11 ferries in double line ahead escorted by three 'E' boats and 4 aircraft. Knowing very little about these ferries I decided to attack them from close range with torpedoes set to zero. When about 500 yards off I thought I was sufficiently close and fired one torpedo at the third ferry in the port column. Just previous to the attack I saw splashes around the periscope and from the odd noises I heard, realised that one of the aircraft was machine gunning the periscope. I kept the periscope up and saw the torpedo explode about a third of the target's length from the bow. At 18.15 I fired three remaining torpedoes at two ferries which were overlapping.

Observed the first torpedo exploding on the bows of the first ferry, which sank within 30 seconds. The other ferry exploded and left only a cloud of black smoke.[8]

In October 1943 *Dzik* sailed from Malta to join the First Submarine Flotilla at Beirut. Her first patrol with the new flotilla was in the Aegean Sea off Monemvasia with Lieutenant Klopotowski in temporary command as Lieutenant Commander Romanowski was ill. On 17 November they intercepted a 40-ton caique carrying olive oil. The caique was sunk and the crew of three was taken on board and transferred later in the day to a smaller caique.

Her next patrol in the Aegean Sea was to be north of Amorgos with Lieutenant Commander Romanowski back in command having recovered from illness. The only confirmed success on this patrol took place on 8 January 1944 when they intercepted the two-masted schooner *Eleni*. The schooner was closed, boarded and found to have a crew of six Greeks and carrying ten German soldiers. Having transferred the prisoners to the submarine the *Eleni* was sunk by demolition charge. The following day, en route for Beirut, they encountered a small caique and, after taking the Greek crew of three on board the submarine sank her by demolition charge.

Dzik made one final patrol that was totally unproductive before being returned to the United Kingdom for refit. After refit she was used primarily for anti-submarine training until transferred to the Royal Danish Navy and renamed *Springeren*.

Parallel to the Mediterranean tour of duty by *Dzik* was the return of *Sokol* under the command of Lieutenant Commander Koziolkowski. They arrived in Malta for service with the Tenth Submarine Flotilla on 12 May 1943. Whilst her early patrols were unproductive her second patrol in July certainly caused some problems for the Commanding Officer. A high fever and severe stomach pains struck down a substantial number of the crew including the First Lieutenant and Navigating Officer. This was put down to bad butter; several tins had to be disposed of due to black spots being found and it tasted very bitter. Also a considerable amount of milk was spoilt. This was all put down to the excessive heat during the patrol.

After the capitulation of Italian forces *Sokol* was to become involved in intercepting Italian shipping and dispatching it to friendly ports. On 10 September Lieutenant Commander Koziolkowski was instructed to contact the Italian port authorities at Brindisi to negotiate the movement of merchant vessels to Allied ports. This proved difficult until the approach of the hospital ship *Saturnia* made it possible to contact the escorting minesweeper. Lieutenant G.G. Taylor, RNVR, was put aboard the minesweeper to enter Brindisi, assess the situation there, and make contact with the Italian Naval Officer in Command.

As they waited for the return of Lieutenant Taylor, *Sokol* intercepted the Italian submarine *Vittore Pisani* escaping from Pola. Sub Lieutenant Fritz and two ratings were put aboard and the submarine dispatched to Taranto. Later in the day a second submarine, *Otario*, was intercepted but having no spare crew to put aboard she was allowed to proceed unescorted with instructions to head for Taranto.

Once contact had been made with the Italian Naval Officer in charge at Brindisi negotiations continued and at midnight 12 September the first six merchant ships left en route to Taranto. There were many ships left in Brindisi but the ships' masters claimed they were unseaworthy. There were also a number of warships but the Naval Officer in charge refused to allow them to leave, explaining that they were on standby to remove the King of Italy along with Marshall Badoglio and the whole of the Italian Government who had gathered at Brindisi. It was agreed they could stay for that particular task.

Sokol's next patrol was off Pola in the Northern Adriatic and was very successful. On 4 October they intercepted the 3,080-ton merchant ship *Dea Mazella*. At 08.00 they fired two torpedoes and damaged the merchantman. Having seen her damaged *Sokol* followed her until she sank at 10.45. The next target came on 7 October when they sighted the 7,095-ton Italian merchant ship *Eridania* on requisition to the Germans. Three torpedoes were fired; two hit the *Eridania* and she was seen to sink by the stern after an explosion in the boiler room had created a mass of dark yellow smoke.

Sokol's triumphant return to Malta was a bizarre event. En route from her patrol area she picked up a barrage balloon about ten miles north of Malta. Thus she entered Lazaretto with the balloon in tow like a joyful child returning from the fair. She then transferred to the First Submarine Flotilla at Beirut.

Sokol's first patrol from her new base was successful. On Poland's Independence Day, 11 November, off the island of Amorgos they sighted a 140-ton two-masted schooner with a crew of more than a dozen, all in naval uniform, and flying the German flag. The vessel was engaged by gunfire but the gun jammed after twenty-four rounds and as the returning fire was becoming very accurate, the submarine dived for cover. On reaching periscope depth one torpedo was fired at the target but it passed under the keel. It was, however, sufficient to encourage the crew to abandon ship. The schooner was then boarded by a party led by Lieutenant Fritz who established that she was carrying naval clothing, rifles, ammunition belts, bayonets and boots – all brand-new and stored in the fo'c'sle. After seizing the ship's documents the schooner was dispatched by demolition charge.

As the patrol progressed they intercepted a small caique on 17 November but as it only contained several old Greek men it was allowed to proceed unmolested. The following day saw a different proposition. Patrolling north of Santorini they intercepted the 20-ton caique *Taxiarhi* travelling towards the island.

The submarine surfaced and the occupants of the caique immediately surrendered. They consisted of two Greek seamen and two German soldiers – a sergeant and a private of the Alpine Section of the *Waffen* SS. These were taken prisoner and the caique sunk by gunfire.

19 November found *Sokol* on patrol in Sitia Bay on the northern coast of Crete. At 07.30 that morning they sighted a big, two-masted schooner flying the German flag and crowded with German troops. The submarine surfaced and engaged the schooner by gunfire but after just twenty rounds fired the gun jammed. Three hits from those rounds set the schooner afire; the crew hauled down the German flag and hoisted Greek colours. The schooner fired a distress flare and the shore batteries intervened forcing *Sokol* to dive for cover. The schooner made for the coast and was later seen alongside a rocky coastline unloading the German troops. She was turned beam on to the sea and *Sokol* prepared to attack by torpedo. One torpedo was fired aimed amidships but deviated from a true course, exploding on the rocks. While missing the intended target the explosion of the rock was sufficient to damage the schooner, and all the men who had been landed on the rock disappeared. A further torpedo was dispatched hitting the damaged and listing schooner causing her to blow up and sink. With the exception of the fifteen men who had recently clambered onto the rocks and ten in a small caique in attendance, all the German troops were lost.

Later the same day they sighted another 200-ton schooner in a nearby small bay. She was heavily laden and low in the water with more than 100 men aboard, all of whom appeared to be sunbathing. She was then seen to weigh anchor but not to prepare for sea and a few minutes later three small caiques rendezvoused with her and towed her closer to the shore. An 'E' boat then tied up alongside her and the smaller caiques. The one torpedo fired failed to find the schooner but it did explode on the rocks destroying one of the caiques. The second torpedo again missed the schooner hitting the shore and sinking an accompanying small caique. *Sokol*, driven off by the attentions of the shore batteries, withdrew seaward to re-load her torpedo tubes. They returned to the scene some two hours later fully prepared to continue the attack and found the schooner still in position with the 'E' boat alongside. Just one torpedo was sufficient to sink the schooner and the explosion of that strike is described well by Lieutenant Commander Koziolkowski:

> Torpedo went straight ahead and hit the schooner amidships. Schooner disintegrated – 'E' boat was lifted by the explosion and got 30-degree angle bow up and then gently collapsed. Small caique, the last one of three was stranded on the rock and turned over, broken in half. 'E' boat was still afloat for about 4 minutes and while the whole crew enjoyed her agony, she capsized slowly, showing big Nazi flag painted on the deck and sank.[9]

On her next patrol *Sokol* was off the island of Lemnos on 12 December 1943 when after dark they encountered five schooners. The first, a two-masted vessel, was engaged by gunfire and, after the third round had found the target, a small boat containing six men was seen to leave. Further hits were made and the schooner was sunk after a further ten men had abandoned ship. The second schooner was then engaged, the crew was seen to abandon her in a small boat, and as the submarine passed at close range they sank her by gunfire. As they approached the third schooner it was obvious that the crew had already made off, so she was fired upon from point-blank range; she caught fire, capsized and sank. The fourth schooner was then engaged, the crew immediately abandoned ship and it was dispatched. *Sokol* collected six Greek survivors from a small open boat. The fifth and smallest schooner survived the attack and was allowed to collect the remaining survivors. German records show that this action saw the loss of *Nicolaus Pi790*, *Nicolaus Sy436*, *Nicolaus Sy262* and *Agios Eleimon Sy274*.

Eight more prisoners were taken on 15 December, six Greeks and two Germans, after they had abandoned a 20-ton caique. This vessel was abandoned, still making headway, and was eventually boarded to find a further five Germans hiding on board. The German prisoners were taken aboard the submarine and all the Greek nationals were placed on the caique under the command

168

of Lieutenant Taylor. The caique parted company with the submarine and Lieutenant Taylor sailed it into Turkish-controlled waters where the prisoners were transferred to a pilot boat for repatriation. After the caique had rendezvoused with *Sokol* and the boarding crew was taken off, she was sunk by gunfire.

On her final two patrols *Sokol* was only able to make one further strike. On 12 January 1944 she was south of Milos when they intercepted the 40-ton caique *53*. She closed the target and engaged her by gunfire. After five rounds the caique sank and the five Greek crew members were taken on board the submarine. The following day the Greek survivors were put ashore on the island of Anenes having been provided with a small amount of provisions.

Sokol sailed from Malta on 6 March to return to the United Kingdom where she carried out one North Sea patrol under Polish colours before being returned to Admiralty control.

These two submarines, *Sokol* and *Dzik*, provided admirable service in the Mediterranean. Lieutenant Commander Romanowski, Commanding Officer of *Sokol*, wrote in his final patrol report:

> Our officers and men are very proud to have been part of the famous Tenth and First Submarine Flotillas and that we could add our paltry quota to the magnificent score. All of us regret very much leaving the First Submarine Flotilla, but we hope to join it again.[10]

As they left the Mediterranean, Captain (S) First Submarine Flotilla wrote:

> DZIK and SOKOL now leave the 1st Submarine Flotilla with an excellent record. It is with much regret that we part with Lieutenant Commanders Romanowski and George Koziolkowski and the most efficient submarines, whose exploits have been an inspiration and which have commanded our admiration and confidence at all times and will continue to do so. That their successes have not been even greater has been no fault of the Commanding

Officers, whose enterprise, skill and determination are well known.[11]

The C.-in-C. Mediterranean endorsed these remarks, and the following was originated at the Admiralty:

Both *DZIK* and *SOKOL* have distinguished themselves in the Mediterranean and their efficiency and offensive spirit reflect high credit on the Commanding Officers in particular and the Polish Navy as a whole.[12]

The Royal Norwegian Navy, having lost *Uredd* in February 1943, quickly replaced her with *Ula*. She was commissioned and handed over to Norwegian control on 28 March 1943 under the command of Lieutenant R.M. Sars. She was allocated to the Ninth Submarine Flotilla based at Dundee and on 20 June 1943 sailed on her first war patrol.

After two barren patrols *Ula* sailed on 31 August for her third patrol which included *OPERATION VENUS*. On 5 September she closed the Norwegian coastline in Me Fjord to implement *OPERATION VENUS* and she landed three agents with one-and-a-half-tons of stores at Kvalviken. This was a particularly dangerous operation taking three trips in a small rubber dinghy over a three-hour period before the submarine was able to quietly withdraw to sea using only main motors.

Two more blank patrols followed but on her sixth, off Stadlandet, they found success. *Ula* sailed from Lerwick on 20 November 1943 under the command of Lieutenant S. Valvatne due to Lieutenant Sars being ill. Two days later, as they patrolled off Stadlandet, they hit a problem when the Chief Engine Room Artificer reported a defective port engine that was not repairable at sea. However, this was not enough to persuade Lieutenant Valvatne to abort the patrol. This decision was commented upon by Captain (S) Ninth Submarine Flotilla when he wrote:

His determination to continue his patrol, having weighed up the various considerations, was, in the event, well rewarded.[13]

That reward came later that day, 22 November, when they sighted a small convoy consisting of an armed whaler and trawler escorting a heavily laden merchant vessel. The armed whaler was closest to the submarine and was engaged first. The one torpedo fired hit the target and gave *Ula* the opportunity to attack the merchant vessel. One further torpedo was sufficient to sink the 1,682-ton *Arcturus*. The submarine went deep to 200 feet but was unable to hold her depth and hit the bottom at 250 feet. By blowing numbers 1 and 6 tanks the submarine commenced her ascent but this could not be halted and they broke the surface to see the small trawler searching amongst debris in the area where the other two vessels should have been.

The next two patrols were to experience disappointment for *Ula*. On the first they sighted a convoy of three merchant ships but were unable to manoeuvre into an attacking position. This was followed by an unsuccessful attack on the Bergen-registered vessel *Pan* as both the torpedoes fired malfunctioned. A few days later further torpedo malfunctions were to see the attack on another convoy fail. The next patrol, *Ula*'s eighth, was to patrol the area of Skudesnes Fjord with the hope that they would have no torpedo problems similar to those experienced previously. That was not to occur but neither was luck on their side. On 20 February 1944 whilst off Listafjord they fired a full salvo of torpedoes at a convoy of eight merchant ships and claimed to have sunk one vessel. (German records show the vessel, the *Bussard*, was not hit and made port safely). Later whilst patrolling off the Naze they torpedoed the 898-ton merchant vessel *Ryfylke*. (German records show that the vessel was not hit as the torpedoes were seen to pass the target vessel before exploding).

It was her tenth patrol before *Ula* was to gain any confirmed successes. They sailed on 25 March 1944 and were patrolling off Stadlandet on 4 April when they sighted a convoy of approximately six merchant ships, all under escort. *Ula* closed and fired a full salvo of torpedoes that hit and damaged the 7,603-ton German tanker *Ile* and which was last seen rolled over on her side, stern down. They were then subjected to a series of depth-charge counter-attacks totalling some 114 charges. Fortunately none were too close and no damage was inflicted. Due to the increased anti-submarine activity in the area they moved on and two days later, whilst off Ulvesund, they torpedoed and sank the 1,923-ton German steamer *Wesergau*.

The next patrol was even more spectacular when, on 19 April 1944, whilst patrolling in the North Sea, they sighted the conning tower of the 500-ton U-boat *U974* under the command of *Kapitänleutnant* Heinz Wolff. Just six minutes after the sighting a full salvo of torpedoes was fired with one hitting the *U974* just astern of the conning tower. The U-boat exploded and sank as *Ula*'s Asdic operator reported breaking-up sounds.

This was followed by one inconsequential patrol before *Ula* sailed from Lerwick on 3 October 1944 on her thirteenth patrol. Just one day out from Lerwick she was to experience the 'unlucky thirteen'. Whilst on passage to her patrol area she encountered a friendly aircraft. The officer of the watch fired off a grenade which he believed to be the correct recognition signal. Unfortunately this was not so and the aircraft commenced an attack, forcing the submarine to dive to avoid damage. Even the crash dive was not successful as the first pattern of four depth charges exploded just fifty feet from the submarine when she had only reached ten feet, blowing her back to the surface and causing some superficial damage. The resultant investigation into this incident clearly laid the blame on the submarine. It was not established if *Ula* was in a total attack restriction area or not but the blame was laid squarely upon her. The conclusion by Admiral (Submarines) contained in his report was:

> This incident for which I consider H. Nor. M. Submarine *ULA* can only be held to blame is much regretted. Happily, only insignificant damage was sustained by the submarine, which has such a fine record of enemy sinkings, and valuable lessons have been learnt, not least by Lieutenant Commander R.M. Sars, Royal Norwegian Navy.[14]

Ula carried out two further patrols off the Norwegian coast before the Nazi surrender but no other incident was reported. At the end of hostilities she was transferred to the Royal Norwegian Navy where she served until being decommissioned ready to be scrapped on 14 November 1964.

Utsira joined *Ula* in the fleet on 24 August 1944 when she arrived at Holy Loch under the command of Lieutenant S. Valvatne to be accepted for service. *Utsira* was to make five patrols before the end of hostilities. On her second patrol she made an unsuccessful attack on a U-boat on 16 December 1944.

On her third patrol, on 11 January 1945, when *Utsira* was off the entrance to Trondheim, she made another unsuccessful attack on a U-boat. Later in the patrol, on 16 January 1944, still off Trondheim, she did achieve success. During the middle watch the radar operator reported shipping that could not be seen from the bridge. The plot was watched as the target vessel moved closer and was eventually identified as a German naval vessel. A full salvo of torpedoes hit and sank the 1,281-ton vessel *V6408* (previously known as the *Skagerrak*).

Her next patrol area was the exit from Folden Fjord and on 5 April she sighted four merchant ships leaving the fjord under escort from ten escort vessels. Having closed and fired a full salvo, they hit and sank the 1,381-ton ex-Norwegian merchant ship *Torridal*. At the moment of attack the submarine broke surface, the crew all ran forward to get the bow down quickly and, with additional water being pumped forward, the submarine was only visible for a few seconds. The escort vessels counter-attacked by depth charge but none were close and no damage was sustained. This was the final sinking by a Norwegian submarine during the conflict and Flag Officer Submarines wrote:

> This is the last of three patrols carried out by *UTSIRA* off Fro Havet since December 1944. All were carried out with the skill and determination that have come to be expected from Lieutenant Commander S. Valvatne, D.S.O., D.S.C., Royal Norwegian Navy since he took temporary command of *ULA* in November 1943 . . . The sinking of S.S. *TORRIDAL* was a fitting conclusion to the successful operation of the Royal Norwegian ships against the enemy.[15]

Utsira was transferred to the Royal Norwegian Navy at the conclusion of hostilities and remained in service until being decommissioned prior to disposal on 9 July 1962.

Three submarines were loaned to the Free French forces and fully manned by their personnel. The first was *Curie* handed over to the Free French Navy on the day she experienced a small battery explosion. This was not serious and less than two weeks later, on 2 May 1943, she sailed into Holy Loch to be accepted as 'completed for service' to commence her work-up period. On 16 September 1943 *Curie* arrived at Algiers to commence service with the Eighth Submarine Flotilla under the command of Lieutenant P.M. Sonneville.

Her time with the Eighth Submarine Flotilla was not to be her best period of service. *Curie* sailed from Algiers on 23 September 1943 for her first Mediterranean patrol off Cape de Noli. On passage to her patrol area she encountered the French cruiser *Montcalm* and was mistaken for an enemy U-boat. *Curie* tried to identify herself by flashing her pennant number but to no avail. The inexperienced crew aboard *Montcalm* opened fire straddling the submarine and forcing her to dive to avoid damage. It was the beginning of an unsuccessful patrol with eight LCTs being sighted but not attacked due to Lieutenant Sonneville believing them to be empty and not suitable for a torpedo attack. On each occasion they were under escort so a gun engagement would have been ill advised.

On her second patrol she carried a party from the Special Boat Squadron with the intention of a demolition attack to disrupt rail services south of Genoa should the opportunity arise. Unfortunately the anti-submarine activity around Nervi was such that this attack was not possible. They also sighted several UJ-boats but these were left unmolested so as not to bring the submarine's presence to the enemy's attention. When it was established that a shore-based attack was not feasible Lieutenant Sonneville attempted to attack a floating crane but as the submarine closed the crane was attacked by Allied aircraft. They also missed the opportunity to attack a small merchant ship as she left harbour, as they were unable to manoeuvre into an attacking position. There were no further opportunities and on returning to Algiers Lieutenant Sonneville wrote:

> This was the end of a long awaited, but quite disheartening, patrol. It seems to me that I lost several opportunities.[16]

Captain (S) Eighth Submarine Flotilla reassured Lieutenant Sonneville by commenting:

> I am sure the *CURIE*, by exercising patience and maintaining her present fine offensive spirit, will be rewarded by a real target.[17]

Flag Officer Submarines commented:

> I think if Sonneville attacked something really important he'd burst in the process.[18]

The next two patrols were as barren as the previous two. On 26 January 1944 *Curie* arrived at Maddalena and transferred to the Tenth Submarine Flotilla with Lieutenant P.J.M.A.F. Chailley taking command. The next patrol off the France-Italy border area was not to see any change in the submarine's fortune as the two attacks made on enemy shipping were both unsuccessful. This was the luck that carried on for the next three patrols as each attack ended in failure. It was not until 21 June 1944 on her eighth patrol that some success came. During a bombardment of shore batteries at Cap Gros, Southern France, they reported gaining fourteen hits on the target before returning fire forced them to withdraw.

This was the only reported success before *Curie* joined the First Submarine Flotilla at Malta. On her first patrol out of Malta, her eleventh in the Mediterranean, she was designated an area of patrol in the Aegean Sea off Cape Sepias. The tenth day of this patrol was to be significant for Lieutenant Chailley and the crew of *Curie*. 2 October 1944 opened with the interception of a 25-ton caique that was stopped and checked. After it was established there were no Germans on board, the caique was allowed to proceed unmolested. This action was not to the pleasure of Captain (S) First Submarine Flotilla who commented that once the submarine had shown herself to the caique she should have sunk it to protect the knowledge of her whereabouts.

The usual pattern appeared to be repeated when later the same day the submarine failed to get into position to attack two ESTE lighters as they passed to landside of the submarine. This missed opportunity was fortuitous, as immediately astern was another convoy that consisted of three merchant ships and included the 1,994-ton troop carrier *Tsar Ferdinand* under destroyer escort. *Curie* closed and surfaced before firing a full salvo of torpedoes that hit and sank the *Tsar Ferdinand* with the loss of nearly 6,000 German troops on board at that time. The next day was to see further success when, as they patrolled north of Skiathos, they sighted another small convoy. On this occasion three torpedoes were fired and the 125-ton patrol vessel *GM03* (previously known as the *Salamis*) was sunk.

Curie made a successful return to Malta to be greeted by the pleasing comments of Captain (S) First Submarine Flotilla who wrote:

> It is gratifying to see that a change of scenery from the Gulf of Lyons to the Aegean has brought about a change of fortune for *CURIE*. This was a most valuable patrol and the losses to the enemy at a time when he needed every possible ship for the evacuation of PIRAEUS. *CURIE* is to be congratulated on her notable contribution to the closing phase of Aegean operations.[19]

This was the last active patrol taken by *Curie* before she was transferred to French control on 26 November 1944.

Two further submarines were loaned to the Free French Navy during hostilities – *Morse* and *Doris*. Whilst loaned during hostilities only *Morse* actually made any contribution and that was just one uneventful patrol east of Orkney. Both were later transferred to French control and joined *Curie*. *Curie* and *Morse* were returned to Admiralty control at Portsmouth on 17 September 1946. *Doris* followed them into Admiralty control on 18

176

November 1947. *Morse* was later sold to the Royal Danish Navy and renamed *Saelen*.

In January 1943 the Greek Naval Authorities were asked to send a crew to Barrow-in-Furness to standby a submarine under construction. That submarine was the *Pipinos* and she was accepted as being completed for service on arrival at Holy Loch on 2 November 1943 with Lieutenant Commander Alexandros Rallis in command. It was always intended that *Pipinos* should operate in the Mediterranean and without any prior patrols she was dispatched. On 2 February 1944 she arrived at Beirut to join the First Submarine Flotilla.

It was on her second patrol off north-western Crete that she was to have her first success. On 13 April 1944 she intercepted the 12-ton caique *Tamiarchis* carrying black-market food and cigarettes. The Greek master was taken on board the submarine and, as the remainder of the crew headed for safety in a small dinghy, the caique was rammed and sank. This course of action received some criticism from Captain (S) First Submarine Flotilla, as there was a ban on sinking caiques less than twenty tons.

The next patrol to the north-west of Milos was to be the last for Lieutenant Commander Rallis. On 28 May 1944 *Pipinos* had a stroke of luck due to missing a target by torpedo. In rough seas Lieutenant Commander Rallis sighted a medium-sized merchant ship but identification was difficult as the target vessel was silhouetted against the sun. Not being able to close to an advantageous position, a full salvo of torpedoes was fired from extreme range but none found the target. This was fortuitous, as the ship in question was the Swedish relief vessel SS *Boreland* being engaged as a hospital ship.

On 4 June 1944 Lieutenant Commander Rallis questioned the occupants of a small dinghy off the port of Kyparisi and established that there were no Germans there. As a result *Pipinos* was taken into the harbour for thirty minutes and Lieutenant Commander Rallis described the incident thus:

Entered Kyparisi Bay. There was nothing in the bay. We asked a dinghy from the inhabitants of the picturesque village after having previously ascertained by them there

177

were no Germans around the place. The customs officers and 2 other compatriots approached us full of suspicions. When they perceived that the S/M was Greek, the word was passed around, and the whole village came up to their feet and many boats surrounded us. Men and women were kissing the deck of the S/M and ourselves. With great difficulty I kept the head of the village to restrain the ringing of the church bells for celebrating our visit. We distributed provisions to the inhabitants, and under the quietness of the moonlit night, with great emotion, we heard enthusiastic local patriotic songs sung by men and women. After hearty farewells and cheers from the inhabitants, we left the bay, proceeding towards Monemvasia. I took on board the 26 years old M.N. seaman Adamantios Tsarouchas, feeling sorry to refuse his wish to render his services for the cause of liberating our country.[20]

This visit was much to the chagrin of the Royal Navy Liaison Officer Commander H.L.S. Baker, RN, and he wrote in his report:

I can quite understand that an enterprise of this sort is very pleasing to all concerned; at the same time it cannot be permitted in view of the very considerable and quite unjustifiable risk to the submarine.[21]

Captain (S) First Submarine Flotilla supported this view when he commented:

No doubt this visit had good propaganda value and a beneficial effect on the partisans following so closely on the recent mutiny in the Greek Navy. Nevertheless, to enter what may be an enemy defended port must constitute a considerable risk to the submarine and is to be discouraged. Commander Rallis' services will be greatly missed in the Allied Submarine Service.[22]

With Lieutenant Loundras in command, *Pipinos* had an uneventful patrol off Kos and Stampalia before sailing on 28 July

178

1944 to patrol the Piraeus to Dodecanese shipping route. On 9 August they were off the harbour of Karlovassi, Samos when they saw a small convoy approach the harbour entrance. Unfortunately, the convoy reached the safety of harbour before an attacking position could be obtained. *Pipinos*, not to be outdone, stood off the harbour and waited for the convoy to re-emerge. This patience was rewarded when the 863-ton Italian destroyer *Calatafimi* (being operated by the Germans under the title *TA 19*) sailed from Karlovassi and returned to sea. A salvo of torpedoes was sufficient to sink the *Calatafimi* and give the crew of the submarine the opportunity to watch it break in half and slowly slide beneath the sea.

Her next patrol was full of incident and tested the crew to the full. On 1 September they were off the island of Andimilos when they engaged an unidentified vessel by gunfire. This vessel immediately returned fire to such a degree it was necessary for the submarine to dive to avoid being hit. *Pipinos* was then tracked for some three hours but no attack materialised. On 3 September and again on 6 September they made two unsuccessful torpedo attacks on enemy shipping before disaster struck.

On 7 September patrolling off Santorini, *Pipinos* commenced a surface attack on an unidentified 200-ton armed German caique. As they manoeuvred to fire their remaining torpedo, the caique opened fire and a three-inch shell hit the submarine, which exploded in the conning tower, splitting the lower hatch and rendering *Pipinos* unable to dive. With the central compartment filling with smoke the submarine withdrew to sea at speed using her motors on full power. After they had reached a safe area the engines were used to clear the boat of smoke and fumes. Chief Engineer Kolokouris and Engineer Touloupis worked throughout the night to make good the damage. They managed to fill the hole in the conning tower with a wooden plug and patched the split in the lower conning tower hatch to such a degree that the submarine was able to test dive to a depth of sixty-five feet. This ability to dive was to prove essential on the following morning as they made their way back to Malta. They were proceeding on the surface when they sighted three enemy fighter aircraft and were obliged to dive immediately. This was done successfully and the boat made it back to Malta. This was the final patrol made by *Pipinos* and after one short visit to Mitylene she left Malta in October 1944 for service with the Greek Navy. She was returned to Admiralty control at Malta on 10 December 1957.

The final Allied country to receive submarines in the war effort against Germany was Russia. After some prolonged and difficult negotiations it was agreed to transfer four submarines to the Russian Navy including three 'U' class. Negotiations were so difficult that the Prime Minister sent a personal minute to the First Lord of the Admiralty, which read:

> Do not hesitate to be blunt with these Russians when they become unduly truculent. This is better done by manner and attitude than by actual words, which can be reported, and also by neglect of certain civilities to the superior people when they have been intolerably offensive. They should certainly be given a feeling that we are not afraid of them.[23]

On this occasion they were not loaned new submarines direct from the construction yard but three submarines that had already fulfilled a valuable role in the Royal Navy throughout the conflict. *Unbroken, Unison* and *Ursula* arrived at Rosyth on 6 May 1944 to be transferred to the Russian Fleet and renamed *B2, B3* and *B4* respectively. Even at this late stage the Russian truculence was still in evidence with Vice Admiral Levchenko immediately complaining about the condition of the boats, with particular mention to cleanliness. However, the transfer programme continued with the training of the Russian personnel before Monday, 24 July 1944 when they sailed from Rosyth en route for Polyarnoe and service with the Third Division of the Red Brigade of the Soviet Fleet. There is some misconception amongst British submariners that these boats sailed to Russia and remained in harbour there before being returned and made no contribution to the fight against Axis forces. However, these submarines made a total of six patrols off the northern Norwegian coastline.

B2 sailed from Polyarnoe on 30 September 1944 under the command of Lieutenant Schekin. The intention was to patrol the northern Norwegian waters to intercept shipping involved in the evacuation of German personnel. On 12 October they made the first strike when they torpedoed and sank the German watchship *B6517* before being counter-attacked for about one hour with only superficial damage being inflicted. This was the only success reported for Lieutenant Schekin and *B2* from the three patrols they made.

The second submarine to patrol was *B4* and Captain Third Class Yoselian when they sailed from Polyarnoe on 15 October 1944. On this her first patrol, she is reported to have hit and sunk an unidentified enemy tanker on 17 October off Laksefjorden, northern Norway. Having enjoyed success *B4* remained in the same area and three days later, on 20 October, they intercepted a convoy of four ships under escort. Two of the three torpedoes found their target – an unidentified supply ship of approximately 8,000 tons, which was seen to burst into flames, break in two and sink. Captain Yoselain returned to Polyarnoe to the praise of the Commander of the Red Banner Fleet, who commented:

> The Commanding Officer acted persistently and boldly. His actions are worthy of praise and imitation.[24]

Although subject to such praise this was the only patrol reported for *B4*.

The remaining submarine, *B3*, under the command of Captain Third Class Kabo, sailed on his first patrol on 29 October 1944 but three days out a defective starboard generator affected the submarine power circuit. Captain Kabo returned to Polyarnoe to scorching criticism from Admiral Epokhim who reported:

> The generator accident is evidence of the poor preparation for the battle campaign. With appropriate attention prior to departure the abnormality in the working of the generator should have been cleared up while still at base. On account of this the battle campaign was spoiled.[25]

This type of reaction illustrates the problems that were originally experienced in negotiations to transfer these submarines when nothing appeared to be good enough for the senior Russian naval officers.

Captain Kabo tried his luck again when *B3* sailed on 26 January 1945 for his second patrol with a brief to seek and destroy enemy submarines. The only incident recorded for this patrol was on 30 January when the submarine lost buoyancy and dropped to 200 feet before it was checked by the blowing of numbers 1 and 6 tanks, which forced her to the surface. It was another blank patrol for Captain Kabo and he returned once again to criticism from his senior officers when Admiral Karpuhin wrote:

> Enemy submarines were active in most cases in darkness. Throughout the mission the Commander did not once carry out a search in the dark directly on the shore but remained 20 to 35 miles away. In this way there couldn't be a meeting with the enemy. The submarine '*B.3*' battle mission had no results. The Commander's actions were unsatisfactory.[26]

This was the final patrol carried out by Russian 'U' class submarines before they were returned to Rosyth and Admiralty control on 10 November 1947.

Notes

1. *The Fighting Tenth* by John Wingate, DSC, RN Rtd.
2. National Archives Kew Reference: ADM 199/1852.
3. National Archives Kew Reference: ADM 199/1852.
4. National Archives Kew Reference: ADM 199/1852.
5. National Archives Kew Reference: ADM 199/1340.
6. National Archives Kew Reference: ADM 199/1855.
7. National Archives Kew Reference: ADM 199/1855.
8. National Archives Kew Reference: ADM 199/1853.
9. National Archives Kew Reference: ADM 199/1854.
10. Royal Navy Submarine Museum – Submarine Patrol Reports.
11. National Archives Kew Reference: ADM 199/1854.
12. National Archives Kew Reference: ADM 199/1853.
13. National Archives Kew Reference: ADM 199/1851.

14. National Archives Kew Reference: ADM 199/1851.
15. National Archives Kew Reference: ADM 199/1852.
16. National Archives Kew Reference: ADM 199/1857.
17. National Archives Kew Reference: ADM 199/1857.
18. National Archives Kew Reference: ADM 199/1857.
19. National Archives Kew Reference: ADM 199/1857.
20. National Archives Kew Reference: ADM 199/1850.
21. National Archives Kew Reference: ADM 199/1850.
22. National Archives Kew Reference: ADM 199/1850.
23. National Archives Kew Reference: ADM 1/15679.
24. Russian Naval Archives – Submarine Patrol Reports.
25. Russian Naval Archives – Submarine Patrol Reports.
26. Russian Naval Archives – Submarine Patrol Reports.

VII

SPECIAL OPERATIONS

Spies, Supplies and Sabotage

In the dark the lookout suddenly reported a strange red light flashing on and off irregularly. Very cautiously the UNBEATEN made towards the light. Then they saw the dull red glow lighting up the face of an Italian sentry; he was dragging at his cigarette while pacing the end of the breakwater.

Lieutenant E.A. Woodward, as HMS *Unbeaten*
approached Taranto harbour on 12 December, 1941.[1]

The size of the 'U' class submarines lent themselves to clandestine missions and there were many to report. They became so popular for these missions that C.-in-C., Mediterranean felt it necessary to intervene and instruct that no undercover operations involved in the landing of agents should be undertaken without his personal approval.

The first occasion non-naval personnel were taken on board a submarine was for an introductory trip to gain experience living in such a confined space. On 19 February 1941 *Upright* took on board Lieutenant Dudley Schofield of the Royal Fusiliers together with men of the Special Services Department. It was the following month that combined operations were to commence. On 1 March, *Utmost* (Lieutenant Commander R.D. Cayley) closed the North African coastline at Shebka el Cazel. They launched a boat and brought back Second Lieutenant Fairclough from shore. They returned to the same rendezvous on 28 April and recovered a further Army officer but the arrangements were slightly different on this occasion. The officer was to obtain a rowing boat

184

ashore and row himself out into the Bay of Hammamet as if to go fishing. If everything was in order he was to tie his shirt to an oar and hold it up. If not, he was to do the same with his trousers. All went according to plan; the submarine surfaced and he was transported to Malta. This operation was successfully repeated by *Utmost* on 27 May.

On 24 May 1941 *Upright* (Lieutenant Norman) sailed from Malta with Lieutenant Dudley Schofield and six other ranks aboard with the intention of blowing up an Italian mainline rail link. They were equipped with explosives and a punt to convey them from the submarine. At 02.00 on 28 May the submarine was 800 yards from the enemy coast when the landing party manned the punt. This was found to be very difficult for the landing party as all their training had been in calm waters and the slight swell created a problem. The journey to the beach was erratic as one of the oarsmen was seasick and so the journey of over 800 yards took over an hour to complete. Once ashore the landing party made for the railway line and commenced placing their charges. Unfortunately, before they had completed the task, they heard a train approaching and it was necessary to remove the pressure pads and take cover. Not to be thwarted on this first engagement, the pressure pads and charges were replaced and the landing party withdrew, returning safely to the submarine at 03.55. The submarine stood offshore submerged and at 05.15 a rumbling sound, similar to an explosion, was heard but it was not possible to confirm the source. The mission was considered by the men to have been successful but this was not confirmed by aerial reconnaissance. There were lessons to be learned from the operation and Commander Simpson made the following recommendations as to future operations:

a)   A punt is unsuitable being unnecessarily large and inconveniently immobile. (A skiff was recommended by Lieutenant Schofield.)

b)   The minimum number of Military should be taken on board, and it is considered that two are ample.

c)   The Military should not rely on firearms, since success

185

is dependant upon stealth and the laying of the charge unobserved.

d) Two men can dispose of an isolated sentry quite as well as six; if the enemy are present in force the enterprise should be abandoned.

It is considered that these operations are likely to succeed, and if carried out a short way inside a tunnel may block the single lines for long periods, and present indications are that tunnels are so numerous that they are not all guarded. It is intended to carry out similar operations, using two men and one folbot, which will comfortably carry the necessary weight of men, equipment and explosives.'[2]

Just one month later Lieutenant Schofield was back on Italian ground. Having embarked with Lieutenant Commander Cayley in *Utmost* he led a team of commandos on 24 June to attack and damage the railway line between Naples and Reggio di Calabria. The explosives were set to explode by contact as a train passed the attack location and the team returned to the submarine. The explosives failed to detonate so on the following night Lieutenant Schofield returned to the scene to detonate the explosives and damage the railway line before returning safely to the submarine.

The momentum of sabotage was maintained when Lieutenant Tomkinson in *Urge* closed the Sicilian coastline and landed Lieutenant R. Wilson, Royal Artillery, and Marine W.G. Hughes on a beach near Taormina. As they closed the railway line they saw a white light and went into cover but the light proved to be a signal light and not a guard. They placed their explosives just inside the unguarded tunnel and, as the signal light changed to green, they withdrew heading back to their folbot and *Urge*. The whole operation lasted two hours and fifteen minutes with just twenty-five minutes being taken up in the placing of the explosives and detonators. After fifteen minutes Lieutenant Tomkinson invited Lieutenant Wilson to the bridge as he had seen a train entering the tunnel. He arrived on the bridge just in time to see a large flash followed by the sound of an explosion – proof his task had been completed successfully.

July and August 1941 saw more successes as *Utmost* with Lieutenant Commander Cayley, and *Unique* with Lieutenant Collett, continued to land Military personnel and attack enemy communications. *Unique* made two such attacks within two days landing a two-man folbot party consisting of Corporal R.H. Brown and Lance Corporal J.R.A. Ferguson – both of the London and Scottish Regiment – on both occasions. The first was on the Sicilian coast between Messina and Taormina when they took just twenty-five minutes to land, place their charges and return to the submarine. Three hours later they watched as a train blew up when passing the attack point. The next day, having moved to the Calabrian coast of Italy, the folbot party was again landed between Cape Spartivento and Cap del Armi. In just one hour and twenty minutes the men had landed, placed their charges and returned to the submarine. Unfortunately on this occasion they were not able to confirm success as no train came along during the night and the submarine withdrew to sea with the onset of daylight.

Whilst *Unique* was attacking communications along the southern coast of Italy and on Sicily, *Utmost* was patrolling off the western coast in the Gulf of Eufemia. On 27 July they attempted to land a folbot party but were frustrated by a party of night bathers. Not to be denied this opportunity to attack, a second attempt to land was successful and the resultant explosion destroyed one train together with overhead cables. On re-embarking the landing party, the submarine stood off and watched the explosion and the resultant fire that burned furiously for several hours. A month later, on 26 August 1941, Lieutenant Commander Cayley and *Utmost* found themselves on the eastern coast of Italy and landed their folbot party which destroyed the railway bridge at Trebisacca.

These operations were not always so successful. On 26 August 1941 Lieutenant Commander Wanklyn in *Upholder* landed a folbot party, led by Lieutenant Walker of the Hertfordshire Regiment, three miles east of Sciacca on the Sicilian coast with the intention of blowing up the coastal railway line to Palermo. They landed at 23.00, hid the folbot and set off inland. As they climbed the first slope a dog started to bark, followed by the

187

sound of a pistol shot. Undeterred they carried on and travelled for more than an hour and were more than one mile inland before they saw evidence of the railway line. They watched a train with carriage lights full on pass at least three-quarters of a mile away. As they continued their journey they experienced more dogs barking and more shooting so, with time running out, they reluctantly aborted the action, buried the explosives and made their way back to the submarine.

In addition to these sabotage operations by the folbot section, 'U' class submarines were used to service agent operations in the southern areas of Italy and Sicily. One such operation was undertaken by Lieutenant Tomkinson in *Urge* when, having embarked an agent to be landed near Palermo in Sicily, she sailed from Malta on 22 September 1941. On 24 September the agent was landed by folbot in a suitable place easily identified by a prominent rock formation for the return journey. Arrangements were made for the agent to be collected from the landing point at one minute past midnight on 1 October. He was briefed to smoke a cigar at one minute to midnight, showing the glow seaward whilst shielding it from shore side with his hands. An appropriate challenge and reply were agreed and should he not appear at the agreed time the submarine would return twenty-four hours later when the same arrangements would be implemented.

Urge dispatched Sub Lieutenant B.N.T. Lloyd, RN, in the folbot to make the agreed rendezvous but the agent failed to appear. As they stood by it was noticed that the Cape Gallo Light was burning and a destroyer came through the area, forcing the submarine to dive to avoid detection. After half an hour the agent had not appeared so Sub Lieutenant Lloyd aborted the mission and returned to the submarine. Twenty-four hours later *Urge* again closed the coastline. This time the moon was hidden by cloud and a slight mist made conditions ideal for this type of mission. Once again Sub Lieutenant Lloyd propelled the folbot to the rendezvous position with instructions to return immediately should he suspect anything amiss. As soon as the folbot had been dropped the submarine turned stern-on to the shore giving less of an image to any onlookers. The folbot drew close to the shore at half a minute past midnight just thirty seconds from the rendezvous time, when two automatic rifles opened fire. Fire was returned by pistol shot believed to be from Sub Lieutenant Lloyd having been so equipped. At the same time Leading Signalman Law sighted a small object about three miles out to sea which was identified as a destroyer closing the area fast. The destroyer passed shore-side of the submarine at speed but did not locate her. This confirmed Lieutenant Tomkinson's suspicions that the operation had been compromised and that Sub Lieutenant Lloyd had been hit, so he withdrew to sea.

The initial belief was that the agent had double-crossed the submarine personnel but the reliability of the agent was established a few days later when, in radio communications with Malta, he explained that he had attempted to gain access to the rendezvous point. On each occasion he had been frustrated by enemy attention being given to the beach area. Captain (S) Tenth Submarine Flotilla was of the opinion that the operation was compromised by the previous sabotage actions which had obviously involved submarine operations. These had caused additional attention to be paid to this part of the coastline that compromised this operation.

The next two operations were undertaken by Lieutenant Edmonds in *P36* to service agents operating in occupied France. They were to rendezvous with the fishing vessel *Vincent Mitchelle* off the coast of Brittany and recover four agents. On 27 November 1941 as they reached the rendezvous point they sighted a single white light being shown from the mast of a fishing vessel similar in appearance to *Vincent Mitchelle*. The submarine approached the point from down wind and as the weather was too rough to launch the folbot, the fishing boat was closed to within hailing distance. The vessel was challenged and successfully replied being identified as the *Veach Vad* but the captain was not able to bring her alongside so the transfer was made in her small dinghy by passing two agents at a time to the submarine. Stores were then delivered to the fishing vessel but the captain declined the transfer of fuel due to the weather conditions and refused a rendezvous for the following night, as he wanted to make the fishing grounds. The agents were landed at Dartmouth before *P36* returned to Portsmouth and then onwards to the Mediterranean.

It was on his first patrol, en route from Gibraltar to Malta, that Lieutenant Edmonds carried out the second of his clandestine operations and delivered agents onto the shores of southern France. Prior to sailing he embarked two agents – one being Peter Churchill, the coordinator of resistance in southern France. On 9 January 1942 *P36* closed the French coastline east of Marseilles on a dark, still night. Peter Churchill was landed by folbot and the submarine proceeded easterly to land the second agent, close to Cannes. The submarine then headed for Malta and service with the Tenth Submarine Flotilla.

Clandestine operations for the months of February and March 1942 were left to Lieutenant Commander Tomkinson and *Urge*. On 12 February they sailed from Malta with three agents to be landed off Tunis together with Captain Wilson, Royal Artillery, and Corporal Hughes, both serving with the Special Services Department. This patrol was also to service an agent operating in Sicily, the same agent who had been dropped on an earlier patrol and who Lieutenant Commander Tomkinson distrusted.

On 16 February *Urge* closed to within 2,000 yards of the shore at Cape Kamart in the Gulf of Tunis. At 20.20 the folbot was launched, manned by Captain Wilson who was to land one agent. As they approached the shoreline the sound of the breakers and surf was overwhelming and Captain Wilson instructed the agent on the procedures to ensure a safe landing. However, as they got closer inshore they were caught by a large breaker, which overturned the folbot, dumping the passengers into the sea. The two men landed on the beach in a bedraggled state having lost one oar and a Tommy-gun carried for protection. The folbot followed them ashore and after finding his radio still intact the agent changed his trousers and set off for the railway station to commence his tasks. Fortunately it was raining very heavily at the time which, if needed, would easily account for his condition when he reached the railway station. Captain Wilson returned to the submarine but as the folbot was heavy with water and could not be recovered, it was destroyed and sunk. The weather deteriorated so much that it was not possible to land the remaining two agents and *Urge* set off to service the Sicilian agent.

On 22 February they closed the shore on the eastern corner of Castellammare Bay in north-west Sicily. This operation was to service the agent previously dropped by *Urge* who was involved in suspicious incidents that led to the loss of Sub Lieutenant Lloyd. As *Urge* closed the shore they found the area being patrolled by an E-boat and a trawler obviously intent on intercepting the submarine. Lieutenant Commander Tomkinson anticipated that this was a trap set for him and his boat and withdrew. Whilst the agent's ongoing communications with Malta had given him some credence, this incident persuaded the authorities of his treachery, allowing them to use his subsequent communications accordingly. *Urge* returned to Malta to this comment by Captain (S) Tenth Submarine Flotilla:

> The missions undertaken by *URGE* were accompanied by the hazards of treachery as well as weather. They were carried out with great care and forethought, and so far as was possible with success. The conduct of the patrol shows the reliability of Lieutenant Commander Tomkinson's appreciation and actions.[3]

The experiences of the previous patrol did not deter Lieutenant Commander Tomkinson and on 23 March 1942 *Urge* sailed from Malta having embarked Lieutenant Walker and Sergeant Penn with the intention to sabotage railway communications between Naples and Calabria. On 29 March the sabotage party from Special Service Department was landed in the Gulf of Policastro. The weather was ideal for such an operation with rain and mist making observations difficult. The landing party made their way inland to the main railway line, passing a newly constructed but unmanned machine-gun post, and placed their charges on an open stretch of railway line above a high embankment. They made their way back to the submarine and arrived on board just in time to see an electric train blow up and roll down the embankment. The landing party was ashore for less than one hour to achieve this success.

The sabotage landings were abandoned during the summer months but on 4 August 1942, during operational planning for a high-speed Malta-bound convoy (code-named *OPERATION PEDESTAL*), it was suggested that the Sicilian-based enemy aerodromes could be attacked by commando sabotage raids. A commando unit of the Special Boat Section had recently completed their training and were waiting to be deployed under the leadership of Captain G.E.A. Duncan of the Black Watch. It was decided such an operation would be feasible and it was implemented under the codename *OPERATION WHY NOT*. At a planning meeting three alternative suggestions of proposed targets were discussed. Captain Duncan opposed the initial suggestion of attacking either Gela or Commisso airfields as they were both some distance from the sea and suggested the alternative of Catania, just one mile from the sea. Whilst this was the best-defended target, Captain Duncan explained that his previous experience of German sentries had not impressed him and the importance of the aerodrome was an encouragement to the meeting. It was decided to go ahead and attack Catania aerodrome on 11 August, the night before the convoy would pass through the Sicilian channel.

With the date and place settled, *Una*, under the command of Lieutenant Norman, embarked the detachment of eight men of the Special Boat Section, commanded by Captain Duncan, and sailed from Malta on 9 August 1942. The operation did not go according to plan from the onset; on launching the folbots one was so seriously damaged it had to be destroyed, and three men had to remain on the submarine leaving two boats and six men to head for the landing place. As the operation progressed Lieutenant Norman could see the aerodrome was fully operational with the flare path lit and aircraft taking off and landing. A heavy presence of shore patrols was evident from the flares as they lit their cigarettes. The landing party did not reach the target and were captured before any sabotage could take place, thus thwarting the intended confusion that should have been caused so close to the passing of the Malta-bound convoy. The convoy, which consisted of fourteen merchant ships, passed through the Straits of Gibraltar on 10 August and was attacked continually which resulted in just four merchant ships and one tanker making it to Malta, but even this was a lifeline to the over-stretched inhabitants of this war-torn island.

Lady Luck appeared to desert the Special Services Department and this was to continue on the next sortie into enemy territory. Captain Wilson, Royal Artillery, had recently returned from England and was provided with limpet mines to attach to enemy shipping in their safe havens. He attempted to persuade C.-in-C., Mediterranean to allow him to attack shipping in the harbour at Navarin but Captain Simpson, Captain (S) Tenth Submarine Flotilla was against such an adventure. His reason was that Navarin had been previously attacked from the sea and was well defended. He felt that such an attack presented unnecessary hazards for both submarine and military personnel with little chance of success. Captain Wilson agreed that to attack Crotone would be a viable alternative and so such an attack was planned. On 31 August *Unbroken*, under the command of Lieutenant Mars, sailed from Malta with Captain Wilson and Bombardier J. Brittlebank (one of the survivors of the ill-fated operation to attack Catania aerodrome) on board. Just after midnight on 6 September the landing party pushed off in their folbot. Seventy minutes later flashes were seen coming from the harbour at a time when the landing party should have been in position. Both members of the landing party were captured before they could cause any damage. Subsequent RAF reconnaissance photographs confirmed no damage to enemy shipping.

The landing of agents in enemy territory continued through-out October 1942 with Lieutenant J.W.D. Coombe, RN, now in command of *Utmost*, making two such landings along the western coast of Italy. On 8 and 9 October a total of four agents was landed – two being landed in Lago di Licola, but both were so nervous that it took until almost daylight to persuade them to get into the folbot. The other two agents were Italian nationals and they were landed north of Naples but both were captured and executed.

Having gained experience of operating close inshore to enemy-occupied territory, the submarines were engaged in beach reconnaissance duties immediately prior to the Allied landings in North Africa – (*OPERATION TORCH* due to commence on 8

November 1942). On 31 October *P48* and *Unrivalled* sailed from Gibraltar with military personnel on board to perform beach recces and form beach-marking units for the landing. They were followed on 1 November by *Unshaken* and *Ursula*, similarly equipped. Between 4 and 8 November these four submarines made several folbot landings along the area prior to *OPERATION TORCH* to ensure the landing areas were adequate and to assess the strength of the opposition. These were carried out successfully without detection and on 8 November the submarines acted as beacons for the oncoming troop carriers as *OPERATION TORCH* was implemented and the re-occupation of North Africa commenced.

Another unit of the Special Boat Section consisting of Corporal J. Booth, Seaforth Highlanders, and Marine R.R. Didcott, was embarked in *Umbra* before she sailed from Malta on 2 November 1942. Both these men were survivors of the sabotage raid on the aerodrome at Catania earlier in the year. On 15 November they were landed at the mouth of the Angitola River with the intention of sabotaging the rail link between Naples and Calabria. Lieutenant Maydon commanding *Umbra* described the operation in his patrol report thus:

> It was rather eerie approaching so close to an enemy coast; although very dark, we had the natural misgiving that the submarine was equally visible to any patrols ashore as were the features ashore visible to us. The spur with the electric pylon and the square white house were now clearly visible through binoculars and proved most useful to guide the ship in. It seemed peculiar to hear an enemy dog barking and to see enemy trains with large headlights passing to and fro at such close quarters. The folbot returned and Corporal Booth reported a successful landing but there was a sentry box on the crest of the beach about 20 yards from the landing point. This was empty but a sentry was spotted patrolling some 50 yards beyond. Two double apron barbed wire obstacles had been placed amongst the sand dunes not in view from seaward. In view of these the enterprise was aborted and the party returned to the boat.[4]

194

On 30 November 1942 Lieutenant Lakin brought *Ursula* to within 500 yards of the Italian coastline at Liagueglia intending to mount an attack on the rail tunnel there. Captain R.P. Livingstone and Sergeant S. Weatherall were landed by folbot and Captain Livingstone described the enterprise of three hours' duration in his report:

At 20.20 hours on 30th November 1942 we pushed off from the S/M about 600 yards from the shore and made our landing on the western outskirts of the town. As the main road runs along the shore at this point, there was some difficulty in finding a hiding place for the boat, but we were eventually able to conceal it in the garden of a large villa. We then made our way inland through a series of elaborate gardens and enclosures, and eventually struck the line about 100 yards east of the tunnel entrance. We intended to wait for a train to pass (the line is a single one) and then to follow it into the tunnel so as to have as much time as possible between trains to lay the charges, and also to avoid being caught in the tunnel by a train as they are very brightly lighted.

There was a good deal of movement at this time; people kept coming out of houses and we also detected the presence of a sentry, who was eventually located on top of the tunnel mouth. All this compelled us to lie close for nearly an hour, and as we had arranged, on account of the moon, to rejoin the ship not later that 23.15, there was no time to stalk and kill the sentry as well as to penetrate the tunnel. We were under the impression that the sentry must have seen us and that we were being surrounded, but the neighbourhood quietened down and I am convinced that this was a false alarm. I therefore decided to lay the charges about 100 yards further down the line from the tunnel, where there is a necessary curve, and a rocky cutting renders a block most effective.

Two delay action charges with time fuses were placed inconspicuously on two of the steel posts which carry the electric wires and four charges were laid on the track itself, to be fired by pressure when a train passed over it. We then withdrew, but owing to continuous obstacles were forced out on the main road in the suburbs of the town. As time was running very short and no one seemed to be about, we decided to risk it and walked openly down the road. We passed an Italian soldier and also several other people mysteriously engaged under some trees but although we were prepared to deal with them if necessary, a bold simulation of cheerful innocence enabled us to escape their interest. Reaching the boat, we withdrew without interference and rejoined the ship at 23.20 hours.[5]

The landing party was able to watch the results of its labours when, at about midnight, explosions were heard coming from the attacked location and after several bright flashes the lights further down the line went out – obviously as a result of the explosion damaging the power cables. The following morning found several trains stationary at various points along the track, awaiting line clearance. For the next seven days as *Ursula* patrolled the coastline it was apparent that this one incident had greatly curtailed rail communications in the area as trains were reduced from one or two trains per hour to only three in any one night.

Unbending (Lieutenant Stanley) carried out the next clandestine operation by 'U' class submarines when they sailed from Malta to deliver two agents ashore south of Wadi Udiana in Tunisia. To facilitate the landing, *Unbending* also embarked two military personnel, Sergeant Casey and Private Greghan, Hampshire Regiment. On 28 December 1942 two folbots were floated off, manned by the soldiers, and each carrying an agent. The landing did not go as planned due to poor boatmanship. Private Greghan smashed his folbot on landing and Sergeant Casey smashed his as he attempted to re-launch it to make good their escape. Both soldiers were unable to return to the submarine and were left dressed in uniform, armed and equipped with enough food for forty-eight hours. They had been instructed that in such an eventuality they should conceal themselves together with their means of arrival. Whilst the soldiers did not return, the agents were able to establish themselves and Captain

(S) Tenth Submarine Flotilla was able to report the gratitude of the Military Authorities who considered the operation a success.

January 1943 was not a good month for clandestine operations as the two attempted failed to achieve success. In the first Lieutenant Daniell in *Unison* landed a folbot party on 10 January to rendezvous with chariot personnel returning from an operation to attack Italian cruisers in Maddalena. There was no sign of any personnel and it was subsequently established that *P311* (the submarine that should have delivered the charioteers to Maddalena) was lost before the operation could be carried out.

The end of the month brought another disappointment when Lieutenant Mars in *Unbroken* embarked Commander D.H. Fyfe, RNR, Captain J. Eyre, Royal Engineers and Lieutenant P.M. Thomas, The Buffs, accompanied by six Free French commandos for a special operation code named *FELICE*. The intention was the destruction of a railway bridge near the town of Hammamet. At 19.30 the landing party left the submarine in four folbots. The landing appeared to have been successful but shortly afterwards it was obvious the enemy patrols had been alerted as flares illuminated the beach and Lieutenant Mars reported he could see the folbots on the shore. As these flares also illuminated the submarine it was necessary for her to withdraw. *Unbroken* was not able to recover any of the landing party and returned to Malta. It was later confirmed that the group had failed to damage the intended target.

These types of clandestine operations were also being carried out off the Norwegian coast by home-based submarines. On 5 February 1943 the Norwegian-manned *Uredd* sailed from Lerwick under the command of Lieutenant R.O. Roren, having embarked a sabotage party of six together with 500 pounds of associated stores. *Uredd* was to deliver the landing party to the Norwegian coast in the vicinity of Noviken to implement *OPERATION SEAGULL* and destroy the power plant situated sixty miles east of Bodo. This power plant supplied the Sulitjelma mines, which were regarded as being of great economic importance to the German war effort. The mines were producing about 30,000 tons of copper concentrate, 140,000 tons of pyrites and 9,000 tons of zinc concentrate per annum.

The area chosen for the approach was prohibited to shipping and had been heavily mined. Lieutenant Roren intended to approach along the northern edge of the prohibited area as it was considered this area would not be mined on account of the uneven bottom and strongly shifting currents. This was not so and, as the submarine approached along the northern area of the minefield, she struck a mine and was lost, along with the lives of thirty-nine officers and men. In a letter to the Norwegian Minister of Defence dated 27 February 1943 Admiralty expressed their regret thus:

> It is with very great regret that I have to inform you that the Royal Norwegian Submarine *UREDD* is overdue and must now be considered lost. *UREDD* had rendered most valuable support to the Allied submarine fleet, performing her patrols with skill and notable success and at the time of her loss she was engaged in a special operation entailing hazardous duties off the Norwegian coast.[6]

In June 1985, as a result of a request from Reidar Skarlo, Leader of Submarine Inspection for the Royal Norwegian Navy, their naval units made a search of an area to the northern end of the Flankensperre minefield. This minefield had been extended during the summer of 1942 and was not known to British intelligence at the time *Uredd* sailed on her fateful mission. The *Uredd* was located off Noviken and examination of the wreckage confirmed the damage was consistent with striking a mine. On 13 March 1986 the sunken submarine was designated a war grave.

In the Mediterranean planning was in place for the Allied landings on Sicily in *OPERATION HUSKY*. The landings were not due to take place until 10 July 1943 but the submarine service was fully occupied in gathering intelligence regarding suitable landing places well before that date. The first indication of these operations appeared on 27 February 1943 when *Unbending* and *United* sailed from Malta, quickly followed by *Unrivalled* on 2 March. Each submarine had personnel of the Combined Operations Pilotage Party on board.

These submarines commenced reconnaissance operations of the approaches to the beach along the Sicilian coastline, firstly from the sea and then on to the beaches themselves. All three submarines returned to Malta with the desired information. However, as in many hazardous operations, there were casualties. On 28 February Lieutenant Commander N.J.M. Teacher, RN, failed to return to *Unbending* from a routine reconnaissance in the water. There had been no sound of fighting nor had there been any disturbance on the beach. The submarine's Commander, Lieutenant Stanley, discovered that Lieutenant Commander Teacher had abandoned the swimming suit he had used in practice in favour of one slightly smaller which may have split and flooded. On 4 March *Unbending* was to suffer further losses when Lieutenant N.W. Cooper, RNVR, and Captain G.W. Burbidge, Royal Engineers, failed to return from a folbot expedition.

Lieutenant J.C.Y. Roxburgh in *United* was to have better luck. On 28 February they landed Lieutenant P.R.G. Smith, RN, and Lieutenant D. Brand RNVR, for reconnaissance duties on Gela beach and although they reported hearing sentries ashore, they returned to the submarine after four-and-a-half hours, having completed their task. The following night the officers landed again but on this occasion they failed to return by folbot. Lieutenant Roxburgh searched the area and made the alternative rendezvous point, again without success. During this time he experienced an increase in air activity and feared that the enemy suspected his presence. On 3 March *United* withdrew seaward and reported the loss of these officers only to be told that they had, in fact, returned safely to Malta. Having failed to rendezvous with the submarine, Lieutenants Smith and Brand decided that they would paddle back the seventy-five miles to Malta rather than compromise the operation. They were picked up by MTB five miles from Mellieha after forty-four hours in the water.

Unrivalled failed to achieve any success during her foray into the reconnaissance of Sicilian beaches. On each occasion as they attempted to launch the folbots they floundered and the mission had to be aborted. On return to Malta the Commanding Officer, Lieutenant Turner, reported that he believed that folbots were not ideal for this type of mission and on later missions chariots were used.

These reconnaissance duties were maintained throughout the months leading up to *OPERATION HUSKY* and ended with *Unison, Unrivalled* and *Unruffled* being used as marker vessels for the release points as troops landed on the beaches of Sicily. The only variation to these duties was the introduction of *OPERATION SNAPDRAGON* at the beginning of May 1943. This changed the brief in respect of reconnaissance landings on Sicilian beaches. The strength of the landing parties was increased to facilitate the additional objective of capturing an enemy sentry for interrogation. Both *United* and *Unshaken* made several attempts but all were thwarted. The nearest they came to success was when Lieutenant Whitton and *Unshaken* landed a party of six SAS personnel, under the leadership of Major Appleyard, on 28 May. The group left the submarine at 22.00 in two rubber boats and landed safely on Salina Point. The landing party then climbed the steep cliffs to approach two small huts situated at the top, which they believed to be the sentries' billets. It was a quiet, dark night but the strains of '*O Sole Mio*' led the group to a lone sentry. Four men attempted to overcome the sentry and tried to gag him with their handkerchiefs but to no avail and he let out a piercing yell alerting his colleagues. They rushed from the huts to be repelled by close-range pistol fire. Unfortunately, in the mêlée, a small hand grenade seriously wounded Lance Corporal Hersell. Major Appleyard ordered a return to the boats but the overweight and non-cooperative sentry made it impossible to bring him along so he was abandoned at the top of the cliffs as the landing party made good their escape and returned to the submarine. That was the nearest anyone came to meeting the objective of *OPERATION SNAP-DRAGON*.

As the submarines had become adept as marker vessels for Allied landings in North Africa and Sicily they were called upon one last time in *OPERATION SHINGLE*. *Ultor* and *Uproar* were deployed as beach markers for the Allied landing at Anzio. On completion of these duties they left for a recreational visit on the Isle of Capri.

Whilst all this activity was concentrated in the Mediterranean, the Norwegian-manned submarines, based in Scotland, were carrying the fight to the enemy by supplying the anti-occupation forces in Norway. On 1 September 1943 *Ula*, under the command of Lieutenant R.M. Sars, sailed to complete *OPERATION VENUS* to land three Norwegian nationals to reinforce the resistance movement in Norway and establish a clandestine organisation to report ships' movements. On 5 September they closed the Norwegian coastline off Kvalviken in Me Fjord and at 23.20 surfaced and commenced inflating the landing boats. At 23.25 the first of the agents, described by Lieutenant Sars as 'patriots', landed accompanied by the ship's Navigating Officer and one Able Seaman. A line was established from submarine to beach and supplies were landed by inflated boat pulled to and fro along the line. After three such transfers the final trip, carrying accumulators and the last agents, landed at 01.00. The ship's personnel returned to the submarine and she withdrew from the area at 01.15.

This group was to be supported later by further supplies landed by *Venturer* in November 1944 in *OPERATION HANGMAN*. On Sunday 12 November 1944 Lieutenant Launders took *Venturer* into Me Fjord and grounded the submarine some fifty yards from the chosen landing place. At 23.30 a reconnaissance party, led by Sub Lieutenant P. Brand, RNVR, was put ashore to check the area. Once on land they established a suitable place amongst a cluster of large boulders some twenty-eight metres inshore to cache the supplies. The stores were then transferred to shore in five boatloads. Lieutenant Launders reported the action thus:

> The stores were landed in five boatloads and hidden behind several boulders. The landing and stowage involved considerable hardship on the side of the landing party and the iciness of the boulders resulted in more than one wet skin. By 03.38 all stores were hidden, the party back and boats struck down.[7]

After the completion of these dangerous and demanding clandestine operations the submarines in the Mediterranean entered a period when every new landfall became a joy. On 4 June 1944 the Greek submarine *Pipinos*, under the command of Lieutenant Commander A. Rallis, for the last time before he was relieved, entered the port of Kyparisi on the Peloponnisos coast of Greece. At 23.45 the submarine intercepted a small dinghy in the Kyparisi Bay and, having ascertained from the occupants that there were no German nationals in the village, Lieutenant Commander Rallis closed the port. They were approached initially by two customs men with some caution but as soon as they established that the submarine was Greek-manned the word was quickly passed round the village and they received a joyous welcome.

The experience of *Pipinos* was repeated during the months that followed. On 30 September 1944 Lieutenant Michell in *Vox* approached the harbour of Karlovassi on Samos to see the whole population of the town turn out to greet and invite them to enter the harbour as the Germans had evacuated the island two days earlier. The invitation was reluctantly declined for fear of mines in the small, shallow harbour. Lieutenant Varley in *Vivid* was given a similar welcome when he put in to Mitylene shortly after it had been vacated by German troops. Lieutenant Ogle in *Vigorous* followed up this visit to Mitylene on 3 November 1944 when he described their reception thus:

> The people of Mitylene are extremely hospitable to us and gave us a right royal time. In general our stay was most enjoyable and the inhabitants appeared genuinely glad to see us and happy to entertain us. When we tried to thank them the reply was always 'we have waited four years for this chance'.[8]

During the final months of the Mediterranean campaign the islands of Khios and Mitylene were used as support bases for Allied submarines operating in the Aegean, thus cutting down the time for re-provisioning or re-arming the submarines.

By the end of the war these submarines had more than proved themselves in the art of clandestine approach to enemy coastlines and had assisted in the preparation and implementation of all three major Allied landings in the Mediterranean. They had regularly delivered and maintained undercover operations behind enemy lines and rescued agents in need on more than one occasion. The military authorities, particularly in Malta, were always happy with the contribution made by these small, cheaply produced war machines.

Notes
1. National Archives Kew Reference: ADM 199/1820.
2. National Archives Kew Reference: ADM 199/1819.
3. National Archives Kew Reference: ADM 199/1819.
4. National Archives Kew Reference: ADM 199/1813.
5. National Archives Kew Reference: ADM 199/1819.
6. National Archives Kew Reference: ADM 199/1340.
7. National Archives Kew Reference: ADM 199/1815.
8. National Archives Kew Reference: ADM 199/1876.

VIII

ACCIDENTAL LOSSES OF
SUBMARINES AND LIVES

I have often looked for an opportunity of paying tribute to our
submarines. It is the most dangerous of all services.
Winston Churchill, speaking in
the House of Commons.[1]

The 'U' class submarine served with distinction throughout its
history. Ninety-four vessels were ordered of which seventy-two
were completed and entered service with the British and Allied
navies. Of these, seventeen were lost to the enemy, the majority
of these being lost without any survivors. There were other
submarines and individual men lost to the forces of nature, technical problems, and human error or purely by accident, and this
is the story of those submarines and men.

The incidents that led to the loss of individual lives started on
5 May 1941 when *Upholder*, in harbour at Malta, experienced
the hot run of a torpedo in its tube. In an effort to control the
situation both Lieutenant Christopher Holditch Read, RN, and
Petty Officer James Farley Carter lost their lives. This was
followed one month later by *Unbeaten* when they experienced
the harrowing task of burying, at sea, a fellow crewmember.
Leading Stoker Sturman had been ill prior to *Unbeaten* starting
her patrol but he insisted he had recovered and specially
requested he be allowed to remain with the submarine. They
sailed from Malta on 11 June and during the evening of Friday,
13 June 1941 Leading Stoker Sturman complained of a
headache; he was treated for this and put to bed. Later he was
found unconscious and artificial respiration was applied but by
01.00 on 14 June he had died and was buried at sea at 04.13,

before the submarine dived for daylight running. Captain George Simpson wrote:

> In the opinion of Medical Officers he died through haemorrhage of the brain, a matter which was undoubtedly aggravated by service in submarines due to the various conditions of air pressure in which he spent his daily life.[2]

These small submarines were regularly victims of the forces of nature. When the sea was very rough it became very difficult to retain one's balance whilst serving on the bridge. The first loss of life to nature was that of Sub Lieutenant M.N. Christopher, RNVR, on 17 November 1941. He was Officer of the Watch during the very first patrol of *P38* when he was washed overboard and never recovered. Nature was to take an even greater toll when on 25 November 1942 it struck *Unshaken* as she patrolled in the Gulf of Lions. Severe weather swept across the bridge of the submarine and took with it the Commanding Officer, Lieutenant Oxborrow, together with his lookouts, Yeoman of Signals S.B. Bennett and Able Seaman C. Thorn.

It was not always nature that snatched men from the bridge; it could be caused by operating errors by members of the submarine's crew. At 06.15 on 12 February 1942 *Uproar* was patrolling on the surface off Tripoli. At this time the Commanding Officer Lieutenant Kershaw was on the bridge in company with Lieutenant M.H. Gardner and Sub Lieutenant R. Bucknall when he ordered a 'puff' of air to number one main ballast tank as the submarine was very low in the water. This order appears to have been misunderstood or, according to Lieutenant Kershaw, the operator had a mental aberration, because the main vent to number one main ballast tank was opened wide which allowed it to flood and caused the submarine to dive at a dangerous angle. As a result Lieutenant Kershaw was knocked unconscious and fell into the control room in a wall of water, but Lieutenant Gardner and Sub Lieutenant Bucknall were both washed over the side. The submarine was held at a depth of seventy feet and quickly returned to the surface just twenty yards from the -

incident to find Sub Lieutenant Bucknall swimming in the water. He was recovered from the sea but no trace could be found of Lieutenant Gardner, even though the area was searched until 10.30 when enemy aircraft commenced anti-submarine patrols and forced *Uproar* to withdraw.

Other incidents involved the loss of four submarines and many more lives. In only one of these was it possible to recover the submarine and return it into service. The first incident was the loss of *Unity* off the Tyne. *Unity*, under the command of Lieutenant F.J. Brooks for just ten days, sailed from Blyth at 17.30 on 29 April 1940 in a dense fog. Visibility was down to seventy-five yards on leaving harbour but as she entered the main swept channel, visibility had reduced to no more than thirty yards. Thirty minutes after entering the swept channel a ship's siren was heard straight ahead and, in accordance with maritime rules, the submarine altered course to starboard. As she swung round a new siren was heard fine on the starboard bow. The wheel was put amidships and the submarine, travelling at eight knots, changed to full speed astern and the watertight doors were shut. When the other ship was sighted it was so close that collision was inevitable and *Unity* was struck amidships, just aft of the torpedo tube space. It was obvious the submarine was sinking and the motors were left full astern in an attempt to keep her afloat while the crew was ordered to abandon ship.

The surface ship involved in the collision, the Norwegian ship SS *Atle Jarl*, was also damaged but she quickly lowered two boats to recover the submariners from the sea and ensured the loss of life was kept to a minimum. Only four members of the crew were lost: two were lost in the sea trying to reach the safety of the boats; the other two, Lieutenant J.N.A. Low and Able Seaman H.J. Miller, were last seen in the control room of the submarine, just fifteen seconds before she sank, engaged in shutting the engine-room hatch after the motors had been stopped. The *Atle Jarl* stayed in the area for one-and-a-half-hours in an attempt to recover them but they were never seen again.

The *Atle Jarl* was part of a convoy that entered the swept channel at the same time as *Unity* was leaving it. The convoy's arrival had been reported by signal and had been distributed to all concerned with *Unity* being on the distribution list. The normal practice of all submarines prior to sailing was for the signalman to collect all messages for his boat and produce a signal file for the Commanding Officer's attention. Whilst the signal should have been distributed to *Unity* the signalman has no recollection of this particular signal being collected.

A Board of Enquiry, under the Presidency of Captain Blackman DSO, RN, was held on 16 May 1940 to enquire into the circumstances of the loss of the submarine. The Board investigated the three main subjects leading up to the loss, these being:

(i)   Those leading up to the actual collision.
(ii) The loss of the ship following the collision with SS *Atle Jarl*.
(iii) The matter of the two mislaid signals, one indicating the probable presence of a convoy in the war channel, and the other referring to that signal.

In respect of the circumstances leading up to the collision the Board of Enquiry established that visibility in the war channel was only fifty yards and that *Unity* was proceeding on the surface at eight knots, but not using her siren until the other siren was heard. The Board then heard the testimony of Lieutenant G.E. Hunt who, having been asked to tell the board what happened, said:

I came on the bridge at 7 o'clock, to relieve the Officer of the Watch, Lieutenant Trickey, but Lieutenant Trickey was hoping to sight a war channel buoy and so I did not immediately take over the watch. I stayed on the bridge and helped him to sight it. I cannot be sure of the time because I had not a watch on me. We heard a prolonged blast approximately on the port bow to which Lieutenant Trickey answered with a prolonged blast. The Captain stopped engines. We heard another blast somewhere ahead, which was also answered. I cannot be sure of the bearings because I was listening for the one I heard the first time. We altered course to starboard and then on a bearing approximately Red 50 we saw the bows of the steamer breaking through the fog. Then the Captain went 'full speed astern'. The order to shut watertight doors had previously been given by the Captain. The Captain gave the order 'Collision stations'. 'Prepare to abandon ship'.

The steamer struck us, as far as I can judge, about the port forward hydroplanes. The order to 'Abandon ship' having been given, the men came up the conning tower. We drew apart from the vessel as we stood at sternway and the Captain ordered the motors to be stopped. The port motor still appeared to be going astern and a volunteer was called for to go down below and stop the port motor. Able Seaman Miller, who had come up on the bridge, went down below. The *UNITY* took a slight bow down angle, and the men were ordered off the bridge onto the casing, as the bridge was getting crowded. When we thought that everyone was out of the boat, the order was given to jump into the sea. We had by this time lost sight of the steamer. The *UNITY* seemed to sink very rapidly by the bow.[3]

The Board then commented that whilst the submarine's sailing orders were to proceed 'with despatch' they felt that, in the circumstances, the speed of eight knots was excessive and should have been no more than six. The knowledge that other ships might be using the swept channel, and the presence of enemy forces was unlikely, strengthened that view. They also felt that sound signals should have been used in view of the prevailing conditions. They did, however, agree that the actions of the Commanding Officer had been correct in his endeavours to avoid the collision.

In respect of the actual loss of *Unity*, the Board commented that as the submarine was a small, single-hulled vessel and the collision was at approximately ninety degrees, the loss seemed inevitable and that such ventilation that was left open, in no way contributed to the rapid sinking of the submarine. They reported:

The Board therefore considers that the Commanding Officer acted with promptitude and decision in ordering 'Abandon ship', such promptitude probably saving many lives.[4]

The Board then considered the more contentious issue of the missing signals. They confirmed that the signal from C.-in-C., Rosyth setting out the details of the progress of the Methil-Tyne convoy (reporting that it was due to arrive off Blyth at 19.30 on 29 April) did not reach the submarine's Commanding Officer before sailing. The information was not included in the patrol orders as they had been completed before the signal was received. The matter was not brought to the attention of Lieutenant Brooks, either during his last visit to the Staff Office before sailing, or by Captain (S) Sixth Submarine Flotilla during his last meeting with Lieutenant Brooks. Captain (S) Sixth Submarine Flotilla explained he did not discuss the matter as he had read the signal and noted that it was marked to be distributed to *Unity*.

Having heard all the evidence in respect of the signals, the blame fell on the submarine's Leading Signalman. The Board felt that in spite of his total denial of knowledge he had, in fact, collected them from the Signal Distribution Office prior to sailing and had failed to bring them to the attention of the Commanding Officer. They <u>did</u> absolve the Commanding Officer of blame as their report shows. They wrote:

> The Board considers that Leading Signalman T.H. Moon C/JX 133998 is to blame in that he failed to deliver signals which we consider he must have received. Nevertheless, a certain degree of responsibility must rest with Lieutenant F.J. Brooks, RN, and Captain (S)'s Staff Officer since these officers did not discuss the latest information concerning movements in the war channel; one of the very things for which the last minute meeting at the Staff Office is designed.[5]

The Board summed up their findings thus:

> The Commanding Officer, Lieutenant F.J. Brooks, Royal Navy, should, under the weather conditions prevailing, have been proceeding at a speed of not more than 6 knots, with the siren being sounded in accordance with the Rules for the prevention of collision at sea.

(i) He acted with commendable promptitude by ordering 'Abandon Ship'.

(ii) Leading Signalman T.H. Moon, C/JX 133998, failed to show the Commanding Officer a signal giving the movements of the MT convoy, and that this failure may have been a contributory cause of the accident.

(iii) That the Confidential Books, Signal Publications and other confidential matter sank with the ship, and are therefore not compromised.[6]

The next submarine lost in a collision was *Umpire* and on this occasion the loss of life was even greater. On 17 July 1941 the newly constructed *Umpire*, under the command of Lieutenant M.R.G. Wingfield, RN, and with the motto 'Keep on Keeping on' sailed from Chatham en route for Scotland and operational duties. She joined a northbound convoy to facilitate the journey. Shortly after nightfall on 19 July a defect developed in the port engine and the engine room staff, under guidance from CERA George Stewart Killan, made every effort to make good a repair. This was to no avail and he reported to the Commanding Officer that it was not possible to effect repair whilst at sea. Lieutenant Wingfield reported the matter to the senior officer of the convoy saying that he must reduce speed and would fall astern of the convoy. The convoy commander dispatched a motor launch to act as escort with instruction that the submarine should catch up as soon as possible.

Around midnight *Umpire* was just north of the Sheringham Shoal when she encountered a southbound convoy. The submarine was on the extreme edge of the safe passage with her manoeuvrability greatly reduced by the loss of power. The southbound convoy was all to starboard of the submarine and all was well until the Commanding Officer sighted an armed trawler protecting the starboard flank of the convoy, bearing down on them on a collision course. The rule of the sea in such circumstances is for each ship to steer to starboard to avoid danger but to do so would have put *Umpire* in danger from the main body of the convoy. Immediately to port was the coastal minefield but Lieutenant Wingfield decided that to be the lesser risk and

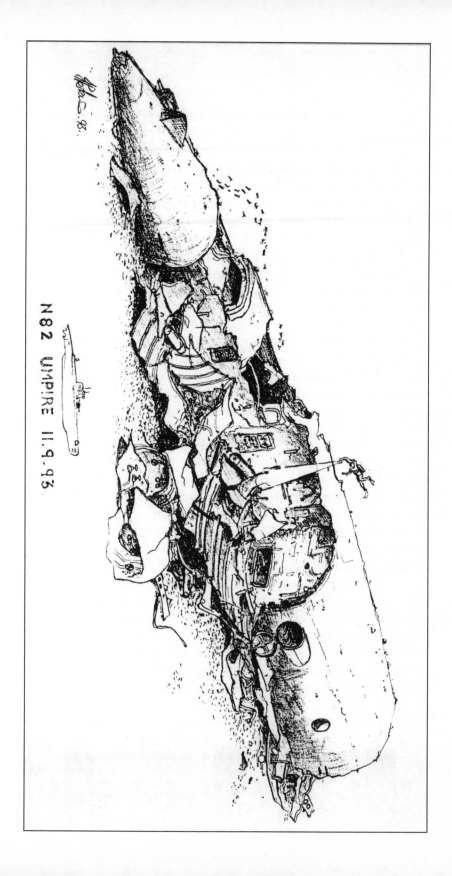

N82 UMPIRE 11.9.93

ordered the submarine to change course to port. Unfortunately, the trawler, *Peter Hendriks*, in accordance with the rules, turned to starboard making collision inevitable. The trawler struck the submarine on the starboard side about twenty-five feet aft of her bow creating a gash just forward of the torpedo room watertight door. The point of impact was important as some quick-thinking by a member of the crew (still unidentified) slammed the watertight door shut, thus saving the remainder of the crew from the onrush of water. As the submarine floated off the trawler, Lieutenant Wingfield, the Officer of the Watch (Sub Lieutenant S.A.G. Godden) and the two lookouts, were swept into the sea. As the submarine went down Lieutenant Wingfield was heard to shout at the trawler, 'You bastard! You've sunk a British submarine.'[7] Fortunately Lieutenant Wingfield was wearing a special Kapok-lined Burberry (a present from his wife), and its floating capabilities saved his life. The crew of the *Peter Hendriks* picked him up some forty minutes later. The remainder of the bridge party were dressed in conventional seagoing garb and were not so lucky.

Inside the sunken, darkened submarine desperate attempts were being made to escape. Petty Officer William Nicholas Treble found himself in the control room and guided the Leading Telegraphist and two Able Seamen to the engine room where CERA Killan was organising the survivors in preparation for escape through the engine-room escape hatch. A quick count showed there were seventeen survivors – sixteen members of the crew and one civilian from Chatham Dockyard. The watertight door was shut and secured and the DSEA equipment was issued but they were short and three men would need to ascend unaided. Whilst it was agreed that those men would be 'towed' to the surface by fully equipped colleagues, none of them were to survive and neither was the civilian who had not received the escape training afforded to the submariners. The last to leave was Petty Officer Treble who described his feelings thus:

> There was I, sitting on the port engine in the darkness – everything deathly silent. All the time we had been in the engine room I had heard no sound of ships overhead so we

had no idea what to expect when we reached the surface. To keep up my spirits I switched on the torch and shone it around the deserted engine room, the greasy oily water reflected the light back at me. To assure myself that it was not some horrible dream I called out 'Is anyone here?' The echo was all the answer I got, and truth to tell I would have had a heart attack if there had been anyone left. I pulled myself together and said aloud, 'The best thing you can do is to get out of here as soon as possible before you lose your reason.' I took a final look around, took a grip on my mouthpiece and was under the water into the twill-trunk. I was shooting through the water, it was dark, but little bubbles passed me. Then suddenly I was on the surface and looking at the dark sky, I saw a light and set off swimming towards it. I had no idea of time, but the light got nearer, and I made it out as a small searchlight sweeping the water. Several times it swept over me and I even considered there was a chance it might be a jerry; the next second I heard an English voice, and then I was looking up into the kindest faces I have ever seen – good-looking, solid, friendly British sailors. They janked me out and on to their deck, where I was greeted by Ronnie Shorrocks and the others, plus an unlimited supply of rum.[8]

Lieutenant P.C. McConnel Banister, First Lieutenant, and Lieutenant E. Young were in the control room and they ensured that the forward watertight door was shut and attempted to stem the water flowing into the submarine, without success. It was coming from the ruptured ventilation shaft and would not be thwarted. The conning tower upper hatch had closed on impact and the control room had not been swamped with water so the two officers checked the conning tower. They found the Able Seaman who had been at the helm at the time of the impact together with the Engine Room Artificer who had been operating the air panel huddled there. The two officers joined them in the small tower and closed the inner hatch securing themselves in the tiny space within the tower. After an unsuccessful attempt to open the outer hatch due to the sea pressure they had to re-think their procedures. They considered that as water was still entering the control room it might be possible to increase the pressure in the tower by opening the inner hatch and allowing the air below to enter. Having done this they felt the air pressure increase but with it came the smell of chlorine gas, making their early escape more desirable. With the increased air pressure the outer hatch was opened and all four men made for the surface. Unfortunately only two of them survived.

The total loss of life was two officers, twenty other ranks and one civilian dockyard employee. The Board of Enquiry held at Chatham found no blame attached to Lieutenant Wingfield and he was offered command of the submarine *Sturgeon*. He retired Captain Mervyn Robert George Wingfield, DSO, DSC and Bar, RN.

Umpire was located in June 1989 by a diving group based in Holt, Norfolk. She was lying on the seabed five miles north of the Sheringham Shoal in some fifty to sixty feet of water.

Disaster was to strike again without warning during the most routine exercise, which caused the loss of a submarine with all thirty-seven members of her crew. On the morning of 24 February 1943 *Vandal*, under the command of Lieutenant J.S. Bridger, slipped her berth on the third day of independent exercises to familiarise the crew with the submarine and test its capabilities before returning that evening to HMS *Forth* at Holy Loch. This final day of exercises was intended for a deep dive to take place in Upper Inchmarnock, provided the Commanding Officer was satisfied with the watertightness of the vessel and the efficiency of the crew. At 08.30 the Pier Master watched as she left her anchorage at Lochranza, a small village north of the island of Arran, and the last time she was seen.

On 25 February 1943 Captain Ionides, Captain (S) Third Submarine Flotilla was informed that *Vandal* had failed to return to Holy Loch and he immediately set in motion investigations to establish her whereabouts. This investigation established that another submarine, *Templar*, operating in the adjacent area, had seen a white smoke candle north of Inchmarnock during the afternoon of 24 February, which may have been from *Vandal*. Later discoveries were to prove that it was not. *Usurper* reported hearing hull tapping at 16.30 that same afternoon not three miles from the sighting of the white candle. *Severn* was immediately dispatched to the area but could find no confirmation of either report. In addition, Captain Ionides dispatched HMS *Cygnet* to carry out an anti-submarine sweep of Kilbrannan Sound and Inchmarnock North and *La Capricieuse* was dispatched to the area with all available diving equipment and medical staff together with the flotilla anti-submarine officer. Air searches were organised and at 14.50 on 25 February the Royal Naval Air Station at Machrihanish reported to Captain (S) Third Submarine Flotilla that a large oil patch had been sighted two miles north-west of Lochranza. This sighting was disregarded by Captain (S) Seventh Submarine Flotilla as not being relevant. The searches were abandoned at noon on 26 February 1943.

On 27 February 1943 a Board of Enquiry was held on board HMS *Forth* under the presidency of Captain J.W. Farquhar, RN, of HMS *Nimrod*. This established that *Vandal* had been in an entirely satisfactory condition for Lieutenant Bridger to proceed with his work-up exercises. They were satisfied with the arrangements made for these exercises but were unable to give any reason for *Vandal*'s failure to surface. They were critical of the procedures to receive submarines from exercise when they wrote:

> It does however seem wrong that a submarine can fail to return to harbour as expected by Commander (S) about 19.00 on 24 February and that no staff officer took any steps to find out where she was until 09.15 the following day. The necessary organisation for checking that submarines do conform to the programme as regards returning to harbour on completion of exercises is lacking. <u>We recommend that this be instituted forthwith</u>. We recommend that the Third Submarine Flotilla organization should be amended to include a method of positively checking in submarines at the time when they can be reasonably expected to return to harbour.[9]

Rear Admiral Barry, Admiral (Submarines) endorsed the report from the Board of Enquiry but added:

It seems unlikely that, even had HMS *Vandal*'s failure to return late p.m. on the 24 February been reported instantly, it would have had any effect on her loss or resulted in the saving of life.[10]

The Liverpool and Glasgow Salvage Company continued searching the area but in August 1943 they advised Captain (S) Seventh Submarine Flotilla that due to the depth of water there was no possibility of finding the submarine and they were to discontinue their search. Throughout the years various searches were made in the area, but all to no avail. After the war, equipment developed at the Admiralty Experimental Establishment at Fairlie was sent to the area in an attempt to locate the submarine, using the most sophisticated equipment designed for mine-hunting, but without success. It was not until 21 June 1994 that *Vandal* was eventually located during a wreck survey of the area by the mine countermeasure vessel HMS *Hurworth* north-west of Lochranza in ninety-five metres of water, less than half a mile from the location of the oil slicks sighted by aircraft from RNAS Machrihanish during the initial searches in February 1943.

The location of the *Vandal* was declared a war grave and the submarine would lie undisturbed. On Saturday 3 May 1997 a memorial cairn stone was unveiled by Flag Officer Submarines Rear Admiral J. Perowne adjacent to the ferry terminal at Lochranza and overlooking the site of *Vandal*'s last resting place.

In August 2003 members of Starfish Enterprise Technical Diving Team located *Vandal* during a dive and established that the forward escape hatch was open but that there was no sign of a ladder or escape trunking. An examination above decks showed that mooring ropes were still on the upper casing neatly coiled about the bollards. All their findings suggest the submarine was on the surface before disaster struck thus adding to the mystery of what happened to HMS *Vandal*. The team members were fully aware of the circumstances surrounding the loss of the submarine and the subsequent events; consequently in reverence to the crew no attempt was made to enter the boat.

The loss of *Vandal* was still fresh in the minds of members of the Third Submarine Flotilla when disaster struck again. Once again during a simple exercise dive the complete crew of thirty-six men was lost. On the morning of 30 May 1943 *Untamed*, under the command of Lieutenant G.M. Noll, sailed from Campbeltown for anti-submarine exercises with the anti-submarine training yacht *Shemara*, commanded by Commander H. Buckle. The morning exercise was completed without incident. Before commencing the afternoon exercise Lieutenant Noll signalled Captain (S) Third Submarine Flotilla reporting that the periscope was leaking and would require attention. At 13.55 the exercise commenced with *Untamed* submerged and towing a small buoy from the bridge to indicate her position. This buoy was normally towed from the bow of the submarine but Lieutenant Noll had indicated he was not able to do this and changed the location to the bridge. At 14.18 a white candle, together with a swirl of water, was sighted. By 14.26 there was no sign of the buoy and Commander Buckle fired one charge to instruct *Untamed* to indicate her position. There was no reply but at 14.50 two yellow candles were seen indicating that the submarine was about to do so. It never appeared and there was no further contact with the submarine that day. Commander Buckle in *Shemara* made several attempts throughout the afternoon to instruct *Untamed* to indicate her position and to surface, but to no avail. Around 16.30 the yacht's listening devices heard a strong whistle effect and the sound of a submarine blowing her tanks but still there was no sighting of the submarine. After 17.15 the submarine's motors were heard stopping and starting but this ceased at 17.45 and no further sound was heard from her. At 17.33 the submarine *Thrasher* arrived and attempted to communicate with *Untamed*, without success. *Shemara* stood by throughout the night having marked the position with a five-hundredweight sinker attached to marker buoys. Oil was seen coming to the surface as late as 18.15 and at 22.12 air bubbles were seen to rise but there were no further indications of life from the submarine. At 00.10 the diving vessel *Tedworth* arrived but conditions deteriorated so much they prevented any diving operations being carried out that day.

It was at 11.15 on 1 June that a diver found the *Untamed* lying on an even keel on a hard, flat, sandy bottom with no obvious signs of damage. Attempts were made to contact the crew by tapping but there was no reply. It was obvious that there were no survivors and thoughts immediately went to raising the *Untamed*. The matter was turned over to the Liverpool and Glasgow Salvage Company to recover the submarine and the bodies of the crew who perished inside her. One of the divers involved in the recovery opened the engine room escape hatch to be confronted by the body of CERA Challenor floating upwards. A glance into the hatch showed bodies packed into the hatch trunking so the diver quickly shut the hatch and recovered the one body. After *Untamed* had been brought to the surface the bodies of all the crew were removed. It was during the clearing of the submarine prior to delivery to Campbeltown that a crucial incident took place. Air was pumped into the partially raised *Untamed* with divers examining the outside to locate any air escaping from the submarine. During this operation the divers reported:

> It's the Ottway log. Seems they withdrew it without the sluice valve being shut. Only three inches across, but that did it, with seawater pressure at 75 pounds per square inch at that depth. Anyway, we've driven a plug into the hole, and the pressure's now holding. Should be clear for you in an hour.[11]

The submarine was later delivered to Campbeltown and a close investigation as to the cause of the loss was launched.

During the days of 8 and 9 July 1943 a thorough inspection of *Untamed* was carried out. This inspection established that the Ottway log had not been fully recovered and the sluice valve was not shut properly. (The Ottway log was an electro-mechanical device used to calculate the submarine's speed through the water by means of a small propeller spinning in a tube that protruded through the bottom of the pressure hull. It could be raised, when necessary for inspection, and the hull sluice valve shut to ensure the submarine stayed watertight. Author's note.) The watertight door between the torpedo stowage compartment and the Petty Officers' Mess had sprung and could not be properly shut. It had been shut initially but could not withstand the pressure of water as it was only tested to 10lbs psi. The submarine, forward of the control-room watertight door, was flooded and contained the bodies of Sub Lieutenant Acworth and Petty Officer Welford. The control room was dry with no person contained. The engine room had contained the remainder of the crew fully prepared to escape. This compartment was fitted with a special quick-flooding connection for flooding at high speed in an emergency. This was shut but the indicator showed 'open'. It was established that various other endeavours had been made to flood the compartment to facilitate escape. Although it was being flooded at such a slow rate that the atmosphere in the compartment would have been foul the pressure would not have been sufficient for CERA Challenor to open the escape hatch.

On 22 July 1943 a Board of Enquiry was established aboard HMS *Wolfe* under the presidency of Captain P.G.L. Cazalet, DSC, RN, with a brief to investigate the foundering of *Untamed* and the circumstances of the death of the ship's company. From the evidence submitted the Board produced a narrative that they accepted was only the probable sequence of events.

The exercises on 30 May 1943 proceeded normally until approximately 14.00 when a rating (probably Petty Officer Welford, the Torpedo Gunner's Mate) withdrew to examine and possibly repair the Ottway log. He did not ensure the sluice valve was shut and consequently the log was forced clear of the gland and water poured into the compartment which was immediately abandoned and the hatch shut and clipped. Petty Officer Welford, in company with Sub Lieutenant Acworth, went into the crew space but in doing so failed to close the starboard bulkhead door to the torpedo tube compartment and the ventilation valves and communication cock which allowed water to continue to pass towards the stern of the boat. The two men were encased in the crew space as the stern bulkhead hatch had been shut and secured.

Some attempts were made to bring the submarine to the surface but at 17.45 all sounds of machinery stopped although oil was sighted coming to the surface at 18.15. At 22.15 all noise from the submarine ceased. During this time all the crew had gathered in the engine room and the compartment was flooded. It is considered that the death of most of the crew took place from carbon dioxide poisoning or from drowning during this period. It was established that at least three men had vomited into their DSEA sets. The slowness of flooding the compartment, together with the large number of men gathered in such a small space, would have rendered the air foul. The post mortem of CERA Challenor showed he died from drowning but there was no post mortem on any other member of the crew.

The Board of Enquiry came to the conclusion that failure of personnel was the contributory cause of the loss and the incorrect drill in removing the log was the initial cause of the disaster. They reported:

> It is considered that the loss of the submarine is directly attributable to failure of the crew to take immediate, obvious and adequate steps to prevent unrestricted flooding. The fact that such an obvious measure as the shutting of a watertight door was neglected, proves that a temporary panic must have prevailed in the submarine.

> Their failure to escape from the submarine can also be attributed to poor drill, ignorance and lack of leadership which was accentuated towards the end, by physical and mental weakness due to CO2 poisoning, the danger of which had not been fully realised.

> Efforts to save the submarine were continued long after it should have been clear that these efforts were futile. This indicates a complete lack of appreciation of the situation and deficient technical knowledge.

> This must be partially attributable to the comparatively short time which can now be devoted to training and the consequent inexperience of a proportion of submarine crews.[12]

They agreed that the watertight door had been found open and swinging but it could not be shut correctly due to distortion. They considered the DSEA flap valve in the engine room showed 'open' when it was, in fact, shut. They reported that the valve had been fitted correctly but the lever had been removed later, most probably to clean, and had been replaced incorrectly. They recommended that the spindle should be constructed in a 'D' section and not square thus ensuring that it would be replaced properly.

The decisions of the Board of Enquiry have been criticised by Captain John Coote, RN Rtd., both in his book '*Submariner*' and in a letter dated 20 March 1993, when he wrote:

> There was an element of whitewash about the official findings; it was also strange that they never called for anyone from *UNTIRING* to give evidence. The appalling quality of the workmanship at Vickers Walker Yard was a contributory factor, with that all-important flap-valve inboard of the main engine-room DSEA flood valve being marked 'Shut' for 'Open'. The official explanation that a rating removed the operating lever to clean it and then replaced it the wrong way round is simply incredible. But our poor state of escape training and lack of knowledge about the inherent danger of breathing pure oxygen under pressure were contributory factors.[13]

With these two disasters occurring so close together there was a suspicion of acts of sabotage taking place at the Vickers-Armstrong Yard. These suspicions were so strongly held that Admiral Submarines, Rear Admiral C.B. Barry wrote to the Secretary of the Admiralty setting out his concerns. His letter read:

> Be pleased to inform the Lords Commissioners of the Admiralty of the following accidents recently suffered by new submarines constructed by Messrs. Vickers-Armstrong Ltd., at their yards at Barrow and High Walker, Newcastle-on-Tyne: -

221

a)   HMS *Vandal* (Barrow)
Launched   23rd November 1942.
Completed and left Yard   20th February 1943.

HMS *Vandal* was carrying out a deep dive in Holy Loch on 24th February 1943 as part of her working up exercises. She failed to surface and has not been located. The cause of loss is not known.

b)   HMS *Unswerving* (High Walker)
Launched   18th May 1943.
Not yet completed.

HMS *Unswerving* partly fell off the blocks P.M. on 21st April 1943. Completion has been delayed from July 1943 to 25th August 1943 in consequence.

c)   HMS *Untiring* (High Walker)
Launched   20th January 1943.
Completed and left Yard   30th May 1943.

HMS *Untiring* was damaged by an explosion in [the] battery tank on 22nd April 1943. The battery has had to be removed and date of completion delayed from 4th May 1943 to 30th May 1943.

d)   HMS *Untamed* (High Walker)
Launched   8th December 1942.
Completed and left Yard   29th March 1943.

After working up, HMS *Untamed* was employed on A/S exercises in Holy Loch. She dived for an ordinary run at 90 feet on 30th May 1943 and shortly afterwards a white smoke candle in the midst of a general disturbance resembling the blowing of a tank or tanks. About half an hour later she fired two or three yellow smoke candles to indicate she wished to surface. She did not surface and is now lying on the bottom in 20 fathoms. It is hoped to raise her, when the cause may be found.

I feel this run of accidents is somewhat suspicious and request that the possibility of malicious intent or even sabotage may be rigorously investigated and a close watch kept on the possible activities of saboteurs in these Yards.'[14]

Untamed was towed to Vickers-Armstrong Yard at Barrow-in-Furness, salved and renamed *Vitality*. On 19 July 1944 she sailed from Barrow-in-Furness under the Command of Lieutenant K.S. Renshaw, RNR, for Holy Loch and work-up exercises. She managed just one war patrol in October 1944 when she patrolled off the Shetland Islands. On 7 August 1945 she was transferred to Reserve Group 'A' at Portsmouth, then sailed to Lisahally where she remained until being sold for scrap in February 1946.

Notes

1. National Archives Kew Reference: ADM 234/380.
2. National Archives Kew Reference: ADM 199/1820.
3. National Archives Kew Reference: ADM 1/12025.
4. National Archives Kew Reference: ADM 1/12025.
5. National Archives Kew Reference: ADM 1/12025.
6. National Archives Kew Reference: ADM 1/12025.
7. Captain M.R.G. Wingfield, DSO, DSC, RN Rtd.
8. *Subsunk* by Captain W.O. Shelford, RN Rtd. By courtesy of Chambers Harrap Publishers.
9. National Archives Kew Reference: ADM 199/1340.
10. National Archives Kew Reference: ADM 199/1340.
11. *Submariner* by John Coote, RN Rtd.
12. National Archives Kew Reference: ADM 1/15066.
13. Letter to Mr. Richard Duffield from John Coote, RN Rtd.
14. National Archives Kew Reference: ADM 1/15478.

IX

IN CONCLUSION

I feel that to continue with the 'U' class just because this would produce greater numbers is not warranted, and on all counts it would be better to have (say) six submarines which could be used to effect than ten 'U' class which could not.
Rear Admiral C. B. Barry, Royal Navy,
Admiral Submarines.[1]

These comments made by Rear Admiral Barry were the result of a review of submarine strength held in June 1943 which recommended that construction of 'U' class submarines be halted. The spare capacity created at the construction yards was to be used to construct the newer 'S' class submarine. The comments were to see the end of 'U' class production but not until the completion of the twenty-eight submarines already in an advanced state of construction. It did mean the scrapping of four, still at an early stage of construction, these being *Upas, Verve, Veto* and *Virile*. It also meant that in January 1944 a further twelve 'U' class submarines, previously ordered, were cancelled.

The end of hostilities led to the end of the production of the 'U' class submarines that had provided meritorious service throughout the war. Their service during the campaign was such that many men who served in them received many awards. A small submarine designed for training and close-waters operations, and produced because they were cheap, was to see service throughout the world from home waters to the Mediterranean, and on to Canada, the West Indies, the Far East and Australasia. Seventy-two submarines were constructed and completed before hostilities ended – the last was *Vagabond*, accepted as completed for service on 27 February 1945.

Seventeen (almost 25 per cent) were lost to the enemy, with a further three being lost in accidents. One other, *Untamed*, foundered with the loss of the complete crew, only to be salvaged and re-enter service as *Vitality*. Two, *Untiring* and *Upstart*, were disposed of as targets for anti-submarine forces during July 1957. The remaining fifty submarines were disposed of as scrap, many having served with Allied navies both during and after the war. The submarines which operated during hostilities have been documented earlier but some were loaned or sold to Allied navies on completion of hostilities to help their respective armed forces rebuild after occupation by Axis forces.

The Greek authorities retained the services of *Pipinos* (previously known as *Veldt*), and in April 1945 *Vengeful* (renamed *Delfin*) joined her. They were joined in July 1945 by *Untiring* (renamed *Xifias*) and by *Upstart* the following month, to be renamed *Amfitriti*. Later, in May 1946, *Virulent* (renamed *Argonaftis*) and *Volatile* (renamed *Triaina*) reinforced them. *Untiring* and *Upstart* were returned to Admiralty control in June 1952, *Veldt* and *Vengeful* in December 1957 with *Virulent* and *Volatile* being retained until October 1958.

Another navy to benefit from the services of these submarines was the Royal Norwegian Navy by taking on loan a further three submarines to join *Ula*, already in their service after being active during hostilities. In October 1946 *Venturer*, *Viking* and *Votary* arrived at Trondheim and were renamed *Utstein*, *Utvaer* and *Uthaug* respectively. The Royal Norwegian Navy retained all four until they were scrapped during 1965.

In October 1946 the Royal Danish Navy, having lost all her submarines when the Danish fleet was scuttled on 29 August 1943 to prevent them being taken by German forces, purchased three submarines. At the end of the war consideration was given to salvaging and modernising the sunken submarines but this plan was abandoned in favour of leasing from the British. Thus on 15 October 1946 *P52* (previously loaned to the Polish Free Navy operating under the name of *Dzik*), *Vortex* (having previously served with the Free French Navy as *Morse*) and *Vulpine* arrived at the naval port of Holmen. They were re-named *U1, U2* and *U3*. They were obviously well received because Commander K.T. Madsen, Royal Danish Navy, wrote in 1994:

> I recall having talked with old submariners who have served in the former British submarines. They all liked the boats and were very confident with their capabilities.[2]

The Commanding Officer of *Vortex*, Lieutenant Donald Hay, RN, recounts the hospitality afforded him and his crew:

> The Danish hospitality has to be experienced to be believed and my officers and I were entertained lavishly both officially and privately.
>
> My officers and I were entertained officially by the Royal Danish Navy to an excellent dinner and I also attended a luncheon given by the Dockyard officials. All officers attended a cocktail party given by Captain Wyburd in his home.
>
> The Danish Allied Committee did much to entertain the officers and ship's company and many spent weekends in the country with Danish families.[3]

In April 1951 these three submarines were renamed *Springeren* (*U1*), *Storen* (*U2*) and *Saelen* (*U3*) in accordance with NATO instructions that all vessels of member countries should have names. They remained in commission with the Royal Danish Navy until the late 1950s when they were returned to Admiralty control and thence to scrap – *Springeren* in October 1957, *Saelen* in January 1958 and *Storen* in January 1959.

As with all shipping movements the delivery of these submarines to their respective scrap dealers was not without mishap and there are many stories of such mishaps. On 29 January 1946 *United* was on passage from Lisahally to the port of Troon in a full gale. They were off the Outer Hebrides when both her main engines broke down and the problem was compounded with her radio equipment being out of order. Fortunately, the *Daniel Willard*, a passing American freighter, sighted her and relayed the distress signal. *United* was then joined by HMS *Loch*

Fada and HMS *Fame* with both ships trying, unsuccessfully, to take the submarine in tow before engineers were able to engage one engine. The two ships escorted the submarine back to harbour.

The next month, February 1946, *Universal* was on tow from HMS *Southdown* from Lisahally to Milford Haven to be scrapped when she broke loose from the tow. The submarine was drifting so dangerously close to the Cantry-Gwaelod reef in Cardigan Bay that the crew of four officers and twenty-four men had to abandon ship, having first secured her by anchor. They were obliged to await the arrival of the tug *Mediator*, which was able to take her in tow and deliver her to Milford Haven to be scrapped.

Virtue sailed from Sydney, Australia, on 23 January 1946 en route to the United Kingdom in company with *Voracious* and *Vox*. The following day *Virtue* experienced engine trouble that proved so serious it was necessary to arrange for her to be towed back to the United Kingdom. This proved so cumbersome that, on arrival at Cochin, India, in May, all three submarines were sold to a local scrap dealer for £3,000 each.

Virulent was another submarine that was sold locally for demolition. On 15 December 1958 she was being towed from Malta back to the United Kingdom when she broke loose from her tow. After many unsuccessful attempts were made to regain her she was eventually taken in tow by local fishermen and towed into the Spanish port of Pasajes. The submarine remained there until she was sold to Spanish ship breakers in April 1961.

The final submarine to be scrapped was the Norwegian *Ula*, scrapped in Hamburg, Germany in December 1965 bringing to an end the era of the 'U' class submarine that commenced on 21 August 1938 when *Undine* was accepted as being completed for service, a total of twenty-seven years' meritorious service.

Officers and men of the 'U' class received many awards, the highest being the Victoria Cross. On 16 December 1941 the *London Gazette* announced the award to Lieutenant Commander Malcolm David Wanklyn – the first awarded to a submariner in the Second World War and the only one to a 'U' class submarine.

This was just four months before *Upholder* was lost with all hands when she was depth-charged off Tripoli by the Italian torpedo boat *Pegaso*. The citation read:

> On the evening of 24 May, 1941, while on patrol off the coast of Sicily, Lieutenant Commander Wanklyn, in command of His Majesty's Submarine *UPHOLDER*, sighted a southbound enemy troop convoy, strongly escorted by destroyers.
>
> The failing light was such that observation by periscope could not be relied on, but a surface attack would have been easily seen. *UPHOLDER*'s listening gear was out of action.
>
> In spite [of] these handicaps, Lieutenant Commander Wanklyn decided to press home his attack at short range. He quickly steered his craft into a favourable position and closed in so as to make sure of his target. By this time the whereabouts of the escorting destroyers could not be made out. Lieutenant Commander Wanklyn, while fully aware of the risk of being rammed by one of the escorts, continued to press on towards the enemy troopships. As he was about to fire, one of the enemy destroyers appeared out of the darkness at high speed and he only just avoided being rammed. As soon as he was clear, he brought his periscope sights on and fired torpedoes, which sank a large troop ship. The enemy destroyers at once made a strong counter-attack and during the next twenty minutes dropped thirty-seven depth charges near *UPHOLDER*.
>
> The failure of his listening device made it much harder for him to get away, but with the greatest courage, coolness and skill he brought *UPHOLDER* clear of the enemy and safe back to harbour.[4]

In addition to the Victoria Cross, Lieutenant Commander Wanklyn was awarded the DSO and two Bars.

The total number of awards made to officers and men of the British-manned 'U' class submarines was one Victoria Cross, thirty-four Distinguished Service Orders, sixty-seven

Distinguished Service Crosses, 239 Distinguished Service Medals and 234 Mentions in Dispatches. Personnel of the Allied navies operating in 'U' class submarines were awarded three Honorary Distinguished Service Orders, nine Distinguished Service Crosses, twenty-two Distinguished Service Medals and eighteen Mentions in Dispatches. In addition Royal Navy personnel operating in submarines manned by the Allied navies were awarded with three Dutch Bronze Crosses, two Croix de Guerre, three Greek War Crosses, seven Polish Military Crosses, three Norwegian War Medals and three King Haakon VII Liberty Crosses (Norway). The identity of all the recipients of awards is listed in the appendices. Whilst all these awards were in respect of the conflict with Axis forces the courage of the submariner can also be highlighted by two separate awards made in respect of conduct in other dangerous situations.

On 16 August 1940 the *London Gazette* announced awards for bravery resulting from the sinking of *Unity* after collision with the Norwegian ship SS *Atle Jarl*. Lieutenant John Niven Angus Low, Royal Navy, and Able Seaman Henry James Miller, P/J 55387 were awarded EGM (GC) Post. These being posthumous awards of the George Cross, they substituted for the posthumous award of the Empire Gallantry Medal. The recommendations for these decorations included the following passage:

> Lieutenant John Niven Angus Low, R.N., and the other rating Able Seaman Henry James Miller were last seen, fifteen seconds before "*Unity*" sank, in the Control Room, engaged in shutting the engine room door after having stopped the main motors.
>
> Lieutenant Low acted with heroism throughout. He passed the order to shut watertight doors, himself closing some and personally seeing to the closing of others. He heartened the crew by calling out 'There is no need to get into a panic, boys.' He helped to pull some of the ratings through the galley door. He assisted in closing the forward Control Room door. He was last seen in the forward Compartment. It is clear therefore that up to the final point when the order came by voice-pipe to try and stop the

229

Motors he had, in an orderly and calm manner not only heartened his men, but had himself closed or seen to the closing of several watertight doors, had pulled several men through the galley door and had collected the men and seen to their going up the ladder on to the deck. The position at the moment of the *Unity*'s sinking was this. Lieutenant Low was still below – alone. He was at that moment joined by Able Seaman Miller, who had heard that Lieutenant Low had called for someone to stop the Centre Motor (the other having clearly been stopped by Lieutenant Low himself); Miller came down the ladder and joined his Lieutenant. Knowing the submarine to be in immediate danger of sinking, and knowing that, in that event, they must be drowned by the sudden inrush of water, the one kept on carrying out his Commanding Officer's order with the same thorough and unwavering courage which he had exhibited down below from the very start, while the other deliberately went below to assist his Lieutenant at a moment when he knew that any chance of regaining the deck was so infinitesimal as not to be worth even considering.[5]

On 27 January 1942 the *London Gazette* announced the award of the British Empire Medal to Chief Petty Officer William Nicholas Treble, D/J 95987 and Chief Engine Room Artificer George Killan, D/MX 46543 for services when *Umpire* was sunk. The recommendations for the decorations read:

The qualities of leadership, the standard of professional knowledge and coolness in a desperate situation displayed by these two ratings are strongly recommended for recognition. Their example and courage was an inspiration to the remainder of the crew.[6]

These are probably the ideal words to describe all the officers and men who have ever served in the submarine service and a fitting way to end the history of these 'small submarines'.

Notes

1. National Archives Kew Reference: ADM 199/373.
2. Letter from Commander K.T. Madsen, Royal Danish Navy.
3. National Archives Kew Reference: ADM 1/19843.
4. National Archives Kew Reference: CAB 106/312.
5. National Archives Kew Reference: ADM 1/11525.
6. National Archives Kew Reference: ADM 1/11505.

APPENDIX I

GALLANTRY MEDALS AWARDED TO OFFICERS AND MEN SERVING IN BRITISH 'U' CLASS SUBMARINES

Victoria Cross

Name	Rank	Submarine
Wanklyn, Malcolm David	Lieutenant Commander	*Upholder*

Distinguished Service Order

Name	Rank	Submarine
Boyd, Robert	Lieutenant	*Untiring*
Cayley, Richard Douglas	Lieutenant Commander	*Utmost*
Chapman, Paul Charles	Lieutenant	*Upstart*
Daniell, Anthony Robert	Lieutenant	*Unison*
Gordon, Cecil	Lieutenant	*Universal*
Harrison, Peter Robert Helfrich	Lieutenant	*Ultimatum*
Hunt, George Edward	Lieutenant	*Ultor*
Kershaw, John Bertram de Betham	Lieutenant	*Uproar*
Lakin, Richard Barklie	Lieutenant	*Ursula*
Launders, James Stuart	Lieutenant	*Venturer*
Mars, Alastair Campbell Gillespie	Lieutenant	*Unbroken*
Maydon, Stephen Lynch Conway	Lieutenant	*Umbra*
Norman, Compton Patrick	Lieutenant	*Una*
Norman, Edward Dudley	Lieutenant	*Upright*
Phillips, George Chesterman	Lieutenant Commander	*Ursula*

Piper, Aston Dalzell, RNR	Lieutenant	*Unsparing*
Roxburgh, John Charles Young	Lieutenant	*United*
Stanley, Edward Talbot	Lieutenant	*Unbending*
Stevens, John Samuel	Lieutenant	*Unruffled*
Tomkinson, Edward Philip	Lieutenant Commander	*Urge*
Wanklyn, Malcolm David	Lieutenant Commander	*Upholder*
Woodward, Edward Arthur	Lieutenant Commander	*Unbeaten*
Wraith, John Somerton	Lieutenant	*Upright*

Bar to Distinguished Service Order

Name	Rank	Submarine
Cayley, Richard Douglas	Lieutenant Commander	*Utmost*
Hunt, George Edward	Lieutenant	*Ultor*
Launders, James Stuart	Lieutenant	*Venturer*
Maydon, Stephen Lynch Conway	Lieutenant Commander	*Umbra*
Stevens, John Samuel	Lieutenant	*Unruffled*
Tomkinson, Edward Philip	Lieutenant Commander	*Urge*
Wanklyn, Malcolm David	Lieutenant Commander	*Upholder*
Woodward, Edward Arthur	Lieutenant Commander	*Unbeaten*

Second Bar to Distinguished Service Order

Name	Rank	Submarine
Cayley, Richard Douglas	Lieutenant Commander	*Utmost*
Wanklyn, Malcolm David	Lieutenant Commander	*Upholder*
Woodward, Edward Arthur	Lieutenant Commander	*Unbeaten*

Distinguished Service Cross

Name	Rank	Submarine
Akeroyd, Richard Hewson	Lieutenant	*Unsparing*
Allen, David Bennett	Lieutenant	*Urge*
Archdale, Edward Folmer	Lieutenant	*Unbroken*
Band, Brian Hugh	Lieutenant	*Upholder*
Boyall, Anthony John	Lieutenant	*Upshot*
Boyd, Robert	Lieutenant	*Utmost*

Challis, Frederick Danford Gordon	Lieutenant	*Unique*
Chalmers, Andrew Thomas	Lieutenant	*Venturer*
Clark, George Gordon, RNR	Temporary Lieutenant	*Una*
Clayden, Stanley William	Lieutenant	*Unruly*
Coates-Walker, Ronald, RNR	Temporary Lieutenant	*Universal*
Collett, Anthony Foster	Lieutenant	*Unique*
Crawford, Michael Lindsay Coulton	Lieutenant	*Upholder*
Daniell, Anthony Robert	Lieutenant	*Upright*
Drummond, James Ralph	Lieutenant	*Upholder*
Duff, Malcolm John Luxmoor	Lieutenant	*Unbending*
Fenton, John Munro Crosland	Lieutenant	*Unbroken*
Forbes, Eric Keith, RCNVR	Lieutenant	*Ultimatum*
Fyfe, John Paton	Lieutenant Commander	*Unruly*
Greene, John Dennis	Lieutenant	*Ursula*
Haddow, John Renwick Haig	Lieutenant	*Unbroken*
Herrick, Laurence Edward	Lieutenant	*Ultimatum*
Hezlet, Arthur Richard	Lieutenant Commander	*Unique*
Howard, John Edwin Ernest Denny	Lieutenant	*Unison*
Lakin, Richard Barklie	Lieutenant	*Utmost*
Lambert, Charles Walderne St. Clair	Lieutenant	*Unbeaten*
Lascelles, Oliver	Lieutenant	*Unruffled*
Launders, James Stuart	Lieutenant	*Umbra*
Maccoy, Alan Harold, SANF(V)	Lieutenant	*Umbra*
Mars, Alastair Campbell Gillespie	Lieutenant	*Unbroken*
Menzies, Ian Robert, RNVR	Lieutenant	*Upstart*
Michell, John Martin	Lieutenant	*Vox*
Norman, John Harsent, RNVR	Temp. Sub-Lieutenant	*Upholder*
Oakley, John Philip Holroyde	Lieutenant	*Uproar*
Oxborrow, Charles Ernest	Lieutenant	*Utmost*
Piper, Aston Dalzell, RNR	Lieutenant	*Ursula*
Place, Basil Charles Godfrey	Lieutenant	*Unbeaten*
Poole, James Malcolm Stuart	Lieutenant	*Urge*
Prideaux, Andrew George	Lieutenant	*Unrivalled*
Ransome, John Sandeman Deane, RNR	Temp. Sub-Lieutenant	*Urge*

Rowe, Barry Loraine Dudley	Lieutenant	*Ultor*
Ruck-Keene, Francis	Lieutenant	*Upholder*
Sallis, Richard Thomas	Lieutenant	*Unseen*
Seaburne-May, Ronald Max	Lieutenant	*Unruffled*
Swanston, David	Lieutenant	*Upright*
Tattersall, Michael Dent, RNVR	Lieutenant	*Unswerving*
Taylor, Charles William, RNR	Lieutenant Commander	*Vampire*
Thirsk, Paul Stamford, RNVR	Temporary Lieutenant	*Unbroken*
Turner, Hugh Bentley	Lieutenant	*Unrivalled*
Varley, John Cromwell	Lieutenant	*Vivid*
Westmacott, Herbert Patrick	Lieutenant	*Unshaken*
Whitton, Jack	Lieutenant	*Unshaken*
Wilson, Donald Rupert, RANVR	Lieutenant	*Untiring*
Wingate, John Allan	Lieutenant	*United*

Bar to Distinguished Service Cross

Name	*Rank*	*Submarine*
Crawford, Michael Lindsay Coulton	Lieutenant	*Unseen*
Fyfe, John Paton	Lieutenant	*Unruly*
Harrison, Peter Robert Helfrich	Lieutenant	*Ultimatum*
Hunt, George Edward	Lieutenant	*Ultor*
Lambert, Charles Walderne St. Clair	Lieutenant	*Unbeaten*
Launders, James Stuart	Lieutenant	*Venturer*
Piper, Aston Dalzell, RNR	Lieutenant	*Unbeaten*
Poole, James Malcolm Stuart	Lieutenant	*Urge*
Rowe, Barry Loraine Dudley	Lieutenant	*Ultor*

Second Bar to Distinguished Service Cross

Name	*Rank*	*Submarine*
Piper, Aston Dalzell, RNR	Lieutenant	*Unbeaten*

Distinguished Service Medal

Name & Number	Rank	Submarine
Allen, Charles Edward P/J 103446	Acting Petty Officer	*Ursula*
Anderson, Charles KX 80375	Leading Stoker	*Ursula*
Anderson, Frederick Christie M 28823	Chief Engine Room Artificer	*Umbra*
Anderson, William E. D/JX 136036	Petty Officer Telegraphist	*Upholder*
Ansell, Hector Frederick C/J 62829	Chief Petty Officer	*Upright*
Armstrong, Harry C/JX 145754	Acting Chief Petty Officer	*Ultor*
Ashford, William George C/KX 82966	Stoker Petty Officer	*Urge*
Attewell, Percy William Pointer P/J 104715	Petty Officer	*Unrivalled*
Bailey, George Walter Claud P/J 105751	Petty Officer	*Unison*
Bailey, Joseph D/JX 77768	Stoker Petty Officer	*Ultor*
Ball, Ernest Frederick P/MX 54367	Engine Room Artificer	*Upright*
Barker, Alan D/JX 135280	Petty Officer	*Venturer*
Barnett, William George P/KX 80133	Stoker Petty Officer	*Unison*
Bell, Joseph C/JX 141130	Acting Petty Officer	*Unruffled*
Bennett, William C/JX 150767	Petty Officer	*Universal*
Bird, George C/JX 236852	Able Seaman	*Untiring*
Birnie, Peter D/JX 135218	Leading Telegraphist	*Unbeaten*
Bishop, John Eric P/JX 361825	Able Seaman	*Ultor*
Blake, Leopold P/JX 142985	Acting Leading Telegraphist	*Upholder*

Board, Norman Douglas P/MX 55599	Engine Room Artificer	*Upholder*
Bond, Raymond Walters John P/JX 137669	Leading Signalman	*Unique*
Bonsall, Victor P/JX 183946	Able Seaman	*Ultor*
Booty, William John P/J 113514	Acting Chief Petty Officer	*Unbending*
Bramhall, James Henry P/SSX 22392	Able Seaman	*Unbroken*
Brammer, Bernard D/JX 176650	Acting Leading Seaman	*Unsparing*
Bravery, Albert James MX 45993	Engine Room Artificer	*Ursula*
Britton, Charles Beresford C/MX 45233	Chief Engine Room Artificer	*Venturer*
Broadbent, Cecil D/MX 55525	Chief Engine Room Artificer	*Untiring*
Buckingham, Edwin JX129701	Petty Officer	*Ursula*
Buckingham, Fred Foster C/JX 133254	Petty Officer Telegraphist	*Umbra*
Burden, Arthur Edward P/MX 47296	Chief Engine Room Artificer	*Una*
Burgoyne, Charles Llewellyn C/MX 51007	Engine Room Artificer	*Upholder*
Byrne, John Stanley C/SSX 33942	Acting Leading Telegraphist	*Venturer*
Cake, Albert Charles D/JX 135328	Leading Telegraphist	*Uproar*
Cameron, John Lees D/JX 152912	Petty Officer	*Unsparing*
Cavanagh, Michael C/JX 143179	Acting Chief Petty Officer	*Vox*
Chapman, Clifford P/KX 79256	Leading Stoker	*Upholder*
Chidwick, Charles Walter C/KX 81539	Leading Stoker	*Urge*
Chisholm, William Heron C/JX 142524	Petty Officer Telegraphist	*Sokol*
Clabby, John P/KX 75337	Stoker Petty Officer	*Utmost*

Clarke, Robert D/KX 79557	Stoker Petty Officer	*Una*
Clarkson, George D/KX 80319	Stoker Petty Officer	*Unseen*
Claxton, Roy Alfred C/JX 140185	Acting Chief Petty Officer	*Ultor*
Clements, Sydney James D/JX 129907	Petty Officer	*Ursula*
Coakley, Cornelius D/JX 137361	Acting Petty Officer	*Unsparing*
Cochrane, Norman P/JX 156654	Acting Petty Officer Telegraphist	*Universal*
Cockburn, Thomas Bethune C/JX 134985	Leading Telegraphist	*Utmost*
Couldridge, Frank William C/JX 186403	Able Seaman	*Unbeaten*
Cox, Alfred Henry Hewlett P/K 66097	Stoker Petty Officer	*Venturer*
Crook, Andrew Thomas C/MX 51378	Chief Engine Room Artificer	*Unseen*
Cryer, George Frederick Herbert C/JX 156271	Leading Telegraphist	*Unbroken*
Cummins, Gilbert Frederick P/JX 139686	Leading Telegraphist	*Upholder*
Dannatt, Robert P/JX 283275	Acting Chief Petty Officer	*Universal*
Davidson, Robert Wallace P/JX 143409	Acting Leading Seaman	*Upholder*
Day, George Oliver C/JX 133839	Petty Officer	*Unison*
Deacon, Thomas Ernest C/KX 84144	Leading Stoker	*Upright*
Deffley, George Gilbert D/SSX 17555	Acting Leading Seaman	*Vampire*
Dominey-Frost, Richard P/JX 171484	Able Seaman	*Vox*
Don, Robertson Chalmers P/JX 158621	Telegraphist	*Ultimatum*
Drury, Norman William C/JX 128288	Acting Petty Officer Telegraphist	*Unbeaten*
Duckers, Donald D/JX 213687	Able Seaman	*United*

Evans, Samuel Joseph Lindop P/MX 46521	Chief Engine Room Artificer	*Unshaken*
Fairclough, John Roger D/K 66502	Stoker	*Utmost*
Fall, Charles George C/KX 116958	Acting Leading Stoker	*Unbroken*
Farr, Charles Edward P/JX 126235	Petty Officer	*Unruffled*
Fisher, Ronald Alfred C/MX 49885	Chief Engine Room Artificer	*Ultor*
Florence, William James P/M 22627	Chief Engine Room Artificer	*Ursula*
Forbes, George Dallas D/JX 161397	Acting Leading Seaman	*Unbeaten*
Ford, Donald William C/JX 137661	Acting Chief Petty Officer	*Unrivalled*
Forrest, Thomas Edmonstone P/MX 57335	Engine Room Artificer	*Vivid*
Fowkes, Reginald Eric P/MX 78857	Engine Room Artificer	*Unruly*
Frame, Frederick James D/M 38773	Engine Room Artificer	*Upholder*
Garnham, Walter Edgar D/SSX 23807	Acting Petty Officer	*Universal*
Gaskin, Charles C/MX 49759	Chief Engine Room Artificer	*Unruly*
Gilders, Walter Richard P/JX 267599	Able Seaman	*Upstart*
Glenn, Ernest Arthur P/J 115182	Chief Petty Officer	*Unseen*
Gregory, Ernest D/J 87852	Petty Officer Telegraphist	*Utmost*
Gregory, Frederick William C/KX 80267	Acting Stoker Petty Officer	*Upholder*
Groves, Laurence Frank C/J 101563	Leading Seaman	*Urge*
Grubb, Andrew P/KX 91257	Acting Leading Stoker	*Unbending*
Haimes, Cyril D/MX 90759	Engine Room Artificer	*Ultor*
Hall, Henry George William P/JX 156454	Acting Leading Seaman	*Unbending*

Hambly, Reuben Charles D/JX 129924	Petty Officer	*Ultimatum*
Harris, James George C/M 18337	Chief Engine Room Artificer	*Unique*
Harrison, Kenneth P/MX 55714	Chief Engine Room Artificer	*Vox*
Hatherly, William Murray C/JX 138060	Petty Officer	*United*
Hawkins, Edwin Charles D/KX 86461	Stoker Petty Officer	*Upstart*
Hayward, Leslie George Joseph P/MX 50132	Chief Engine Room Artificer	*Unswerving*
Head, Percival Arthur Thomas P/SSX 29670	Acting Leading Seaman	*Venturer*
Hedgecock, Frederick Thomas J. P/J 95686	Able Seaman	*Unison*
Hellyer, Reginald C/MX 47775	Engine Room Artificer	*Urge*
Hemmings, Royston Ernest D/BD/X 1647	Acting Leading Seaman	*Venturer*
Hicks, Albert Edward C/MX 50803	Engine Room Artificer	*Utmost*
Hiles, Ronald P/JX 156018	Acting Leading Signalman	*Unruffled*
Hill, Frederick Henry D/J 110524	Petty Officer	*Unison*
Hinds, Alfred Charles C/J 104901	Chief Petty Officer Telegraphist	*Upright*
Holland, Horace Henry P/MX 52950	Act. Chief Engine Room Artificer	*Voracious*
Hollis, Alfred Stephen D/JX 143782	Acting Chief Petty Officer	*Venturer*
Horsley, John William C/JX 137828	Petty Officer	*Upstart*
Hough, Leonard Bertram D/SSX 17401	Acting Chief Petty Officer	*Upstart*
Howells, Cecil Brinley C/SKX 114	Acting Leading Stoker	*Unruffled*
Hughes, Benjamin D/J 107296	Petty Officer	*Urge*
James, Thomas George Leslie D/JX 154312	Acting Leading Seaman	*Umbra*

James, Sidney D/SSX 32094	Leading Seaman	*Unswerving*
Jarvis, Arnold Horace D/KX 118387	Stoker	*Unrivalled*
Jenkins, Tudor James D/JX 133685	Telegraphist	*Unique*
Jennings, Thomas Edward D/JX 140195	Petty Officer	*Umbra*
Jones, Stacey Baker P/J 95513	Able Seaman	*Utmost*
Kettle, Cyril C/KX 80337	Acting Leading Stoker	*Utmost*
Kidd, Joseph D/J 106499	Acting Chief Petty Officer	*Unshaken*
Kilpatrick, William Gibb D/MX 50071	Chief Engine Room Artificer	*Unsparing*
King, Frank P/MX 58181	Act. Chief Engine Room Artificer	*Venturer*
Kirk, John C/KX 85225	Leading Stoker	*Ultimatum*
Kissane, Laurence Michael P/J 113061	Petty Officer	*Unbending*
Larner, Harry James C/JX 138852	Petty Officer	*Unruly*
Laurance, John Spencer C/MX 50281	Engine Room Artificer	*Unbeaten*
Lawrence, Albert Victor Jack C/JX 167342	Able Seaman	*Unseen*
Leadbetter, Leslie P/JX 138746	Petty Officer Telegraphist	*Unswerving*
Leaf, Sydney Jack C/MX 54031	Engine Room Artificer	*Unbeaten*
Lee, Arthur Stephen Kingston P/J 113443	Petty Officer	*Utmost*
Lee, William Frank D/JX 129908	Petty Officer	*Unbroken*
Lewis, Charles Henry D/WRX 664	Leading Telegraphist	*Venturer*
Lewis, Howard D/MX 51405	Engine Room Artificer	*Unbroken*
Lewis, Joseph Norman Victor C/JX 134555	Petty Officer Telegraphist	*Unruffled*

Lindsay, Harold P/JX 137859	Acting Chief Petty Officer	*Umbra*
Low, Alexander C/SSX 16667	Able Seaman	*Upright*
Mallett, Alfred James D/JX 130986	Leading Seaman	*Ursula*
Malone Francis C/KX 85452	Acting Stoker Petty Officer	*United*
Mann, Alfred George C/J 95585	Able Seaman	*Unique*
Martin, Frederick Philip C/J 113749	Chief Petty Officer	*Una*
Miller, David Andrew D/JX 164986	Able Seaman	*Urge*
Miller, William D/JX 153162	Leading Seaman	*Vampire*
Moon, Thomas Harold C/JX 133998	Yeoman of Signals	*Utmost*
Moore, Rhyeas Vincent C/KX 130325	Acting Leading Stoker	*Unruly*
Mowatt, Alexander Orchiston P/SSX 21589	Leading Seaman	*Ultor*
Murray, Philip James P/JX 151721	Acting Leading Telegraphist	*Umbra*
McKenzie, John Laybourne P/MX 75125	Chief Engine Room Artificer	*Votary*
McNeil, Malcolm D/MX 73392	Engine Room Artificer	*Ultimatum*
McPherson, John Allan C/KX 83440	Leading Stoker	*Unique*
Niblett, Francis Edward P/M 37225	Chief Engine Room Artificer	*Ursula*
Nimmo, Hugh Ferguson P/MX 55931	Engine Room Artificer	*Unrivalled*
Norris, Jesse C/JX 142500	Leading Seaman	*Urge*
Norris, Raymond Dean P/J 107443	Chief Petty Officer	*Unbeaten*
Norwood, Roy Frederick C/JX 134461	Acting Chief Petty Officer	*Ultimatum*
Osborn, Herbert George Arthur C/JX 134094	Acting Leading Seaman	*Urge*

Partleton, John Edward C/J 108856	Acting Leading Seaman	*Upholder*
Paul, Reginald Henry D/JX 134650	Petty Officer Telegraphist	*Unseen*
Peck, William Arthur C/J 112719	Chief Petty Officer	*Uproar*
Pert, Robert Sherret C/JX 223911	Acting Leading Seaman	*Umbra*
Phillips, Philip Maurice Leonard C/JX 128040	Petty Officer	*Vivid*
Pitman, Richard D/J 107819	Petty Officer	*Ursula*
Porter, Percy Andrew Clarke P/JX 126832	Petty Officer	*Unseen*
Powell, Harry Stanley Baden C/JX 155976	Able Seaman	*Unruffled*
Ray, William Henry D/M 38397	Engine Room Artificer	*Unruffled*
Richardson, Edward Frederick P/JX 141872	Acting Petty Officer	*Unruffled*
Richardson, Sidney C/KX 83298	Leading Stoker	*Umbra*
Robertson, John Millar P/MX 54597	Engine Room Artificer	*Umbra*
Robins, Russell Denis D/JX 139799	Acting Leading Seaman	*Untiring*
Rogers, Roy Williams George D/SSX 26082	Telegraphist	*Urge*
Rose, David George P/JX 139958	Able Seaman	*Utmost*
Ross, George Eric C/JX 133570	Petty Officer Telegraphist	*Una*
Round, Arthur Dennis P/KX 82218	Stoker Petty Officer	*Unsparing*
Rowley, John Kenneth C/SSX 21371	Able Seaman	*Urge*
Sammon, William C/MX 73601	Engine Room Artificer	*Umbra*
Sayce, Thomas Albert C/SSX 28609	Able Seaman	*Uproar*
Scott, George Bell P/JX 131208	Leading Telegraphist	*Unseen*

Selby, Francis Gordon C/JX 145558	Leading Seaman	*Upholder*
Seller, John C/JX 127467	Petty Officer	*Vampire*
Shanahan, James D/JX 131173	Able Seaman	*Utmost*
Sharp, Frederick Charles C/KX 81692	Stoker Petty Officer	*Unbroken*
Sheldon, Thomas Frederick P/JX 125570	Petty Officer Telegraphist	*United*
Simmonds, George Ernest P/JX 217354	Able Seaman	*Unrivalled*
Simmonds, Rex P/J 108490	Leading Signalman	*Upholder*
Sims, George Frederick D/J 111989	Petty Officer	*Untiring*
Sizer, Frank D/J 96997	Acting Chief Petty Officer	*Unbroken*
Smith, Arthur Charles P/JX 167433	Able Seaman	*Upright*
Smith, Horace Baden C/SSX 18530	Able Seaman	*Ultor*
Smith, John P/JX 235722	Able Seaman	*Unruly*
Stalker, James Burton C/JX 125988	Petty Officer	*Unshaken*
Standley, John Norman P/KX 152191	Acting Leading Stoker	*Venturer*
Stanley, Patrick Joseph P/KX 92269	Stoker	*Unbeaten*
Stephens, Donald Joseph P/JX 217674	Able Seaman	*Unruffled*
Stewart, Kenneth Charles C. C/M 38818	Chief Engine Room Artificer	*Upstart*
Stockton, Joseph Robert D/JX 146792	Leading Telegraphist	*Unbending*
Stockwell, John Edward F. C/SSX 124546	Stoker	*Unbeaten*
Strangward, Peter Charles Parr C/JX 141445	Acting Chief Petty Officer	*Ultimatum*
Surridge, Sidney Frank C/KX 139152	Stoker	*Ultor*

Swainston, John George P/JX 125082	Petty Officer	*Upholder*
Swift, Edward Joseph P/J 107665	Leading Telegraphist	*Ultimatum*
Tamplin, Morris Ivor D/J 111084	Petty Officer	*Unique*
Teft, Albert D/JX 190704	Able Seaman	*Universal*
Thomas, Ernest Alfred C/J 99723	Acting Chief Petty Officer	*Utmost*
Thomas, William Josiah D/K 65098	Stoker Petty Officer	*Uproar*
Timms, Francis George D/M 39372	Chief Engine Room Artificer	*Ultimatum*
Toms, Charles Herbert D/M 35358	Chief Engine Room Artificer	*Urge*
Tout, Leon D/M 39447	Chief Engine Room Artificer	*United*
Travers, Sidney Eustace D/J 107209	Acting Chief Petty Officer	*Unruly*
Trewhela, John James P/J 92052	Petty Officer	*Ultor*
Turner, William Robert D/J 110765	Acting Petty Officer	*Upholder*
Twist, Henry Ernest D/JX 225829	Telegraphist	*Urge*
Upton, Walter P/SSX 15635	Acting Leading Seaman	*Unbeaten*
Voyzey, Francis James D/JX 149558	Acting Leading Seaman	*Una*
Waldron, Horace P/SSX 19242	Able Seaman	*Ultimatum*
Walker, Reuben D/KX 93943	Leading Stoker	*Upstart*
Walls, Gerald Desmond P/JX 136741	Petty Officer	*Unruffled*
Walters, Norman George D/JX 159213	Leading Seaman	*Vivid*
Wanstall, William Henry S. C/JX 149247	Petty Officer Telegraphist	*Unrivalled*
Wareing, Robert D/KX 97075	Leading Stoker	*Untiring*

Watson, Charles Glover C/JX 159446	Petty Officer	*Unbeaten*
Watson, James Alexander P/JX 131355	Acting Chief Petty Officer	*Upright*
Watson, Norman C/JX 130944	Petty Officer	*Ursula*
Watts, Henry Roland Joseph P/J 129967	Petty Officer	*Urge*
West, William Harold P/MX 50131	Engine Room Artificer	*Upright*
Wickens, Joseph Richard D/JX 164991	Acting Chief Petty Officer	*United*
Willey, John Gatenby C/JX 130133	Petty Officer Telegraphist	*Unbroken*
Williams, James D/SSX 22211	Able Seaman	*Umbra*
Williams, John Henry D/JX 142219	Acting Leading Telegraphist	*Upright*
Williams, Robert P/MX 59350	Engine Room Artificer	*Universal*
Willoughby, Arthur P/J 109024	Acting Chief Petty Officer	*Untiring*
Wilson, Richard Douglas P/MX 56274	Engine Room Artificer	*Utmost*
Woolley, Ernest Clifford William C/J 98058	Able Seaman	*Upright*
Wright, Geoffrey Harry Anthony C/KX 79996	Stoker Petty Officer	*Unbeaten*
Wynne, Eric Puckering P/KX 75809	Acting Leading Stoker	*Una*
Yeo, George Amos D/JX 129805	Petty Officer	*Unbeaten*
Young, Leslie John Abel C/J 101714	Able Seaman	*Upholder*

Bar to Distinguished Service Medal

Name & Number	Rank	Submarine
Curtis, Alfred William Reginald P/J 110997	Petty Officer	*Urge*
Harding, William James D/J 96730	Chief Petty Officer	*Unbeaten*
Hollis, Alfred Stephen D/JX 143782	Acting Chief Petty Officer	*Venturer*
Jackman, Charley John P/J 110919	Chief Petty Officer	*Urge*
Mallett, Alfred James D/JX 130986	Petty Officer	*Una*
Manuel, Leslie Thomas John C/MX 47540	Chief Engine Room Artificer	*Unbroken*
Miller, David Andrew D/JX 164986	Able Seaman	*Upholder*
Poulter, Arthur P/JX 130942	Acting Chief Petty Officer	*Unsparing*
Rycraft, Harold Charles P/M 27337	Chief Engine Room Artificer	*Utmost*
Simons, Thomas William C/J 114129	Petty Officer	*Utmost*
Swainston, John George P/JX 125082	Acting Chief Petty Officer	*Upholder*
Thomas, Ernest Alfred C/J 99723	Acting Chief Petty Officer	*Unruffled*
Wood, Norman Leslie Robert C/MX 47345	Chief Engine Room Artificer	*Unbending*

George Cross

Name & Number	Rank	Submarine
Low, John Niven Angus	Lieutenant	*Unity*
Miller, Henry James P/J 55387	Able Seaman	*Unity*

APPENDIX II

GALLANTRY MEDALS AWARDED TO OFFICERS AND MEN OF THE ALLIED NAVIES SERVING IN 'U' CLASS SUBMARINES

Honorary Distinguished Service Order

Name Service	Rank	Submarine
Karnicki, Boris Free Polish	Lieutenant Commander	*Sokol*
Soede, Henri Max Louis Frederick Emile Dutch	Lieutenant Commander	*Dolfijn*
Valvatne, Sigurd Norwegian	Lieutenant	*Ula*

Distinguished Service Cross

Name Service	Rank	Submarine
Chailley, Pierre Jean Free French	Lieutenant	*Curie*
Klopotowski, Andrzej Free Polish	Lieutenant	*Sokol*
Koziolkowski, Jerzy Karol Free Polish	Lieutenant Commander	*Sokol*
Loundras, Constantinos Greek	Lieutenant Commander	*Pipinos*

Romanowsky, Boleslaw Szymon Free Polish	Lieutenant Commander	*Dzik*
Sandved, Sam Block Norwegian	Sub Lieutenant	*Ula*
Stromsland, Sverre Norwegian	Sub Lieutenant	*Ula*
Valvatne, Sigurd Norwegian	Lieutenant	*Ula*

Bar to Distinguished Service Cross

Name Service	Rank	Submarine
Koziolkowski, Jerzy Karol Free Polish	Lieutenant Commander	*Sokol*

Distinguished Service Medal

Name Service	Rank	Submarine
Bjotveit, Gerhard Norwegian	Chief Petty Officer	*Ula*
Bouvand, Raymond Free French	Senior Motor Mechanic	*Curie*
Buszman, Rudolf Free Polish	Petty Officer	*Dzik*
Daoukos, Nikolaou Greek	Petty Officer	*Pipinos*
Deboos, Marc Free French	Motor Mechanic	*Curie*
De Nooy, Rudi Dutch	Leading Telegraphist	*Dolfijn*
Domicz, Tadeusz Free Polish	Chief Petty Officer	*Sokol*
Gasowski, Franciszek Free Polish	Petty Officer	*Dzik*
Hoel, Bjarne Asbjorn Norwegian	Leading Seaman	*Ula*
Knutsen, Einar Norwegian	Chief Engine Room Artificer	*Ula*

Magdziarek, Stepan Free Polish	Petty Officer	*Dzik*
Nielsen, Knut Eeg Norwegian	Leading Seaman	*Ula*
Nowacki, Feliks Free Polish	Chief Electrician	*Sokol*
Pajak, Jan Free Polish	Leading Signalman	*Sokol*
Przadak, Feliks Free Polish	Chief Petty Officer	*Sokol*
Roznowski, Ryszard Free Polish	Petty Officer	*Dzik*
Sienkiewicz, Stanislaw Free Polish	Chief Engine Room Artificer	*Sokol*
Svanberg, Kristoffer Norwegian	Leading Seaman	*Ula*
Szewczyk, Marian Free Polish	Acting Petty Officer	*Sokol*
Wilhelmsen, Ragner Norwegian	Engine Room Artificer	*Ula*
Ziajka, Jozef Free Polish	Petty Officer	*Dzik*

APPENDIX III

SUBMARINE PENNANT NUMBERS

'U' class submarines were initially given pennant numbers as identification but on the insistence of the Prime Minister, Winston Churchill, all submarines still in commission not having adopted an appropriate name or under construction were named. Throughout the text each submarine has been identified by that name to assist in any identification problems; the pennant numbers originally allotted to those submarines are set out below.

Name	Number	Name	Number
Ultimatum	P34	Ultor	P53
Umbra	P35	Unbroken	P42
Unison	P43	United	P44
Universal	P57	Unrivalled	P45
Unruffled	P46	Unruly	P49
Unseen	P51	Unshaken	P54
Unsparing	P55	Unswerving	P63
Untiring	P59	Uproar	P31
Upstart	P65	Usurper	P56
Uther	P62		

ABBREVIATIONS

Asdic	Allied Submarine Detection and Investigation Committee, which became the acronym for the device to detect submarines underwater. It could also be used by submarines to communicate with each other whilst submerged.
CERA	Chief Engine Room Artificer.
C.-in-C.	Commander-in-Chief, an Admiral with responsibility for a fleet operating in a particular area e.g.: C.-in-C. Mediterranean.
COPP	Combined Operations Pilotage Party.
DSEA	Davis Submerged Escape Apparatus.
Folbot	A two-man collapsible canoe.
FO (S)	Flag Officer, Submarines.
Hydrophone	An instrument for detecting sound through water.
HE	Hydrophone effect, i.e. the sound of an engine or propeller.
HP blow	High-pressure blow.
HSD	Higher Submarine Detector – a skilled Asdic operator.
OOW	Officer of the Watch.
'Q' Tank	The emergency quick diving tank which, when flooded, added ten tons to the weight of the submarine.

BIBLIOGRAPHY

The Fighting Tenth by John Wingate, DSC, RN, Rtd.
Periscope Patrol by John Frayn Turner.
Submariner by Captain John Coote, RN Rtd.
Seedies List of Submarine Awards for World War II.
Submarines of World War Two by Ermino Bagnasco.
Naval Staff History Volumes One and Two.
Weekly Intelligence Reports.
The Ships of the Royal Navy and those of the Government Navy
    1814-1962 from the Office of Naval History, Holland.
Original submarine patrol reports held at the Royal Navy
    Submarine Museum, Gosport.
Original ships' logs and patrol reports held at the Public Record
    Office, Kew.
Original patrol reports from the Russian Naval Archives,
    Moscow.

ACKNOWLEDGEMENTS

Line drawings: Mrs Joan Slate

Translators: Doctor Hilary Turner – Greek

                       Mrs Cory Owen – Dutch

                       Mrs Kristin Bohinen – Norwegian

                       Miss Camilla Herd – Danish

                       Ms Annette Beattie – Danish

                       Ms Cara Marchant – Russian

Access to Material: Lieutenant G.A. Newton, RN – Obtaining patrol reports for submarines in the service of the Russian navy.

                       Mrs Margot Novorol – Information and photographs of Polish Submarines.

                       Mrs Marie-Christine Campbell – Information and photographs of *Pipinos*.

                       Dr O. ten Hove, Afdeling Maritime Historie – Information on *Dolfijn*.

                       Captain M.R.G. Wingfield, DSO, DSC, RN Rtd. – Memoirs on the *Umpire*.

                       Margaret Bidmead and the late Gus Britton.

                       Royal Navy Submarine Museum.

Julie Ash, National Archives Kew.

Ronnie Coates-Walker, DSC, RNR Rtd. Memoirs and photographs of HMS *Universal.*

Dave Barlow, Scottish Branch of Submarine Old Comrades Association.

INDEX

Atle Jarl – 3, 23, 206, 207, 229
Aalborg – 105
Abba – 145
Abdullah – 129
Abdy, Lieutenant D. – 57, 62
Acciaio – 111
Acworth, Sub Lieutenant – 219
Adalia – 161
Admiral Scheer – 31, 158
Agia Anna – 152
Agios Eleimon, Sy274 – 168
Agios Georgius Hydra – 162
Agios Ionna – 139
Agios Matheus – 152
Albatros – 107
Alep – 128
Alfa – 63
Alga – 83
Alice Robert – 143
Altmark – 20
Amabile Carolina – 98
Amfitriti – 10, 225
Ammiraglio Milo – 71
Ammiraglio Saint Bon – 68
Ammiraglio Vespucci – 124
Amsterdam – 85
Andrea Sgarallino – 126
Andrew, Lieutenant B.J.B. – 94, 106,
    107, 115, 116
Angela – 101
Anita – 147
Antonietta Laura – 48
Antoniotto Usodimare – 70
Appleyard, J.G., Major, 2nd SAS
    Regiment – 200
Aquila – 80, 81
Aquino, Tenente de Vassalo – 120, 161
Aquitania – 63
Arcturus, 1,682 tons – 171
Arcturus, 2,586 tons – 49

Ardito – 98
Argonaftis, see *Virulent* – 14
Ariosto – 70
Armando Diaz – 45
Arsia – 54
Arta – 48
Artesian – 137
AS49 – 129
Asien – 34
Asmara – 116
Assunta de Gregori – 74
Astree – 140
Attilio Regolo – 86
Audace – 94
Aversa – 130
Aviere – 157
Azrou – 109

B2, see *Unbroken* – 10
B3, see *Unison* – 10
B4, see *Ursula* – 3
B6517 – 181
Baalbek – 102
Bacchus – 134
Baker, Commander H.L.S. – 178
Balzano – 79
Banister, Lieutenant P.C.M. – 213
Bannar-Martin, Lieutenant R. – 35
Barbarigo – 55
Barbiano – 45
Barletta – 90
Barlow, Lieutenant T.E. – 79, 81, 82,
    116, 119, 126
Barry Rear Admiral C.B. – 15, 16, 215,
    221, 224
Bennett, S.B., Yeoman of Signals – 90,
    205
Beppe – 84
Berta – 151
Bivona – 106

Blackman, Captain RN – 207
Block, Oberleutnant H., – 36
Bois Rose – 103
Bologna – 108
Bombardiere – 96
Booth, J., Corporal, Seaforth
    Highlanders – 194
Boreal – 103
Boreland – 177
Boyd, Lieutenant R. – 33, 130, 132,
    134, 140, 144
Brakema, Lieutenant H.J. – 160
Brand, Lieutenant D. – 199
Brand, Sub Lieutenant P. – 201
Brandenburg – 126
Brarena – 55
Bridger, Lieutenant J.S. – 32, 214, 215
Brindisi – 116
Brittlebank, J., Bombardier – 193
Brooks, Lieutenant F.J. – 206, 209
Brooks, Lieutenant J.E. – 42
Brown, Lieutenant J.F.B. – 7, 20, 21,
    22, 23
Brown, R.H., Corporal, London &
    Scottish Regiment – 187
Bryant, Captain B. – 37, 38
Buckle, Commander H. – 217
Bucknall, Sub Lieutenant R. – 69, 205
Burbridge, G.W., Captain, Royal
    Engineers – 199
Bussard – 171
Byrne, J., Telegraphist – 122

Caique 53 – 169
Caique 238 – 127
Caique Cal 93 – 139
Caique CHA113 – 149
Caique GN61 – 146
Caique GN62 – 146
Caique KAL 14 – 146
Caique SY547 – 137
Cairns, Lieutenant R.D. – 149, 152
Calatafimi – 179
Cap Blanc – 144
Capitaine Damiani – 52
Capo Vita – 45
Carabiniere – 70
Carlo del Greco – 67
Carlo Margottini – 102
Carlo P – 101
Carnaro – 163
Carter, J.F., Petty Officer – 49, 204

Casey, Sergeant, Hampshire Regiment
    – 196
Castelverde – 93
Cayley, Lieutenant R.D. – 44, 45, 54,
    56, 66, 67, 184, 186, 187
Cazalet, Captain P.G.L. – 219
Cerere – 140
Cesena – 112
Cesira Curreri – 92
Chailley, Lieutenant P.J.M.A.F. – 175
Challenor, Chief Engine Room Artificer
    – 218–220
Chalmers, Lieutenant A.T. – 37
Chamberlain, Neville – 18
Champagne – 126
Chapman, Lieutenant P.C. – 33, 136,
    140, 141
Chateau Yquem – 114
Cheveson, Admiral Arthur – 1, 23
Chico, Valentino, Petty Officer – 68
Chietti – 137
Christopher, Sub Lieutenant M.N. –
    205
Churchill, Sir Winston – 11, 12, 204
Churchill, Peter – 190
Circe – 56, 70
Ciri Menotti – 120
Citta di Bergamo – 103
Citta di Catania – 115
Citta di Palermo – 156
Citta di Spezia – 116
Clairvoyant – 140
Climene – 106
Coates-Walker, Lieutenant R. – 119
Collett, Lieutenant A.F. – 44, 46, 54,
    75, 187
Collins, Lieutenant B. – 93
Conte Rosso – 52, 53
Coombe, Lieutenant J.W.D. – 193
Cooper, Lieutenant N.W. – 199
Coote, Captain J. – 221
Corridoni – 120, 161
Cortopassi, Dario, Seaman Electrician –
    112
Cosala – 100
Cosenza – 103
Cr. Columbo – 124
Crawford, Lieutenant M.L.C. – 30, 31,
    97, 100, 102, 105, 130, 133, 134
Cunningham, Admiral Sir Andrew – 41
Cunningham, Admiral Sir John – 144
Curie – 10, 32, 174, 175, 176

Curtatone – 52
Cygnet, HMS – 215

Dalmatia – 69
Daniell, Lieutenant A.R. – 100, 101, 103, 105, 106, 109, 115, 197
Darling, Lieutenant G.P. – 47
Day, G.O. Petty Officer – 115
Dazzi, Carlo, Boatswain – 117
Dea Mazella – 166
Delfin, see *Vengeful* – 14
Diana – 140
Didcott, R.R., Royal Marines – 194
Djebel Dira – 94
Dolfijn – 10, 32, 44, 120, 160, 162, 163
Donohoe, Able Seaman – 100
Dora C – 118
Doris, see *Vineyard* – 14
Douglas, HMS – 30
Doxa – 147
Drache – 133
Dubrovnik – 132
Duckers, D., Able Seaman – 96
Duilio – 63
Duisburg – 43
Duncan, G.E.A., Captain, Black Watch – 192
Dzik – 102, 134, 163, 164, 169, 170, 225

Eaden, Lieutenant J.H. – 24
Edda – 97
Edmunds, Lieutenant H.N. – 70, 189, 190
Egle – 160
Eleni – 164
Emilio Morandi – 95
Encounter, HMS – 24
Enotria – 62
Enrica – 108
Enrichetta – 85
Enrico Costa – 54
Epokhim, Admiral, Russian Navy – 181
Eridania – 166
Eritrea – 101
Esperia – 62
Evans, Sub Lieutenant J. – 121, 122, 123
Evengelistria – 137
Eyre, J., Royal Engineers – 197

F9 – 19
F541 – 130

Fabio Filzi – 67
Fabiola – 117
Fairclough, Second Lieutenant, COPP – 184
Fame, HMS – 227
Faron – 132
Farquhar, Captain J.W. – 215
Fawkes, Captain G.B.H. – 118
Federico – 56
Felicia – 46
Ferguson, J.R.A., Lance Corporal, London & Scottish Regiment – 187
Fiore, Ernest, Torpedoman – 68
Flegetonte – 117
Flett, P.F. – 73
FMA 06 – 144
Foggia – 105
Force – 35
Forth, HMS – 214, 215
Francesco Barbaro – 82
Friedrichshaven – 34
Fritz, Sub Lieutenant – 165, 166
Fyfe, Commander D.H. – 197
Fyfe, Lieutenant J.P. – 105, 107, 108, 109, 111, 133, 134, 135

Galilea – 44
Gallantry Medals, see Appendices
Galloway, Lieutenant R.M. – 54, 56
Gardner, Lieutenant M.H. – 69, 205
Garibaldi, Romolo, Seaman – 68
Genova – 97
George L M Russ – 31
Gertrud – 142
Giacomo C – 106
Giovanna – 81
Giovanni de Verazzano – 84
Giovanni delle Bande Nere – 73
Giovanni G – 110
Giovinezza – 50
GK 61 – 148
GM03 – 176
Gneisenau – 25
Godden, Sub Lieutenant S.A.G. – 212
Gordon, Lieutenant C. – 118, 131, 133, 144, 145, 147
Gorizia – 70
Gran – 94
Greghan, Private, Hampshire Regiment – 196
Groppo – 90
Grotte de Bethlehem – 33

Guglielmotti – 71
Guiseppe Garibaldi – 56
Guiseppina – 157
Gustavo, Giusti, Signalman – 119, 120

Habist II – 33
Haddow, Lieutenant J.R.H. – 150, 151
Halliday, Lieutenant A.C. – 77, 80, 84, 85
Halliday, J., Leading Signalman – 115
Hardy – 148
Harrison, Lieutenant P.R.H. – 66, 68, 71
Harvey, Lieutenant E.M. – 20
Harwood, Admiral Sir Henry – 76
Hay, Lieutenant D. – 226
Head, P.A.T. Leading Seaman – 37
Heddernheim – 21
Hemingway, Lieutenant R.J. – 70
Hennevelt, H.J., Seaman First Class – 160
Henri Desprez – 108
Heraklea – 46
Herrick, Lieutenant L.E. – 116, 126, 131, 137, 138
Hersell, Lance Corporal – 200
Hezlet, Lieutenant A.R. – 44, 62, 64
Horton, Admiral Max – 65, 126
Hughes, W.G., Royal Marines – 186, 190
Humanitas – 161
Hunt, Lieutenant G.E. – 105, 109, 111, 117, 126, 130, 133, 136–138, 141, 143, 144, 148, 207
Hurworth, HMS – 216

Ile – 171
Ile de Beaute – 126
Impero – 113
Ingeborg – 129
Ingram, Captain D.C. – 133, 135
Ionides, Captain H.M.C – 31, 214, 215
Iseo – 113

Jackson, Lieutenant Commander A.S. – 19
Jay, Sub Lieutenant R.L. – 69
Jones, J., Able Seaman – 84
Jordan, S.V., Chief Petty Officer – 20

K3 – 28, 159
Kabo, Captain 3rd Class, Russian Navy – 181, 182

Karnicki, Lieutenant Boris – 26, 27, 155, 156
Karpuhin, Admiral, Russian Navy – 182
Kershaw, Lieutenant J.B. de B. – 25, 66, 69, 72, 205
Kett, Lieutenant W.H. – 127, 130, 136, 139, 141
Killan, G.S., Chief Engine Room Artificer – 210, 212, 230
King, Lieutenant J.P. – 115
Kirk, E., Petty Officer – 57
Kita – 126
Klopotowski Captain A. – 5, 164
Kolokouris, A., Chief Petty Officer – 179
Koziolkowski, Lieutenant Commander G. – 121, 123, 165, 168, 169
Kreta – 126
KT7 – 106

L'Angelo Raffaelo – 102
La Capricieuse – 215
La Havraise – 144
Lakin, Lieutenant R.B. – 90, 91, 195
Launders, Lieutenant J.S. – 34, 35, 36, 38, 201
Laura C – 55
Laurence, Rear Admiral N.F. – 2, 3
Law, E.C., Leading Signalman – 189
Le Foce – 133
Le Jacques Coeur – 105
Le Tre Maria Sorelle – 100
Leipzig – 19
Leonardo Palomba – 81
Levchenko, Vice Admiral, Russian Navy – 180
Leverkusen – 49
Libau – 158
Libeccio – 67
Liberia – 81
Lince – 117
Lisbon – 99
Littorio – 67, 77
Livesay, Lieutenant J.F. – 50
Livingstone, R.P., Army Captain – 195
Lloyd, Sub Lieutenant B.N.T. – 188, 189, 191
Loch Falda, HMS – 226
Loreto – 85
Loundras, Lieutenant C. – 178
Low, Lieutenant J.N.A. – 23, 206, 229, 230

Lower, D., Able Seaman – 121
Lucania – 69
Lucrino – 122
Luigi Di Duca Degli Abruzzi – 67
Luigi Verni – 101
Luni – 98
Lupa – 83
Lussin – 62

Maas, Lieutenant J.B.M.J. – 162
Macedonia – 93, 102
Maddalena – 95
Madden, Admiral Sir Charles – 1
Madsen, Commander K.T. – 226
Malachite – 160
Manfredo Camperio – 80
Manunta, Tenente de Vassalo Giovanni
    – 120
Marco Foscarini – 106
Margherita, 69-ton schooner – 94
Margherita, 140-ton minesweeper – 98
Maria Immacolata – 72
Maria Pompei – 66
Marigola – 66
Marin Sanudo – 72
Mars, Lieutenant A.C.G. – 79, 84, 97,
    104, 115, 193, 197
Martin, Lieutenant D.S.R. – 69
Martin, Lieutenant J.D. – 72, 99
Martin, W., Engine Room Artificer – 60
Matara – 138
Maydon, Lieutenant S.L.C. – 68, 69,
    74, 76–78, 80, 81, 85, 88, 91, 92,
    95, 194
Mediator – 227
Messaryas Nomikos – 116
Michelino – 98
Michell, Lieutenant J.M. – 146, 148,
    151, 152, 202
Milano – 106
Miller H.J., Able Seaman – 23, 206,
    208, 229, 230
Missouri, USS – 153
Montcalm – 174
Montemagno, Carlo, Midshipman –
    112
Moon, T.H., Leading Signalman – 209,
    210
Morris, Lieutenant R.W. – 60
Morse, see *Vortex* – 14
Mott, Lieutenant D.R.O. – 114, 128
Mussolini, Benito – 155, 156
Muzzio Attendolo – 79

Napoli – 69
Neptunia – 63, 64
Netztender 44 – 132
Nicolaus – 163
Nicolaus, Pi790 – 168
Nicolaus, Sy262 – 168
Nicolaus, Sy436 – 168
Nieder Sachsen – 136
Niko Matkovich – 110
Nimrod, HMS – 215
Ninetto G – 73
Nioi – 129
Noll, Lieutenant G.M. – 15, 217
Norman, Lieutenant C.P. – 72, 73, 192
Norman, Lieutenant E.D. – 44, 45, 185
Nuovo Domenico – 95

Oceania – 63, 64
Oddie, Lieutenant E.R.J. – 17
Ogle, Lieutenant J.C. –
    34,147,150,151,202
Olbia – 110
Onestas – 93
Operation Felice – 197
Operation Halberd – 65
Operation Hangman – 201
Operation Husky – 111, 198, 200
Operation Pedestal – 192
Operation Seagull – 159, 197
Operation Shingle – 200
Operation Snapdragon – 200
Operation Torch – 41, 86, 88, 193, 194
Operation Venus – 170, 201
Operation Vigorous – 76
Operation Why Not – 192
Otario – 121, 165
Oxborrow, Lieutenant C.E. – 31, 90,
    205

P31, see *Uproar*
P32 – 9, 53, 57
P33 – 9, 53, 55, 57
P34, see *Ultimatum*
P35, see *Umbra*
P36 – 9, 67, 70, 73, 75, 189, 190
P37, see *Unbending*
P38 – 9, 67, 70, 71, 205
P39 – 9, 67
P41, see *Uredd*
P42, see *Unbroken*
P43, see *Unison*
P44, see *United*
P45, see *Unrivalled*

P46, see *Unruffled*
P47, see *Dolfijn*
P48 – 9, 86, 93, 194
P49, see *Unruly*
P51, see *Unseen*
P52, see *Dzik*
P53, see *Ultor*
P54, see *Unshaken*
P55, see *Unsparing*
P56, see *Usurper*
P59, see *Untiring*
P61, see *Varangian*
P62, see *Uther*
P63, see *Unswerving*
P65, see *Upstart*
P66, see *Ula*
P67, see *Curie*
P311 – 197
Paccinotte – 131
Pallas – 144
Pan – 171
Panunzio, Contrammiraglio Tommaso – 121
Parry, Petty Officer – 129
Pasubia – 102, 104
Pearce, W., Signalman – 29
Pegaso – 73, 228
Penerf – 105
Penn, Sergeant, COPP – 191
Perowne, Rear Admiral J. – 216
Perseo – 51
Peter – 137, 150, 151
Peter Hendriks – 9, 26, 212
Petrarca – 100
Petrel – 148
Phillips, as Lieutenant Commander G.C. – 18–20
Phillips, as Captain G.C. – 122, 131
Phoenix, HM Submarine – 65
Piemonte – 89
Pietro Querini – 54
Piper, Lieutenant A.D. – 117, 127, 128, 129, 135, 136, 137, 145
Pipinos – 14, 32, 177, 178, 179, 180, 202, 225
Pisani – 72
PLM 20 – 72
Ploch, Johannes, Seaman – 68
Pomo – 110
Pozarica – 80
President Dal Piaz – 145
Pronte – 85
Protinus – 21, 22

Raimondo Montecuccoli – 56
Rallis, Lieutenant Commander A. – 177, 178, 202
Rampino – 68
Rastrella – 116
Ravenna – 82
Raw, Captain S.M. – 42, 43
Read, Lieutenant C.H. – 49, 204
Redden, M.E., Flight Sergeant – 103
Redentore – 99
Regent, HM Submarine – 45
Regina – 104
Remo – 111
Renshaw, Lieutenant K.S. – 223
Ringulv – 109
Romanowski, Lieutenant Commander B. – 163, 164, 169
Roren, Lieutenant R.O. – 158, 197, 198
Rosolino Pilo – 79
Rostro – 81
Roxburgh, Lieutenant J.C.Y. – 89, 95, 96, 109–111, 199
Ruhr – 46
Ryfylke – 171

Sabbia – 44, 161
Sacro Cuore – 91, 92
Saelen, see *Vortex*
Sahib, HM Submarine – 93
Sainte Marguerite – 91
Sainte Marguerite (Ringulv) – 109
Salamis – 176
Salomea – 151
Salvatore, Tenente di Vascella – 111
Sampiere Corso – 145
San Francisco di Paola – 113
Santa Maria – 107
Sapphire, HMS – 90
Sars, Lieutenant R.M. – 170, 172, 201
Saturnia – 123, 165
Saumur – 141
Scharnhorst – 25
Schekin, Lieutenant, Russian Navy – 181
Schofield, D., Lieutenant, Royal Fusiliers – 184–186
Schoneboom, Oberleutnant Dietrich – 130
Scipio Africanus – 123
Sebastiano, Capitano Gallia – 113
Sejro – 21
Severn, HM Submarine – 215
Sevillona – 147, 148

SF121 – 151
Shadwell, Captain L.M. – 159
Shemara – 15, 217
Shorrocks, R.G., Stoker Petty Officer – 213
Siebel Ferry 284 – 145
Silver, Lieutenant R. – 75
Silvia Tripcovitch – 44
Sim, J., Able Seaman – 93, 94
Simmonds, G., Able Seaman – 29
Simpson, Commander G.W.G. – 43, 47, 49, 51, 64, 74, 92, 185, 193, 204
Sirio – 67, 68
Sirius – 38
Skarlo, Reidar, Royal Norwegian Navy – 198
Smith, Lieutenant P.R.G. – 199
Soede, Lieutenant H. Van Oostrum – 120, 160
Sofia – 152
Sokol – 9, 25, 26, 121, 123, 124, 155–157, 165–170
Sonneville, Lieutenant P.M. – 174, 175
Southdown, HMS – 227
Sparviero – 102
Sportivo – 97
Spratt, Lieutenant – 115
Springeren – 10, 165, 225, 226
St. Lucien – 105
Standard – 36
Stanley, Lieutenant, E.T. – 82, 83, 84, 98, 101, 103, 196, 199
Starfish Enterprise Technical Diving Team – 216
Stephano Galleano – 161
Stevens, Lieutenant J.S. – 80, 81, 85, 86, 89, 93, 98, 99, 102, 108
Stockholm – 36
Storen, see *Vulpine*
Straw, Sub Lieutenant H. – 129
Sturgeon, HM Submarine – 214
Sturman, Leading Stoker – 55, 204
Suzanne – 142, 147
Svelberg – 92
Swanston, Lieutenant D. – 45, 120, 139

TA19 – 179
Talbot, HMS – 73
Tamiarchis – 177
Tanais – 145
Tattersall, Lieutenant M.D. – 138, 142, 143, 146, 151

Taxiarhi – 166
Taylor, Lieutenant C.W. – 143, 145, 149, 150, 151
Taylor, Lieutenant G.G. – 123, 165, 169
Teacher, Lieutenant Commander N.J.M. – 199
Tedworth – 217
Tembien – 71
Templar, HM Submarine – 214
Tenedos – 145
Teodolinda – 99
Terni – 109
Theonie – 162
Thomas, P.M., The Buffs – 197
Thor – 34
Thorn, C., Able Seaman – 90, 205
Thrasher, HM Submarine – 217
Tirpitz – 31, 39, 158
Titania – 84
Togo – 90
Tomkinson, Lieutenant E.P. – 25, 51, 55, 63, 66, 67, 72, 74, 186, 188–191
Tommaseo – 107, 108
Torpille – 33
Torridal – 173
Touloupis, Engineer – 179
Tre Sorelle – 118
Treble, W.N., Petty Officer – 212, 230
Trento – 70, 77, 78
Triaina, see *Volatile*
Trichero – 71
Trickey, Lieutenant – 207
Triglav – 104
Truant, HM Submarine – 75
Tsar Ferdinand – 176
Tsarouchas, Adamantios, Seaman – 178
Tullio – 109
Tuna, HM Submarine – 28
Turner, Lieutenant H.B – 29, 92, 93, 97, 98, 102–107, 112, 121–123, 130,199

U1, see *Springeren*
U2, see *Vulpine* and *Storen*
U3, see *Vortex* and *Saelen*
U35 – 18
U73 – 88
U374 – 68
U431 – 130
U616 – 130

U771 – 36
U864 – 37
U974 – 172
Ugo – 118
UJ2106 – 145
UJ2201 – 103
UJ2204 – 103
UJ2205 – 105
UJ2208 – 128
UJ6078 – 144
UJ6705 – 140
Ula – 10, 32, 33, 170–173, 201, 225, 227
Ultimatum – 9, 66, 68, 69, 71, 73, 77, 78, 127, 130, 136, 139, 141, 142
Ultor – 9, 105, 109, 111, 117, 126, 127, 130, 133, 136–139, 141, 143, 144, 148, 200
Umbra – 9, 33, 68, 69, 74, 76, 77, 80–82, 85, 86, 88, 91–93, 95, 103, 194
Umpire – 8, 9, 26, 39, 210, 214, 230
Una – 8, 9, 67, 69, 72, 73, 77, 85, 86, 99, 100, 192
Unbeaten – 8, 25, 31, 32, 46, 50, 53, 55, 63, 64, 68, 71, 72, 184, 204
Unbending – 9, 28, 29, 78, 82–84, 98, 101–103, 196, 198
Unbroken – 9, 10, 79, 84, 94, 97, 104, 106, 107, 114, 180, 181, 193, 197
Undaunted – 8, 25, 46, 50, 53
Undine – 2, 17, 18, 19, 39, 227
Unger di Lowenberg, Capitano di Fregato C. – 56
Union – 8, 25, 46, 54, 56, 57
Unique – 8, 24, 25, 42–44, 46, 54, 62, 75, 76, 82, 187
Unison – 9, 10, 76, 77, 80, 84, 85, 100, 101, 103, 105, 106, 109, 115, 119, 180–182, 197,200
United – 9, 76, 79, 80–82, 86, 88, 95–97, 109–111, 198–200, 226
Unity – 2, 3, 7, 18, 20–23, 39, 206–208, 229, 230
Universal – 10, 118, 119, 131, 133, 144, 147, 227
Unno van Fischel, Oberleutnant – 68
Unrivalled – 9, 29, 82, 92–95, 97, 98, 102–105, 107, 112, 113, 121, 122, 130, 194, 198–200
Unruffled – 9, 28, 76, 80, 81, 85, 86, 89, 93, 98, 99, 102, 108, 115, 116, 200

Unruly – 9, 105, 107, 108, 109, 111, 122, 133–135, 139
Unseen – 9, 30, 31, 82, 93, 97, 100, 102, 104, 105, 116, 117, 126, 130, 133
Unshaken – 9, 31. 34, 82, 86, 88, 90, 104, 106, 107, 110, 112, 116, 117, 120, 127, 194, 200, 205
Unsparing – 10, 15, 16, 113, 115, 117, 127–129, 135, 136, 143, 145, 150
Unswerving – 10, 15, 138, 142, 143, 146, 151, 222
Untamed, see Vitality
Untiring – 10, 15, 33, 130, 132, 134, 140, 144, 221, 222, 225
Upas – 224
Upholder – 8, 25, 42, 43, 48, 49, 52, 53, 55, 56, 62–64, 66,67, 68, 71, 73–75, 187, 204, 228
Upright – 8, 9, 13, 24, 41, 42, 44, 56, 64, 65, 67, 184, 185
Uproar – 9, 26, 66, 69, 72, 77, 116, 126, 131, 137, 138, 200, 205, 206
Upshot – 14
Upstart – 10, 33, 136, 140, 141, 225
Urchin – 8, 9, 25, 155
Uredd – 9, 27, 28, 31, 32, 39, 156, 158, 160, 170, 197, 198
Urge – 8, 25, 46, 51, 54, 55, 63, 66, 67, 72, 74, 186, 188, 190, 191
Ursula – 2, 3, 7, 18–21, 24, 41, 44, 63–65, 82, 84, 86, 88, 90, 91, 94, 161, 180, 181, 194–196
Urtica – 14
Usk – 8, 25, 42, 46, 47, 53
Usurper – 10, 114, 128, 214
Uthaug, see Votary
Uther – 10, 33
Utmost – 8, 13, 24, 41, 44–46, 54, 56, 65–67, 76, 86, 90, 184–187, 193
Utsira – 14, 173, 174
Utstein, see Venturer
Utvaer, see Viking

V6408 – 173
Vagabond – 14, 224
Valentino Coda – 109
Valfiorita – 111
Valvatne, Lieutenant S. – 170, 173
Vampire – 14, 143, 145, 146, 149, 150, 225
Vandal – 10, 15, 17, 32, 39, 214–217, 222
Vang – 35

Varangian – 10, 33
Variance, see *Utsira*
Varley, Lieutenant J.C. – 145, 147, 152, 153, 202
Varne II – 14
Varne I, see *Ula*
Veach Vad – 189
Veldt, see *Pipinos*
Vengeful – 14, 225
Venturer – 14, 34–38, 201, 225
Vergilio – 132
Verve – 224
Veto – 224
Vidas, Capitano Antonio – 117
Vigorous – 14, 34, 147, 150–153, 202
Viking – 14, 35, 36, 225
Viminale – 98
Vincente Mitchelle – 189
Vineyard – 14, 176
Virile – 224
Virtue – 14, 149, 152, 227
Virulent – 14, 227
Visigoth – 13, 14, 150–152
Vitality – 10, 15, 32, 217–219, 222, 223, 225
Vittore Pisani – 121, 124, 165
Vittorio Veneto – 67
Vivid – 14, 145, 147, 152, 202
Volatile – 14, 225
Voracious – 14, 152, 227
Vortex – 14, 176, 177, 225, 226
Votary – 14, 15, 225
Vox – 14, 146–148, 151, 152, 202, 227
Vox I, see *Curie*
Vulcania – 64, 124
Vulpine – 14, 225, 226

Walker, Lieutenant, Hertfordshire Regiment – 187, 191

Wanklyn, Lieutenant Commander M.D. – 43, 48, 49, 52, 55, 56, 62, 65, 66, 68, 71, 73–75, 187, 227, 228
Watson, Lieutenant A. – 115
Watson, Lieutenant D.E.O. – 31
Weatherall, S., Sergeant – 195
Welford, Petty Officer – 219
Wesergau – 172
Whiteway-Wilkinson, Lieutenant R.D. – 55,57
Whitton, Lieutenant J. – 34, 90, 104, 106, 107, 110, 112, 116, 117, 120, 127, 200
Willard Daniel – 226
Williams I.G., Able Seaman – 46
Wilson, Able Seaman – 129, 130
Wilson, R., Lieutenant, Royal Artillery – 186, 190, 193
Wingfield, Lieutenant M.R.G.S. – 26, 210, 212, 214
Winter, Lieutenant H. – 28, 29
Wolfe, HMS – 219
Wolff, Kapitänleutnant Heinz – 172
Wolfram, Korvettenkapitän R.R. – 37
Wood, Lieutenant N.R. – 153
Woodward, Lieutenant E.A. – 50, 54, 55, 63, 64, 68, 71, 72, 184
Wraith, Lieutenant J.S. – 56, 65, 67
Wyburd, Captain, Royal Danish Navy – 226

Xifias – 10, 225
Yoselian, Captain 3rd Class, Russian Navy – 181
Young, Lieutenant E. – 213
Zeffiro – 51
Zeila – 103
Zenobia Martini – 97